P9-BYW-007

STEVE TURNER

THE BEATLES A HARD DAY'S WRITE

THE STORIES BEHIND EVERY SONG

MJF BOOKS
NEW YORK

This book is dedicated to the memory of
T-Bone Burnett and Larry Norman in memory
of many hours of Beatle-talk over the years.

Published by MJF Books
Fine Communications
322 Eighth Avenue
New York, NY 10001

The Beatles: A Hard Day's Write
LC Control Number: 2011927638
ISBN 978-1-60671-109-5

First published by Carlton Books Limited 1994

Text copyright © Steve Turner 1994, 1999, 2005, 2009
Design copyright © Carlton Books Limited 1994, 1999, 2005, 2009

This edition is published by MJF Books in arrangement with Carlton Books Limited.

All rights reserved. No part of this publication may be reproduced or transmitted in any form or by any means, electronic or mechanical, including photocopy, recording, or any information storage and retrieval system, without the prior written permission of the publisher.

Printed in China

MJF Books and the MJF colophon are trademarks of Fine Creative Media, Inc.

OGP 20 19 18 17 16 15 14 13 12

THE BEATLES
A HARD DAY'S WRITE

CONTENTS

PREFACE 4
INTRODUCTION 6

PLEASE PLEASE ME 18
I Saw Her Standing There; Misery; Ask Me Why; Please Please Me; Love Me Do; PS I Love You; Do You Want To Know A Secret?; There's A Place

WITH THE BEATLES 40
From Me To You; Thank You Girl; She Loves You; I'll Get You; It Won't Be Long; All I've Got To Do; All My Loving; Little Child; Don't Bother Me; Hold Me Tight; I Wanna Be Your Man; Not A Second Time; I Want To Hold Your Hand; This Boy; I Call Your Name

A HARD DAY'S NIGHT 70
A Hard Day's Night; I Should Have Known Better; If I Fell; I'm Happy Just To Dance With You; And I Love Her; Tell Me Why; Can't Buy Me Love; Any Time At All; I'll Cry Instead; Things We Said Today; When I Get Home; You Can't Do That; I'll Be Back

BEATLES FOR SALE 90
I Feel Fine; She's A Woman; Eight Days A Week; I'm A Loser; No Reply; I Don't Want To Spoil The Party; I'll Follow The Sun; Baby's In Black; Every Little Thing; What You're Doing

HELP! 110
Yes It Is; I'm Down; Help!; The Night Before; You've Got To Hide Your Love Away; I Need You; Another Girl; You're Going To Lose That Girl; Ticket To Ride; Tell Me What You See; You Like Me Too Much; It's Only Love; I've Just Seen A Face; Yesterday

RUBBER SOUL 130
Day Tripper; We Can Work It Out; Drive My Car; Norwegian Wood; You Won't See Me; Nowhere Man; Think For Yourself; The Word; Michelle; What Goes On; Girl; I'm Looking Through You; In My Life; Wait; If I Needed Someone; Run For Your Life

REVOLVER 154
Paperback Writer; Rain; Taxman; Eleanor Rigby; I'm Only Sleeping; Love You To; Here, There and Everywhere; Yellow Submarine; She Said, She Said; Good Day Sunshine; And Your Bird Can Sing; For No One; Doctor Robert; Got To Get You Into My Life; I Want To Tell You; Tomorrow Never Knows

SGT PEPPER'S LONELY HEARTS CLUB BAND 184
Penny Lane; Strawberry Fields Forever; Sgt Pepper's Lonely Hearts Club Band; With A Little Help From My Friends; Lucy In The Sky With Diamonds; Getting Better; Fixing A Hole; She's

Leaving Home; Being For The Benefit of Mr Kite!; Within You Without You; When I'm Sixty-Four; Lovely Rita; Good Morning, Good Morning; A Day In The Life

MAGICAL MYSTERY TOUR / YELLOW SUBMARINE 214
All You Need Is Love; Baby, You're A Rich Man; Hello Goodbye; Only A Northern Song; All Together Now; Hey Bulldog; It's All Too Much; Magical Mystery Tour; The Fool On The Hill; Flying; Blue Jay Way; Your Mother Should Know; I Am the Walrus; Lady Madonna; The Inner Light; Hey Jude

THE BEATLES 240
Back In The USSR; Dear Prudence; Glass Onion; Ob-La-Di Ob-La-Da; Wild Honey Pie; The Continuing Story of Bungalow Bill; While My Guitar Gently Weeps; Happiness Is A Warm Gun; Martha My Dear; I'm So Tired; Blackbird; Piggies; Rocky Raccoon; Don't Pass Me By; Why Don't We Do It In The Road?; I Will; Julia; Birthday; Yer Blues; Mother Nature's Son; Everybody's Got Something To Hide Except Me And My Monkey; Sexy Sadie; Helter Skelter; Long Long Long; Revolution; Honey Pie; Savoy Truffle; Cry Baby Cry; Revolution 9; Good Night; Don't Let Me Down

LET IT BE 284
Two Of Us; Dig A Pony; Across The Universe; I Me Mine; Dig It; Let It Be; I've Got A Feeling; One After 909; For You Blue; The Long And Winding Road; Get Back; The Ballad of John and Yoko; Old Brown Shoe; You Know My Name

ABBEY ROAD 302
Come Together; Something; Maxwell's Silver Hammer; Oh Darling; Octopus's Garden; I Want You; Here Comes The Sun; Because; You Never Give Me Your Money; Sun King; Mean Mr Mustard; Polythene Pam; She Came In Through The Bathroom Window; Golden Slumbers; Her Majesty; Carry That Weight; The End

LIVE AT THE BBC 324
I'll Be On My Way

ANTHOLOGY 1–3 150
Free as a Bird; Real Love; Christmas Time (Is Here Again); In Spite of All the Danger; You'll Be Mine; Cayenne; Cry for a Shadow; Like Dreamers Do; Hello Little Girl; You Know What To Do; If You've Got Trouble; That Means a Lot; 12-Bar Original; Junk; Not Guilty; What's the New Mary Jane; Step Inside Love; Los Paranoias; Teddy Boy; All Things Must Pass; Come and Get It.

CHRONOLOGY 358
DISCOGRAPHY 1962 – 66 364
DISCOGRAPHY 1967 – 70 368
BIBLIOGRAPHY 372
INDEX 374
PICTURE CREDITS 380
COPYRIGHT CREDITS 381
ACKNOWLEDGEMENTS 382

PREFACE

This book tells the stories behind the Beatles' songs, which I've defined as songs written and recorded by the Beatles. It looks at the how, why and where of the songwriting and traces the inspiration back to source.

Having said that, this is not a book about how the Beatles recorded the songs, nor about who played what on which sessions. Mark Lewisohn has done that job definitively in *The Complete Beatles Recording Sessions.* Neither is it a book of in-depth musical analysis. For this approach, see *Twilight Of The Gods* by Professor Wilfrid Mellers (Schirmer Books, 1973) or *The Songwriting Secrets Of The Beatles* by Dominic Pedler (Omnibus Press, 2003).

Also exemplary is *Revolution in the Head* by Ian MacDonald (Fourth Estate, 1994). MacDonald takes the same song-by-song approach that this book takes and his insights and depth of knowledge about popular music of the sixties are unparalleled.

This is also not a book that explains what the Beatles 'were really trying to say'. Although I've given outlines of many songs and have referred to psychological factors that I believe influenced the standpoint of the writing, I've left the task of interpretation to others. If you do want to know what Paul was saying, read a book like *Paul McCartney: From Liverpool To Let It Be* by Howard DeWitt (Horizon Books, 1992) or, if you want to catch the drift of John's intellectual development, read *The Art and Music of John Lennon* by John Robertson (Omnibus, 1990) or *John Lennon's Secret* by David Stuart Ryan (Kozmik Press, 1982).

What I have tried to do is simply to tell the story of how each song came into being. It could have been a musical inspiration, such as trying to write in the style of Smokey Robinson. It could have been a phrase that just wouldn't go away, like the 'waves of sorrow, pools of joy' line that compelled John to write 'Across The Universe'. Or it could have been an incident like the death of socialite Tara Browne which led to the writing of a section of 'A Day In The Life'.

My primary source has been the words of the Beatles themselves. I was fortunate enough to meet John, interviewing him and Yoko at the Apple office in Savile Row in the summer of 1971, shortly before *Imagine* was released. I remember complimenting him on the personal nature of his new songs that had come after an intense period of therapy. "My songs have always been personal," he responded. "'Help!'

was personal. 'You've Got To Hide Your Love Away' was personal. 'I'm A Loser' was personal. I've always been on that kick."

I didn't meet Paul until 1992 when I was asked to help Linda in the writing of the text for her photographic book *Linda McCartney's Sixties: Portrait Of An Era*. I had hoped that Paul would contribute his own memories but he decided that he couldn't just dip into a project like this and yet didn't have the time to make a full commitment. He did, however, point out some discrepancies in the stories I had collected so far which I was then able to change.

The most reliable comments on the songs being those made by the Beatles themselves, I've drawn extensively on the published interviews I have personally collected since beginning my first Beatles' scrapbook in 1963. Those that I had missed, I searched out at the National Newspaper Library and the National Sound Archives in London. There were seven invaluable written accounts which I found myself coming back to repeatedly and without which I wouldn't have known where to start. In order of publication these were: Alan Aldridge's interview with Paul McCartney published as *A Good Guru's Guide To The Beatles' Sinister Songbook* in the *Observer* magazine, London, on November 26, 1967; *The Beatles* by Hunter Davies, 1968; *Lennon: The Greatest Natural Songwriter of our Time* by Mike Hennessey in Record Mirror, October 2, 1971 (reprinted in Hit Parade, April 1972); *Lennon Remembers* by Jann Wenner, 1971; *I Me Mine* by George Harrison, 1980, *The Playboy Interviews* with John Lennon and Yoko Ono, 1981 and *Paul McCartney: Many Years From Now* by Barry Miles (1997). There were also two radio series which shed light on the songwriting: Mike Read's *McCartney On McCartney*, broadcast on BBC Radio 1 during 1989, and *The Lost Lennon Tapes*, an American production featuring demo tapes from John's private collection which Yoko had allowed to be broadcast for the first time.

As informative as all these were, they didn't tell me the whole story. Many of the anecdotes are already well known. I wanted to interview the people who were around when the songs were written, or who had even been the subject of songs. I also wanted to track down the newspaper stories which had provided ideas, the books from which they'd taken lines and the places which had inspired them. I wanted to surprise even the remaining Beatles themselves because I knew that they didn't know who Mr Kite really was or what happened to the girl whose story inspired 'She's Leaving Home'.

The definitive book on this subject won't be written until John's and George's journals, letters and work books are made public and Paul and Ringo sit down in front of a microphone and share everything they remember about the 208 songs which the Beatles recorded. The chances are, though, that John's material will remain locked in vaults for the foreseeable future because much of it refers to people still living and Yoko believes that it is too sensitive to release. The six-part television series *The Beatles Anthology* and the accompanying 'biography' of the Beatles was disappointing to anyone expecting the remaining members of the Beatles to tell hitherto-untold stories.

That's why it was worth compiling this book. It may be the closest we'll ever get to understanding how the Beatles conjured up their songwriting magic.

Steve Turner

London, November 1998 and March 2005

INTRODUCTION

I once worked out that if you added up the number of days that the Beatles existed as recording artists, the midpoint of their career came when John Lennon had to defend himself over his comparison between the group and Jesus. It was a highly symbolic half way post because it marked the beginning of the end of their life as a touring act and their transition from highly polished practitioners of show business into serious artists. It also marked the beginning of their life as spokesmen for a generation.

The songs explored in this book are from throughout their lives together on record; from the period largely characterised by Beatlemania; concert tours; Cuban heel boots; hair on foreheads (but not faces) and songs that were hummable and predominantly about boys who liked girls or girls who liked boys, to their more cerebral and experimental period.

When the Beatles first went into EMI's Abbey Road Studios in 1962, their ambitions were no greater than any other group that had grown up on rock'n'roll. They wanted to produce good, catchy songs that would get them into the pop charts and make them money. Their role model was Elvis. Three years later, when they cut *Rubber Soul*, they'd already topped Elvis and made their fortune. They were now more interested in Ravi Shankar, states of altered consciousness and being appreciated as artists.

John Lennon and Paul McCartney were the first major pop stars to have benefited from an extended education. Before the Beatles, pop music was a career for those who'd failed in academia and fancied their chances at making it on their looks and voices alone. Although John never excelled in exams and aborted his art studies, he had at least been to college. Paul hadn't been to college but he'd been to one of the best grammar schools in Liverpool and had studied for his A-levels.

The difference this made was that, as time went on, they were able to see what they did as musicians and composers as being like what Chaucer, Picasso and Dylan Thomas had done. They could identify with the creative approaches of these artists and the battles

"Here are a few that we made earlier": the Beatles compare and contrast the sleeves to some of their peerless music catalogue.

mono
DISC

they fought to extend the scope of their art forms. In 1963 John made the prescient comment: "This isn't show business. It's something else. This is different from anything that anybody imagines. You don't go on from this. You do this, and then you finish."

The early songs in their catalogue were not lyrically profound although they were invariably musically complex, always adding fresh chord changes and key shifts that they'd learned from an obscure record or an older more experienced musician. They consciously worked within the expectations of the existing pop market and took their cues from already successful songs that they would atomise to discover how they worked. "We were just writing pop songs a la Everly Brothers, a la Buddy Holly," John once explained. "They were pop songs with no more thought to them than…to create a sound. And the words were almost irrelevant."

When they started there was no thought of being confessional or of exploring the world of ideas. There were times when events suggested storylines but the influences were much more likely to come from other songs than from events in their lives. John later admitted that he kept his personal observations and experiments in language for his poems and short stories. Some of these were later published in his two books, *In His Own Write* and *A Spaniard in the Works*. "I was already a stylised songwriter on the first album," he said. "To express myself I would write…personal stories which expressed my personal emotions. I'd have a separate, songwriting John Lennon who wrote songs for the sort of meat market, and I didn't consider the lyrics to have any depth at all. They were just a joke."

When the Beatles dressed in black leather and played in cellar clubs their sets were dominated by songs recorded by Elvis, Buddy Holly, Gene Vincent, Little Richard and the Everly Brothers. Later they developed an interest in American girl groups such as the Shirelles and the Chiffons and the new Motown sound of the Miracles and Marvin Gaye. The songwriting team they admired the most was Gerry Goffin and Carole King, the authors of hits like 'Will You Still Love Me Tomorrow,' 'Chains,' 'One Fine Day,' 'Take Good Care Of My Baby,' and 'Please Don't Ever Change.'

"First of all, Paul and I wanted to be the Goffin and King of England," said John, and in their early compositions it's possible to

The band pictured at EMI's headquarters at Manchester Square, London, with a host of silver discs. Even by 1963, the band were setting sales records.

see the hallmarks of the Brill Building school of songwriting where hits were written to order during a normal eight-hour day. Like Goffin and King, John and Paul began to write for other artists, offering 'World Without Love,' 'Nobody I Know' and 'I Don't Want To See You Again' to Peter and Gordon, 'Bad To Me' and 'Do You Want To Know A Secret' to Billy J. Kramer and the Dakotas.

Artists clamoured to cover Lennon/McCartney songs. As soon as demo discs were sent to publisher Dick James they were passed on to relevant artists. By 1965 almost every song on a Beatles' album would end up being covered by someone, some of them, like 'Michelle' by the Overlanders, becoming hits in their own right.

The first stage in their songwriting extended from their early work as teenagers who would meet regularly at Paul's family home and scribble lyrics in Liverpool Institute exercise books through the rise of Beatlemania.

By 1964, things were already beginning to change. As they travelled more widely and began mixing with the elite of the young London arts world, their horizons began to extend. Hearing Bob Dylan's early albums showed them the potential within pop and rock to deal with a wider range of emotions and to be more daring with language. It led John to write such soul-baring songs as 'I'm a Loser,' and 'Help.' Dylan showed him how it was possible to carry the spirit of his poetry and creative writing into song.

Paul was affected in different ways. Through his actress girlfriend Jane Asher and her family he was introduced to classical musicians, psychologists, actors, theatre directors, poets and members of London's fledgling 'underground' scene. He visited art galleries, made home movies, experimented with electronic music, went to the theatre and attended lectures. The exposure to a broader range of ideas and art forms was evidenced in the new maturity of songs like 'And I Love Her,' 'We Can Work It Out' and 'Yesterday.'

What made the Beatles' development so exciting during this period was their refusal to be restricted by the limitations routinely accepted by pop musicians. They introduced new instruments (Hammond organ and African drum on *Beatles For Sale*, electric piano, flutes and string quartet on *Help!*, sitar and fuzz bass on *Rubber Soul*), tackled new subjects and incorporated happy accidents into their music.

The mid-Sixties saw a quantum leap in both the musical ideas and lyrical scope of the Beatles' music as they matured as artists.

The band exceeded the normal recording levels, defied the received wisdom on album covers (rarely a smile and not even their name on the front of *Rubber Soul*) and expected producer George Martin to realise their wildest conceptions.

On each album they extended the boundaries of pop, creating the foundation for all pop that has followed. They were blessed with boundless optimism. If they could conceive something in their minds they saw no reason why it couldn't be actualised. It's no accident that the lyric most closely associated with them in these years was 'Yeah! Yeah! Yeah!' For the Beatles, everything seemed attainable.

They began, tentatively at first, to write songs that weren't about love. Although 'In My Life' featured the word love it was really about intimations of mortality. 'Help' was a cry of desolation. 'Nowhere Man' ruminated on the meaning of life. 'The Word,' on *Rubber Soul*, was the group's first 'message song.' They'd reached the point where they were being looked to for guidance and they responded appropriately.

"This is who we are now," said Paul shortly after the album's release. "People have always wanted us to stay the same, but we can't stay in a rut. No one else expects to hit a peak at 23 and never develop, so why should we? *Rubber Soul*, for me, is the beginning of my adult life."

The three year journey from *Please Please Me* to *Rubber Soul* was the most extraordinary in 20th century pop and we're still coming to terms with the legacy. The northern entertainers who many thought would go the way of Tommy Steele and the Hula Hoop instead became one of the most powerful creative forces in modern music. Faddish songs seem hollow once the fad has died out but the pleasure produced by a Beatles song never seems to diminish.

The second half of the Beatles' career saw them pushing the popular song form as far as they could then imagine it going. I can still remember my surprise on first hearing 'Paperback Writer' because the words of the title were so unlike anything I'd heard in a chart song before. Pop songs were about girls and cars and dancing, not about paperback books or prospective authors.

From 1966 onwards the Beatles didn't seem to consider any subject as inappropriate. At least half the songs on *Revolver* were nothing to do with love and their primary inspiration was no longer the work of other artists. They grabbed song ideas from overheard conversations, anecdotes, newspaper headlines, esoteric books, posters, dreams, TV commercials, paintings and everyday occurrences. They were equally voracious musically, listening to Asian music, avant-garde jazz, musique concrete and experimenting with the possibilities of tampering with magnetic tape.

Revolver, Sgt. Pepper's Lonely Hearts Club Band and the soundtracks for *Magical Mystery Tour* and *Yellow Submarine* all developed from the pursuit of altered states of consciousness. *The Beatles* (*The White Album*), although mostly written during a meditation course in India, marked a return to basics – comic book stories, guttural blues, folk style guitar – and a break with their recent psychedelic past. *Let It Be*, another film soundtrack, was an attempted return to the music that had first inspired them. *Abbey Road* reprised their good points while showing that they were still capable of surprise.

This period of their career saw George Harrison emerging as a composer and John playing less of a central role in the Beatles as Yoko Ono loomed larger in his life. In 1964 and 1965 John had been

From 1966 onwards, the Beatles devoutly pursued altered states of consciousness.

a major contributor to the group's hit singles. After *Sgt. Pepper,* Paul came to dominate. 'Hello Goodbye,' 'Magical Mystery Tour,' 'Lady Madonna,' 'Hey Jude', 'Get Back' and 'Let It Be' were all written by Paul. The partnership that produced 'She Loves You' and 'I Want To Hold Your Hand' was over.

Almost forty years after the band stopped playing together, their songs still mean a lot to us. For those of us who grew up with them they are like old friends that we never tire of meeting. Because they brightened up our lives and perhaps even helped in awakening our intellectual and spiritual curiosity our feelings towards them are forever warm. Finding out where they came from helps us find out where we came from.

Overleaf: They may have matured into the most ferocious creative minds in popular music but the Beatles began life as happy-go-lucky, chirpy Northern lads.

PLEASE PLEASE ME

One of the great strengths of the Beatles was that by 1962, the year they cut their first record, they were already seasoned performers, well-versed in American soul, gospel, rhythm and blues and rock'n'roll. Most of what they knew had been learned the hard way. They knew how songs were constructed because, unable to afford sheet music, they had to decipher lyrics and work out chord changes by listening to records over and over again. Having played rock'n'roll to adoring teenagers at the lunch-time Cavern Club sessions in Liverpool, as well as to inebriated German businessmen in Hamburg, they also knew how to excite, calm and seduce an audience.

John and Paul had been together for five years; George had been with them for almost as long. Ringo was a recent member, having replaced Pete Best on drums, but they'd known him since 1959 and his previous position with Rory Storm and the Hurricanes meant that he had played the same venues as they had.

At this time, the Beatles' material was standard beat group fare – the best-known songs by the best-known rock'n'roll artists. Top of their list was Elvis Presley. They covered almost 30 of the songs he'd recorded, as well as numbers by Chuck Berry, Buddy Holly, Carl Perkins, Gene Vincent, Fats Domino, Jerry Lee Lewis, Larry Williams, Ray Charles, the Coasters, Arthur Alexander, Little Richard and the Everly Brothers. Studying the music of these artists taught John and Paul the basics of songwriting.

When they came together at Paul's house to write their own material, it was a case of reassembling the familiar chords and words to make something distinctively theirs. This is how a bass riff from a Chuck Berry number came to be incorporated into 'I Saw Her

Please Please Me hit Number 1 in Britain but failed to chart in the US, where it was went under the name *Introducing The Beatles*.

Standing There', a song about seeing a girl at the Tower Ballroom in New Brighton, and explains how the sound of Roy Orbison's voice came to be the inspiration behind 'Please Please Me', the Beatles' first Number 1 single.

Sometimes their songs were 'about' incidents from their lives but often the words, like the chords, were borrowed from what had gone before. At this stage, the words were important to create sounds and impressions, rather than to convey a message.

Most of their debut album was recorded in a single session on February 11, 1963. It was released on March 22, 1963, and reached the top spot in the British charts. In America it was titled *Introducing The Beatles* and released on the little-known Vee Jay label. The US version didn't include 'Please Please Me' or 'Ask Me Why' and failed to make the charts.

I SAW HER STANDING THERE

Producer George Martin's original idea had been to tape a Beatles' show at the Cavern Club in Liverpool but it was later decided to get the group to play their live show in the studio and cut the album in a day. This was done on February 11, 1963, when in a 15-hour session the Beatles recorded ten new tracks to which were added both sides of their first two singles.

'I Saw Her Standing There' was the perfect song with which to open the Beatles' first album because it set the group firmly in the context of sweaty ballrooms, full of dancing teenage girls. They decided to keep the 1-2-3-4 'intro' as this added to the impression of a raw Liverpool beat group captured in live performance.

Originally titled 'Seventeen', the song tells the simple story of a boy who sees a girl dancing at the local ballroom and, after deciding that her looks are 'way beyond compare', determines never to dance with anyone else again. As the story unfolds there is a wonderful

I SAW HER STANDING THERE

Written:	Lennon/McCartney
Length:	2' 55"
UK release:	*Please Please Me* album, March 22, 1963
US release:	*Introducing The Beatles* album, July 22, 1963
US single release:	December 26, 1963, as B-side of 'I Want To Hold Your Hand'

'I Saw Her Standing There' set the Beatles firmly in the world of sweaty ballrooms and dancing teenage girls. It was a classic, almost ideal debut single.

mixture of youthful arrogance and insecurity portrayed. There is no hint that the narrator has considered the possibility of rejection and yet, in that unforgettable beat group rhyme, we're told that as he 'crossed the room' his heart 'went boom'.

Paul started composing this song one night in September 1962 while driving back to his home in Allerton, Liverpool. He liked the idea of writing about a 17-year-old girl because he was conscious of the need to have songs which the group's largely female audience could easily relate to. "I didn't think a lot about it as I sang it to myself," he said four years later. "Originally the first two lines were 'She was just seventeen, Never been a beauty queen'. It sounded like a good rhyme to me at the time. But when I played it through to John the next day, I realized that it was a useless line and so did John. So we both sat down and tried to come up with another line which rhymed with 17 but which meant something."

After a while, John came up with 'you know what I mean', which, as Paul recognized, could either be dismissed as a filler or accepted as sexual innuendo, 16 being the legal age of sexual consent. It was also a very Liverpudlian phrase that neatly avoided the borrowed Americanisms which littered most English rock'n'roll of the time.

Mike McCartney photographed his brother and John sitting by the fireplace in Forthlin Road working on this song. Paul was sitting in front of a small black and white television and John was beside him wearing his horn-rimmed spectacles. They were both playing acoustic guitars and a Liverpool Institute exercise book was open in front of them on the floor with the crossings out in the song clearly visible.

Paul later explained in an interview with *Beat Instrumental* that the bass riff was stolen from Chuck Berry's 1961 song 'I'm Talking About You'. "I played exactly the same notes as he did and it fitted

our number perfectly," he confessed. "Even now, when I tell people about it, I find few of them believe me. Therefore, I maintain that a bass riff doesn't have to be original."

In December 1961, Paul had started dating Iris Caldwell, sister of the local beat singer Rory Storm, whose group the Hurricanes featured Ringo Starr as drummer (he joined the Beatles in August 1962). Just like the girl in 'I Saw Her Standing There', Iris was only 17 at the time when Paul saw her dancing the twist at the Tower Ballroom in New Brighton (situated 25 minutes out of Liverpool). She was a trained dancer and Paul was apparently impressed with her legs, which were displayed in fishnet stockings, and the fact that she was already working professionally in show business.

Paul became a frequent guest at the Caldwell family home at 54 Broad Green Road, Liverpool 15, which was known to the local beat groups as Hurricaneville. He became close to Iris' mother, Violet, and would often drop in with John to sit around and write songs. "Paul and I dated for a couple of years," says Iris. "It was never that serious. We never pretended to be true to each other. I went out with lots of people. I was working away in different theatres at the time but if I was back home then we would go out. There were never any promises made or love declared."

According to Iris, Paul intended giving 'I Saw Her Standing There' to her brother Rory to record. "He thought it would be a good song for him but it wasn't dealt out that way. Brian Epstein didn't want Rory to have it."

By late 1962, 'I Saw Her Standing There' was part of the Beatles' stage act, one of the earliest Lennon and McCartney songs slipped between those of Buddy Holly and Little Richard. During the recording at Abbey Road in February 1963 the song was new enough for Paul to sometimes forget the sequence of the verse endings 'How could I dance?', 'She wouldn't dance' and 'I'll never dance'.

'I Saw Her Standing There' was one the very first original compositions that the Beatles slipped into their sets alongside rock'n'roll covers

The first cover version of the song was by the English rock'n'roll singer Duffy Power in 1963. In America, it became the flip side of 'I Want To Hold Your Hand', the single released in January 1964 that was the Beatles' first US Number 1. It was one of five songs which the Beatles performed on the celebrated *Ed Sullivan Show* of February 9, 1964, which was watched by 70 million people, then the largest US TV audience ever recorded. In November 1974, John performed the song with Elton John at Madison Square Garden.

MISERY

By January 1963, with 'Love Me Do' a British Top 20 hit under their belt, the songwriting confidence of the McCartney/Lennon team (as they were initially credited) had grown, but when plans were made to record their first LP, they were suddenly under pressure to come up with some new songs .

Although not all the songs were going to be their own compositions – they had chosen material by American songwriters to fill almost half the album – they were determined to stamp their own mark on the recording and not become yet another British act making a living out of cover versions. In the climate of the times, this was a bold move. Traditionally, British rock'n'roll acts didn't record their own songs but, aping the US sound, covered promising American singles before they were released in the UK. Cliff Richard, Britain's top home-grown pop star when the Beatles signed to EMI , had broken the mould slightly by recording songs written by Ian Samwell, a former member of his backing group, but no one in the UK had succeeded in producing genuinely British-sounding rock'n'roll.

It was against this background that Paul and John began to pull together the five new unreleased songs for their debut album *Please Please Me*. Backstage at the King's Hall, Glebe Street, Stoke-on-Trent, where they were playing a concert on January 26, 1963, they huddled together and wrote 'Misery', with John as the major contributor. Just as Paul had shown unbounded confidence that he would get to dance with the girl in 'I Saw Her Standing There', John kicked off his career as an album artist by complaining about a girl who had left him and made him lonely. 'The world is treating me bad' was the song's portentous first line. "Allan Clarke and Graham Nash of the

Hollies helped on that song," remembers Tony Bramwell, then an employee of Brian Epstein. "John and Paul were desperate to get it finished and got stuck on one of the lines and Allan and Graham began throwing in suggestions. The boys wanted to get it ready for Helen Shapiro."

Allan Clarke can remember the day well but not the lines or words that he helped throw in. "It was just four guys together sitting in a room," he says. "John and Paul were plunking along writing this song and we helped with a couple of words. Everyone thought that the Hollies and the Beatles were in competition with each other but we weren't really."

Within days they had made a tape and sent it to Norrie Paramor of EMI's Columbia label for him to consider for Shapiro, who they

The Beatles took the brave decision to record a debut album composed largely of self-penned material.

MISERY

Written:	Lennon/McCartney
Length:	1' 50"
UK release:	*Please Please Me* album, March 22, 1963
US single release:	*Introducing The Beatles* album, July 22, 1963

knew would shortly be recording in Nashville. Indeed, Paul told Alan Smith, the editor of *New Musical Express*, that it was a song written to be covered: "We've called it 'Misery' but it isn't quite as slow as it sounds. It moves along at quite a steady pace and we think Helen Shapiro will make quite a good job of it."

Just 16 at the time, Helen had been having Top 10 hits in Britain since early 1961 and the Beatles were due to debut on the cinema circuit as one of seven support acts on her 14-date February tour. It would only be in the final shows, with 'Please Please Me' a Top 10 sensation, that the Beatles were upgraded, although even then they only got to close the first half. Package tours still formed part of the British entertainment scene at the time, despite being a hangover from the days of variety shows where singers followed jugglers and magicians on to the stage. For this tour, the Beatles had time to deliver four songs and were sandwiched between comedy turns.

"I got on great with them," remembers Helen, "and John was like a brother to me. Very protective. He and Paul certainly offered 'Misery' to me first, through Norrie, but I didn't know anything about it until I met them on the first day of the tour (February 2, Bradford, Yorks). Apparently he'd turned it down even though I hadn't heard it." The offer was taken up by another artist on the same tour, Kenny Lynch, a black singer from Britain, whose biggest success to date had been a Top 10 hit with a cover of the Drifters' 'Up On The Roof'. 'Misery' wasn't a hit for him but it gave him the distinction of being the first non-Beatle to record a Lennon and McCartney song.

The 'la-la-la-la-la' outro appeared to allude to Pat Boone's 'Speedy Gonzales', a single that had entered the British charts in July 1962 and didn't leave until October.

ASK ME WHY

ASK ME WHY
Written: Lennon/McCartney
Length: 2' 27"
UK single release: January 11, 1963 as B-side of 'Please Please Me'
US single release: February 25, 1963 as B-side of 'Please Please Me'

Written in the spring of 1962, with John as the major contributor, 'Ask Me Why' was a lightweight love song from the Beatles' set at the Cavern Club that year, and was premiered on the BBC radio programme *Teenagers' Turn* on June 11, 1962. It was one of four songs which they took to their first recording session on June 6, 1962, at EMI Studios in Abbey Road, north London, but George Martin didn't think it was strong enough to be their debut single. Re-recorded in February 1963, it was released in Britain as the B side of 'Please Please Me'.

'Ask Me Why' was in the running to be the Beatles' debut single but eventually appeared as the B-side of 'Please Please Me'.

PLEASE PLEASE ME

'Please Please Me' was one of those innocent-sounding pop songs with a subversive subtext. Some critics have seen it as a plea for equality in sexual pleasure. Robert Christgau, music editor of New York's *Village Voice*, has more controversially claimed that it's about oral sex. Under pressure in 1967 over alleged drug references in their work Paul commented: "If they had wanted to they could have found plenty of double meanings in our early work. How about 'I'll Keep You Satisfied' or 'Please Please Me'? Everything has a double meaning if you look for it long enough."

Iris Caldwell remembers Paul coming over to her house one night and reading her the words to the just-completed song. "He used to pick up my brother's guitar and play it but that night he didn't bother," she says. "He just read out the lyrics. They didn't seem to make any sense to me at the time and I thought they were absolutely awful." The song's origins were certainly innocuous, the chorus having been suggested by the 1932 Bing Crosby song 'Please', written by Leo Robin and Ralph Rainger, which starts off by playing with the homophones 'pleas' and 'please': 'Oh please, lend your little ear to my pleas, Lend a ray of cheer to my pleas, Tell me that you love me too'. Later, John recalled that his mother, Julia, sang this to him as a child, adding that he'd always been fascinated by the dual use of the 'please' sound.

When John came to write this song, in his front bedroom at 251 Menlove Avenue in Liverpool ("I remember the day and the pink eyelet on the bed"), he imagined Roy Orbison singing it because he'd just been listening to the hit single 'Only The Lonely'. It's easy to imagine Orbison singing the original slow version of 'Please Please

Although some critics claimed that 'Please Please Me' was a song about oral sex, it was originally inspired by a 1932 number sung by Bing Crosby.

Me'. With his pallid, dough-like features and permanent shades, Orbison might have looked an unlikely pop star, but he was a brilliantly soulful singer and wrote his own songs. He was someone whom John in particular could relate to because his lyrics explored dark moods of loss and loneliness – and he wore glasses.

Within months of 'Please Please Me' being released as a single and reaching the Number 2 spot in the British charts, the Beatles were picked to support Orbison on a three-week tour of Britain. "We never talked to each other about songwriting on that tour," remembered Orbison years later. "The basic thing they wanted to know at that time was how I thought they would get on in America. I told them to let people know they were British and to get on something like the Ed Sullivan Show. If they did that, I said they could be just as big in America as they were in Britain. I said that in an article for *New Musical Express* which came out during the tour. I thought it was important that they let people know they were British because we hadn't heard much from Britain except for the Blue Streak missile and the Profumo scandal."

His exact words, recorded in May 1963, were: "The Beatles could well be tops in America. These boys have enough originality to storm our charts with the same effect as they have done here, but it will need careful handling. They have something that is entirely new even to us Americans and although we have an influx of hit groups at home I really do believe they could top the charts...It's a change to see new stars who are not just watered-down versions of Elvis Presley. This seems to be a sound they have made famous all on their own and I really think it is the greatest. Though you know it as

PLEASE PLEASE ME

Written:	Lennon/McCartney
Length:	2' 03"
UK single release:	January 11, 1963
UK chart position:	2
US single release:	February 25, 1963
US chart position:	3

Merseyside music, I am sure this will be hailed as the new British sound in America."

Orbison didn't discover that John had written 'Please Please Me' in emulation of his style until producer George Martin mentioned it to him in June 1987 at an Abbey Road celebration for the 20th anniversary of *Sgt Pepper's Lonely Hearts Club Band*. "He told me that it sounded so much like me that they had to change it a little bit," Orbison commented. "That's a nice thing to find out."

In March 1963 John had revealed that they had intended 'Please Please Me' as a B side for their first single until Martin complained about this similarity. "He thought that the arrangement was fussy, so we tried to make it simpler," said John. "In the weeks following (the 'Love Me Do' session), we went over it again and again. We changed the tempo a little. We altered the words slightly and we went over the idea of featuring the harmonica, just as we'd done in 'Love Me Do'. By the time we came to record it, we were so happy with it that we couldn't wait to get it down."

The Beatles' fondness for Orbison was to survive the Sixties. John described the sound of his last single, 'Starting Over', as 'Elvis Orbison' and in 1988 George Harrison joined Orbison, Bob Dylan, Tom Petty and Jeff Lynne in recording the critically-acclaimed *Traveling Wilburys* album.

The Beatles toured the UK in 1963 as support to Roy Orbison, whose music was influential on them throughout their entire career.

LOVE ME DO

In Britain, 'Love Me Do' was the Beatles' first hit and, like the group's image, it was all pretty strange to a generation which had spent the last two or three years listening to insipid pop performed by men with short haircuts and big grins.

An early song written by Paul, the lyrics of 'Love Me Do' were as basic as could be, with most words consisting of only one syllable and 'love' being repeated 21 times. 'I love you forever so please love me in return' was the song's entire lyrical statement. What set it apart from the teen love songs of the time was a gospel-blues tinge to the singing – a feeling that was heightened by John's harmonica and the slightly mournful close harmonizing. (John's fondness for gospel was confirmed when he listed R&B and gospel as his 'tastes in music' in the *New Musical Express* of February 15, 1963.)

During 1962, the American star Bruce Channel had enjoyed a British hit with 'Hey Baby' which featured a harmonica solo by

LOVE ME DO

Written:	Lennon/McCartney
Length:	2' 22"
UK single release:	October 5, 1962
UK chart position:	4
US single release:	April 27, 1964
US chart position:	1

Nashville session musician Delbert McClinton. John was impressed by this and, when he met McClinton in June 1962 at the Tower Ballroom, New Brighton, where the Beatles were playing support for Channel, he asked him how he played it.

"John was very interested in harmonica and, when we went on to play another couple of dates with the Beatles, he and I hung out a lot together," says McClinton. "He wanted me to show him whatever I could. He wanted to know how to play. Before our time together was over he had his own harmonica ready in his pocket." It was only three months later that the Beatles recorded 'Love Me Do', in which John was able to include a distinctive harmonica break.

John went on to play harmonica on the next two singles, 'Please Please Me' and 'With Love From Me To You', as well as on six other tracks including 'Little Child' (*With The Beatles*) and 'I Should Have Known Better' (*A Hard Day's Night*). The last time he used it on record was on 'I'm A Loser' (*Beatles For Sale*) recorded in August 1964. By that time he reckoned it had turned into a Beatles' gimmick.

'Love Me Do' was included on the group's first four-track extended play record which had sleeve notes written by Tony Barrow, a Lancashire journalist who was then working as the Beatles' press officer. Barrow's comments on the four tracks ('From Me To You', 'Thank You Girl', 'Please Please Me' and 'Love Me Do') were remarkably prescient.

"The four numbers on this EP have been selected from *The Lennon and McCartney Songbook*," he wrote. "If that description sounds a trifle pompous perhaps I may suggest you preserve this sleeve for ten years, exhume it from your collection somewhere around the middle of 1973 and write me a very nasty letter if the pop people of the Seventies aren't talking about at least two of these titles as 'early examples of modern beat standards taken from *The Lennon and McCartney Songbook*'."

In 1967, when every Beatle song was believed to be drenched in meaning and they had been elevated into 'spokesmen for a generation', Paul commented to Alan Aldridge in an interview for The *Observer* "'Love Me Do' was our greatest philosophical song... for it to be simple, and true, means that it's incredibly simple."

Even as late as 1967, when they were seen as spiritual gurus to a generation, Paul was calling 'Love Me Do' the Beatles' "greatest philosophical song".

PS I LOVE YOU

Written in 1961, 'PS I Love You' was another early song by Paul which the Beatles considered recording as their first single. In Britain, it became the B-side of 'Love Me Do'. In America, almost two years later, it became a single in its own right and made the Top 10.

It had become fairly routine for British beat groups of the time to play stints in German night clubs, where there was a great demand for the new American-style music but few musicians around who could actually play it. In April 1961, the Beatles – John, Paul, George, Pete Best (drums) and Stuart Sutcliffe (bass) – started a gruelling 13-week residency at the Top Ten Club in Hamburg, Germany, playing for over five hours each night, seven days a week. It was the best apprenticeship they could have had. The continuous playing of other artists' songs taught them how songs were constructed and the pressure to entertain taught them what worked and what didn't.

Paul's girlfriend at the time was Dorothy 'Dot' Rhone, an elfin Liverpool teenager who worked for a chemist and lived at home with her parents. She was a shy but sweet girl whom Paul had been dating for a while and who had become a regular guest at his family home in Liverpool. "She was very much in love with Paul," remembered her friend Sandra Hedges. "He in turn would jealously guard her by placing her amid the group while they were playing." Dot became close to Cynthia Powell, John's girlfriend from art school, and during the Easter holidays the two girls decided to visit their boyfriends in Germany, Cynthia staying with Astrid Kirchner, Stuart Sutcliffe's girlfriend, and Dot staying with Paul on a houseboat.

After Dot had returned to Liverpool, Paul wrote this song which she assumed was for her although, years later, Paul denied that he

PS I LOVE YOU
Written: Lennon/McCartney
Length: 2' 05"
UK single release: October 5, 1962 as B-side of 'Love Me Do'
US single release: April 27, 1964 as B-side of 'Love Me Do'

George and the rest of the Beatles, whose line-up still included Pete Best and Stuart Sutcliffe, played a tough 13-week residency in Hamburg in 1961.

had anyone specific in mind. Written in the form of a letter, 'PS I Love You' was the precursor of Paul's other letter songs, 'Paperback Writer' and 'When I'm 64'. Paul's relationship with Dot was picked up after returning from Hamburg but ended in the summer of 1962 just as the Beatles began recording. At the time, she was sharing a flat with John's girlfriend Cynthia Powell at 93 Garmoyle Road, Liverpool, close to Penny Lane.

Paul came round late one night and broke the news to Dot. Cynthia remembered her collapsing in tears. "Poor little defenceless Dot," she wrote in her book *A Twist Of Lennon*. "She wouldn't hurt a fly but had been hurt so much that she couldn't even tell me without renewed convulsions and outbursts of uncontrollable crying. As it happens, she didn't need to tell me anything. Only one thing would have done that to Dot and that was Paul giving her the push...he was too young to settle down. He wanted desperately to be footloose and fancy free and I suppose he let Dot down very gently under the circumstances."

DO YOU WANT TO KNOW A SECRET?

Around the same time that Paul finished with Dot Rhone, Cynthia discovered that she was pregnant. On August 23, 1962, she and John did the conventional thing by getting married at a registry office in Mount Pleasant, Liverpool. The best man at this small affair attended by Paul, George, and a handful of relations was manager Brian Epstein, who offered the newlyweds the privacy of a ground floor flat he rented at 36 Faulkner Street to start their married life. This

'Do You Want To Know A Secret?' was based on a song that John's mother had picked up from Disney's 1937 film *Snow White and the Seven Dwarves*.

DO YOU WANT TO KNOW A SECRET?
Written: Lennon/McCartney
Length: 1' 59"
UK single release: *Please Please Me* album, March 22, 1963
US single release: *Introducing The Beatles* album, July 22, 1963

wasn't Epstein's main home but a place in the city centre that he kept for his own discreet homosexual liaisons.

Cynthia remembered being ecstatic at the unexpected wedding gift as they hadn't given much thought to where they would live and there was no time in the busy Beatles' schedule for a honeymoon. "It was the first apartment I'd ever had that wasn't shared by 14 other art students," John later admitted.

It was while living here that John wrote 'Do You Want To Know A Secret?', the secret in question being that he had just realized that he was really in love. As with 'Please Please Me', it had its genesis in a song his mother used to sing to him, which she in turn had picked up from Walt Disney's 1937 film *Snow White And The Seven Dwarfs*. In one of the opening scenes in the film, Snow White is working as a kitchen maid and, as she stands by the castle well, she begins to sing to the doves: 'Wanna know a secret?, Promise not to tell?, We are standing by a wishing well' ('I'm Wishing', words and music by Larry Morey and Frank Churchill).

In an interview with *Musician* magazine, George Harrison was later to reveal that the musical inspiration for the song came from 'I Really Love You', a 1961 hit for the Stereos.

John made a demo of 'Do You Want To Know A Secret' on an acoustic guitar while sitting in a bathroom (a fact that became obvious because of the flush of a toilet at the end of the song). This was offered to another Epstein artist, Billy J Kramer, who took it with him to Germany as part of his stage act. Kramer's real name was Billy Ashton and he was Epstein's third signing following on closely from Gerry and the Pacemakers. Epstein then acquired the Big Three, the Fourmost, Tommy Quickly and Cilla Black, all of them Liverpool acts.

Kramer came back from Germany convinced that 'Do You Want To Know A Secret?' wasn't a crowd pleaser but EMI liked it enough to offer him a recording contract after hearing a test tape of it. It went on to become a Number 2 hit for him in Britain during the summer of 1963, the first time a Lennon and McCartney song by another artist had made the Hit Parade.

Although John had written it with his own voice in mind, when the Beatles recorded it, the song was offered to George. "I thought it would be a good vehicle for him," John said, "because it only had three notes and he wasn't the best singer in the world."

THERE'S A PLACE

Just as 'Misery' indicated the feelings of isolation and rejection which would become a major preoccupation in John's songs, so 'There's A Place' introduced what was to become a recurring theme of finding comfort in his thoughts, dreams and memories. In 'There's A Place', John deals with his life's sorrow by retreating into the safety of his inner thoughts and, in a more sophisticated way, this is what he would do in later songs such as 'Strawberry Fields Forever', 'Girl', 'In My Life', 'Rain', 'I'm Only Sleeping' and many others. "The usual Lennon thing," he said of 'There's A Place'. "It's all in your mind."

"He was a combination of introversion and extroversion," says Thelma McGough who as Thelma Pickles dated John while they were both at Liverpool School of Art. "He appeared very extrovert and yet it was all front. He was actually very deep but he'd keep that pretty well hidden until you were on your own with him."

Although John spoke as though the song was entirely his, Paul has since claimed that the original idea for it came from him, the title being derived from the *West Side Story* song 'There's A Place For Us' (1957) which he had in his Forthlin Road record collection.

Musically, John admitted that 'There's A Place' was his attempt at "a sort of Motown, black thing", referring to what was then a hot new sound emerging from Detroit on Berry Gordy's fledgling independent record label. Motown hits were mostly written by production line writers and performed by groups trained in the label's own school – it was dance music driven by inventive bass lines, gospel-style splashes of tambourine and vocal harmonies. Among the Beatles' favourite acts were Barrett Strong, the Miracles (featuring Smokey Robinson), the Marvelettes, Marvin Gaye and 'Little' Stevie Wonder.

In fact the Beatles were to play a crucial role in popularizing the Motown label, initially by recording Motown songs such as 'Please Mr Postman', 'You've Really Got A Hold On Me' and 'Money' and later by dropping the names of new Motown artists and records in interviews. Explaining the success of his label to *Record World* in 1964 Berry Gordy said: "It helped when we had several songs of ours recorded by the Beatles. I met them and found out that they were great fans of Motown and had been studying Motown music, and they went on to become some of the greatest songwriters in history. We were absolutely delighted."

THERE'S A PLACE

Written:	Lennon/McCartney
Length:	1' 52"
UK release:	*Please Please Me* album, March 22, 1963
US release:	*Introducing The Beatles* album, July 22, 1963

The Beatles' early image could be comedic but 'There's A Place' had a depth that belied their slapstick antics.

WITH THE BEATLES

The Beatles had five years to prepare for their first album and five months to prepare for their second. After years of meeting up at Paul's house, with hours of spare time on their hands, they were now forced to write in hotel bedrooms, on tour buses and in dressing rooms – anywhere they could snatch a quiet moment.

Such pressures cause some songwriters to dry up, but it proved to be a positive stimulus to John and Paul who, as time went on, developed the ability to write Number 1 hits to order.

John and Paul seemed to have an innate sense of what their public wanted to hear. Believing that it was important for each girl in the audience to feel that they were singing personally to her, many of their songs had the word 'you' in the title – for example, 'From Me To You', 'Thank You Girl', and 'I'll Get You'.

However, if in the early days they'd been able to write for an audience they could see and for people they knew on first-name terms, everything changed once they became successful. Suddenly, the police had to devise ingenious ways of smuggling them in and out of venues, and they were even becoming popular in countries they hadn't visited.

Nonetheless, at the height of Beatlemania, often pursued by scores of screaming fans, they still managed to write a steady stream of successful singles. 'I Want To Hold Your Hand', for example, was written with the American market in mind, and propelled them to the top of the Billboard charts, making them the first British recording artists to truly conquer America. Indeed, constant international travel and the move to London were beneficial for their songwriting as it exposed them to a greater variety of influences. Everybody they met seemed to want to turn them on to something new. Through his relationship with the actress Jane Asher, Paul was becoming more familiar with stage musicals, theatre and classical music. Meanwhile, John was holed up in his Kensington flat listening to imported albums by black American groups like the Miracles, the Shirelles and the Marvelettes.

With The Beatles, their second album, was a much more considered recording than their first, with sessions spread over a three-month period. It went to Number 1 in Britain shortly after its release in November 1963 and became the first pop album to sell over a million copies. A version of *With The Beatles*, titled *Meet The Beatles*, was released in America in January 1964 and also went to Number 1.

For *With The Beatles*, the band managed to maintain a steady stream of hit singles despite the distractions of Beatlemania.

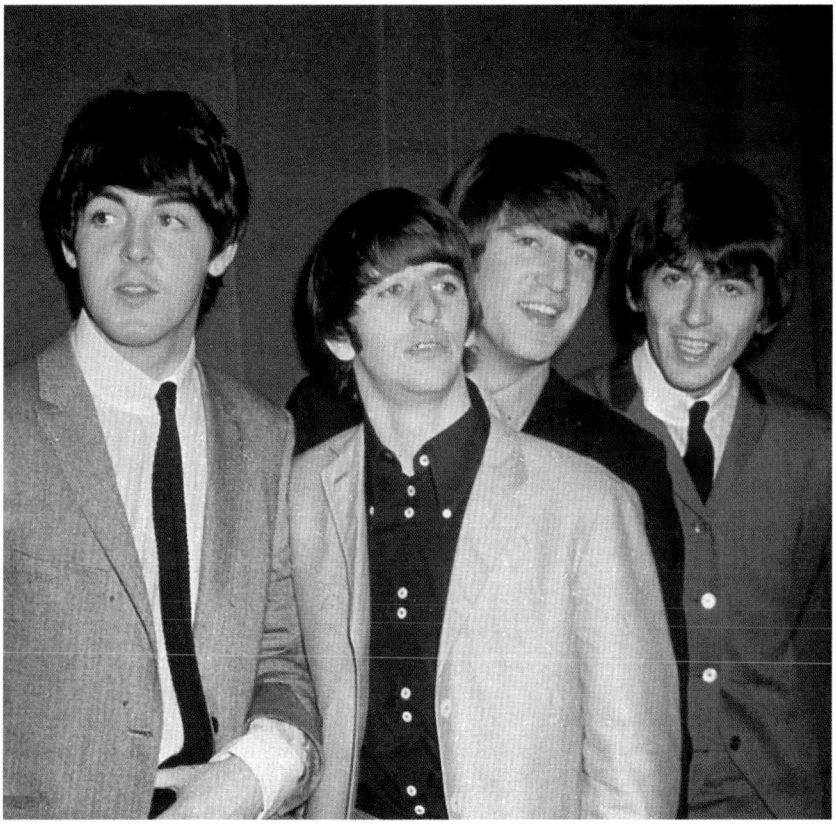

FROM ME TO YOU

'From Me To You', the Beatles' third single, was written on February 28, 1963, while travelling by coach from York to Shrewsbury on the Helen Shapiro tour. Helen can't remember them actually writing it, but can recall it being played to her when they arrived at Shrewsbury in the afternoon ready for their evening concert at the Granada Cinema. "They asked me if I would come and listen to two songs that they had," she says. "Paul sat at the piano and John stood next to me and they sang 'From Me To You' and 'Thank You Girl'. They said they sort of knew their favourite but hadn't finally decided, so they wanted me to tell them which one I thought would make the best A side. As it happened I liked 'From Me To You' and they said, 'Great. That's the one we like.'"

The Beatles played the Odeon Cinema in Southport, Lancashire, the next day, the closest the tour would go to Liverpool, and here they were able to play their new song to Paul's father to get his opinion. They knew the lyrics were simple enough but they were

FROM ME TO YOU

Written:	Lennon/McCartney
Length:	1' 57"
UK single release:	April 11, 1963
UK chart position:	1
US single release:	May 27, 1963
US chart position:	41

worried that the music was "a bit on the complicated side" and that "it wouldn't catch on with the fans". It was Paul's dad who convinced them that it was "a nice little tune".

The title was suggested by From You To Us, the letters' column in the *NME*. Paul and John were reading the issue dated February 22, with their tour dates advertised on the front page. They started to "talk about one of the letters in the column", as John revealed in May 1963, when asked about the origins of the song. There were only two letters and it's hard to see which could have provoked comment. One letter complained about 'maniacal laughter' on two recent limbo dance records and the other relished the fact that Cliff Richard appeared to be getting the better of Elvis Presley in the charts. Perhaps it was this last letter that fired the Beatles' own ambition.

Apparently Paul and John started the song by trading lines, making it one of the few Beatle hits that they built from scratch together.

The band donned costumes and visited London's Astoria in Finsbury Park in 1963 for *The Beatles' Christmas Show.*

By 1963 Beatlemania was in full swing and the band regularly had to be smuggled in and out of venues to avoid being mobbed by fans.

The song's great gimmick was the use of the high-pitched 'ooooh' sound, inspired by the Isley Brothers' 1962 recording of 'Twist And Shout'. When Kenny Lynch heard them singing this on the coach, he said to them, "You can't do that. You sound like a bunch of fairies", and they replied, "It's okay. The kids will like it." In April 1963, John commented: "We were just fooling about on the guitar. This went on for a while. Then we began to get a good melody line and we really started to work at it. Before the journey was over we'd completed the lyric, everything. We were so pleased..."

A year later, again talking about how the song was written, John said: "Paul and I kicked some ideas around and came up with what we what we thought was a suitable melody line. The words weren't really all that difficult – especially as we had decided quite definitely not to do anything that was at all complicated.

"I suppose that is why we often had the words 'you' and 'me' in the titles of our songs. It's the sort of thing that helps the listeners to identify with the lyrics. We think this is very important. The fans like to feel that they are part of something that is being done by the performers."

From writing to recording took five days although, as John remembered, "We nearly didn't record it because we thought it was too bluesy at first, but when we'd finished it and George Martin had scored it with harmonica, it was all right."

In April 1963 'From Me To You' became the Beatles' second British Number 1 hit but, released on the Vee Jay label in America, it didn't even make the Top 40.

THANK YOU GIRL

Although John and Paul claimed in the early days to have written over 100 songs together between the summer of 1957 and the summer of 1962, Paul admits that the number was closer to 20. Now that they were stars, though, they could no longer afford to be slow in production, as almost everything they wrote from this point on would have to have hit potential. Between 1963 and 1965, they released at least three singles a year and two albums, an incredible output for a group who were touring, filming, meeting the press and writing most of their own material.

At the time the Beatles came into the industry, pop music was formulaic and rather stale. The B sides of singles tended to be throwaway songs, often written by the producer under a pseudonym so that he could reap the benefits of mechanical royalties, and albums contained one or two recent hits plus a lot of filler material. The Beatles changed all this. Suddenly, every song counted. Each of their singles had a B side which was arguably as good as the A side and each album was chock-full of potential singles. Only rarely did their singles appear on albums.

'Thank You Girl', originally titled 'Thank You Little Girl', was written as a follow-up to 'Please Please Me', with 'From Me To You' actually composed as its B side. In the end, it was 'From Me To You' that sounded like the most natural single and so they swapped the two around. At the time, John seemed quite proud of the song but, in 1971, he dismissed it as "just a silly song that we knocked off" and, in 1980, as "one of our efforts at writing a single that didn't work". Paul appears to agree, "A bit of a hack song," he has said, "But all good practice."

THANK YOU GIRL
Written: Lennon/McCartney
Length: 2'01"
UK single release: April 11, 1963 as B-side of 'From Me To You'
US single release: May 27, 1963 as B-side of 'From Me To You'

SHE LOVES YOU

Although the Beatles had already taken Britain's Number 1 spot twice in 1963, it was 'She Loves You' which took them to the 'toppermost of the poppermost' as they mockingly used to call it. Its sales outstripped anything they'd done before and it went on to be the country's best-selling single of the decade, entering the Top 20 in August 1963 and staying put until February 1964. (In America, it only became a hit after the success of 'I Want To Hold Your Hand'.)

It wasn't simply a commercial triumph. In just over two minutes, the Beatles distilled the essence of everything that made them fresh and exciting. There was the driving beat, the fine harmonizing, the

As hits like 'She Loves You' took the Beatles to the 'toppermost of the poppermost', media interest grew and wacky photocalls became the norm.

SHE LOVES YOU

Written:	Lennon/McCartney
Length:	2' 21"
UK single release:	August 23, 1963
UK chart position:	1
US single release:	September 16, 1963
US chart position:	1

girlish 'wooo' sounds which had gone down so well on 'From Me To You', as well as the bursting enthusiasm of its pace. And on top of this, the distinctive 'Yeah, yeah, yeah' tag which became a gift to headline writers.

The rapid expansion of Beatlemania from regional to national phenomenon can be put down to the Beatles' appearance on *Sunday Night at The London Palladium*, a television show broadcast live from the heart of London on October 13, 1963. Witnessed by a national TV audience of 15 million, screaming fans mobbed the theatre and many of those who packed the streets outside found themselves on the front page of next day's Fleet Street newspapers.

Not only had the Beatles transformed popular music but they had become a phenomenon of post-war Britain. Suddenly they found their photos plastered all over the national papers, not just *Melody Maker*, *New Musical Express* and *Boyfriend*. The single that just happened to be in the centre of this storm was 'She Loves You'.

The song was written by John and Paul in Newcastle after playing the Majestic Ballroom on June 26, 1963. They had a very rare day off before continuing the tour to Leeds on the 28, and Paul remembered being with John at the Turk's Hotel, sitting on separate beds, playing their acoustic guitars.

Their first three singles had been declarations of love with the word 'me' in the title. This time, it was Paul's idea to switch the point of view by making themselves observers of another relationship and addressing the man. Instead of the familiar 'me' and 'you' it became 'she' and 'you'. Paul got the initial idea from Bobby Rydell's then current British hit 'Forget Him' in which the narrator told a girl to forget about a boy who doesn't appear to truly love her.

At first sight, 'She Loves You' is a song about reconciliation. The writer is offering to patch up a broken relationship by passing on messages ('she told me what to say') and offering counsel ('apologize to her').

However, American rock critic Dave Marsh detected 'darker nuances' in the text. In *The Heart Of Rock And Roll*, he wrote: "What Lennon sings boils down to a warning to his friend: You'd better appreciate this woman's friendship, because if you don't, I will." The song remains ambiguous because whether this is really being said as confidential advice to a friend or through gritted teeth to a rival largely depends on how you interpret the tone of voice.

The 'Yeah, yeah, yeah' chorus proved to be a perfect catch phrase for an optimistic era. If Paul's father had had his way, though, things would have been different. On hearing the song for the first time when John and Paul gave it a polish on a quick visit to Forthlin Road, he suggested that they might revise it to 'Yes, yes, yes' because it was more proper. That would have been the Queen's English maybe but not exactly rock'n'roll.

The Beatles were not the first group to use 'yeah yeah'. It was frequently used as an aside in Fifties skiffle music, as well as by Cliff Richard in 'We Say Yeah' (1962) and Elvis Presley in 'All Shook Up' (1957) and 'Good Luck Charm' (1962).

The sixth chord which ends the song was unusual in pop music, although the Glenn Miller Orchestra had used it often on their recordings in the Forties. "George Martin laughed when we first played it to him like that," said Paul. "He thought we were joking. But it didn't work without it so we kept it in and eventually George was convinced."

'She Loves You' was on the surface a positive song of reconciliation, but some critics found an implicit threat in its lyrical leanings.

I'LL GET YOU

'I'll Get You' was written by John and Paul together at John's house as a follow-up to 'From Me To You', and then became the B side of 'She Loves You', a song they wrote days later but which they felt was better. The lyrics, reflective rather than cheerful, appear to owe more to John than Paul and there's a startling similarity between the opening lines ('Imagine I'm in love with you, It's easy 'cos I know') and the opening lines of his 1971 song 'Imagine' ('Imagine there's no heaven, It's easy if you try'). 'I'll Get You' is one of the earliest songs to formulate John's belief in creative visualization – the idea that by imagining changes we want to see, we can actually bring them about. For Paul, who still regards this as one of his favourite Beatles tracks, the use of the word 'imagine' evoked the beginning of a children's fairy tale and offered an invitation into a fictitious world.

One of the song's musical tricks, the shift from D to A minor to break the word 'pretend', was taken from Joan Baez's version of the traditional song 'All My Trials' on her debut album *Joan Baez* (1960). There, the shift takes place in the first line, underneath the words 'don't you cry'.

The Beatles were rapidly becoming more musically sophisticated and 'I'll Get You' saw them stealing a chord change from Sixties icon Joan Baez.

I'LL GET YOU

Written:	Lennon/McCartney
Length:	2' 04"
UK single release:	August 23, 1963 as B-side of 'She Loves You'
US single release:	September 16, 1963, as B-side of 'She Loves You'

IT WON'T BE LONG

With The Beatles was released in November 1963 as Beatlemania swept Britain. Robert Freeman's black and white cover portraits, where half of each face was in shadow, provided a defining moment in Beatle iconography. Whereas the debut album had been recorded in a day, the sessions for *With The Beatles* were spread over three months, allowing the rawness of a live beat music session to give way to more sophisticated pop production. "That was when we discovered double-tracking," John later commented. "When I

John and Paul's word play on 'be long' and 'belong" on this early track was aped many years later by George when he came to write 'Blue Jay Way'.

discovered it, I double-tracked everything. I wouldn't let him have anything single-tracked from then on. He (George Martin) would say, 'Please. Just this one,' and I would say, 'No'."

'It Won't Be Long' was the album's opening track, started by John as a potential follow-up single to 'She Loves You', but discarded because, as John said, "it never really made it". Composed as a love song, this could be the story of John's early life. Lonely and rejected, he sits at home waiting for the girl who has walked out on him to come back and make him happy. As in so many later songs, he contrasts the carefree life he imagines everyone else is having with his own anguish, believing that once he's reunited with his loved one all his problems will be solved.

Thelma McGough, who started dating John a month after his mother died in July 1958, believes that his songs of rejection weren't based on broken romances but on the fact that his father had left him as a child and then his mother had effectively left him again by handing him over to her sister to be brought up. "I lost my mother twice," he was to say, "once as a child of five and then again at 17."

"Rejection and betrayal were his experience of life," says Thelma. "When I met him, the first proper conversation we ever had was all about this because my father had done exactly the same thing and so we felt we had something in common. It was that which helped to draw us close. Also, you have to remember that his mother was run down by a car and, although he appeared very controlled about it, you knew that he was hurting inside. We both felt very let down and abandoned. There was a big difference between Paul and John, although as teenagers they'd both lost their mothers. Paul had a very close-knit family with a network of cousins and aunties. His dad was absolutely wonderful. John's life was very isolated. He lived with Mimi (his mother's sister) who looked after him extremely well but there was no closeness. There was nothing tactile about the relationship."

One of the things that excited John and Paul at the time of writing was the word play that they had introduced around the word 'belong'. Although it was a small innovation for them it was to become a hallmark of their more sophisticated writing. Ironically, when George used 'don't be long' in 'Blue Jay Way' four years later Charles Manson thought he was saying 'don't belong' and took it as a message urging him and others to drop out of society.

IT WON'T BE LONG
Written: Lennon/McCartney
Length: 2' 13"
UK release: *With The Beatles* album, November 22, 1963
US release: *Meet The Beatles* album, January 20, 1964

ALL I'VE GOT TO DO

Half of the 14 songs on *With The Beatles* were written by John and Paul and most of these were written specifically for the album. 'All I've Got To Do', however, was written entirely by John in 1961. The track was, he said, an attempt "to do Smokey Robinson again". His earlier attempt had been with 'Ask Me Why' which was reminiscent of Robinson's 1961 song 'What's So Good About Goodbye'. This time he appears to have used 'You Can Depend On Me' as his model. In 1980, while in the studio recording his vocal track for 'Woman', Yoko commented that John sounded like a Beatle. "Actually, I'm supposed to be Smokey Robinson at the moment, my dear," John answered, "because the Beatles were always supposing that they were Smokey Robinson."

William 'Smokey' Robinson was, in 1963, the 23-year-old leader of the Detroit-based Miracles, a sweet-voiced singer who could also write, arrange and produce songs. Bob Dylan, with perhaps only half of his tongue in his cheek, once referred to him as his favourite living poet. The Beatles also covered his song 'You Really Got A Hold On

ALL I'VE GOT TO DO

Written:	Lennon/McCartney
Length:	2' 04"
UK release:	*With The Beatles* album, November 22, 1963
US release:	*Meet The Beatles* album, January 20, 1964

John composed 'All I've Got To Do' with a very simple motivation in mind: he wanted to write like Motown icon Smokey Robinson.

Me' on this album, which had been a US Top 10 hit for the Miracles in February 1963. "When they recorded that, it was one of the most flattering things that ever happened to me," said Smokey. "I listened to it over and over again, not to criticize it but to enjoy it."

ALL MY LOVING

On April 18, 1963, the actress Jane Asher was in the audience at London's Royal Albert Hall to see the Beatles and other acts in a show which was being recorded by BBC Radio. Although only 17, she was already a successful actress, having appeared in several plays, films and television dramas, besides being a regular guest on BBC Television's pop chart show *Juke Box Jury.* She had been sent to the concert as Britain's 'best-known teenage girl' by the BBC listings magazine *Radio Times*, which wanted to record her comments.

The resulting article, designed to show the effect that the Beatles were having on young people, was published in May 1963, with a photograph of Jane early on in the procedings, looking mature and pensive, contrasted with a later photo of her feigning hysterics. Her comment on the Beatles was: "Now these I could scream for". Little did she know at the time that she would become the best-known of all Paul McCartney's girlfriends and would inspire some of his greatest love songs. She met up with the group after the show at the Royal Court Hotel in Chelsea and it wasn't long before she and Paul became locked in conversation. Shortly afterwards they began dating and, before the end of 1963, Paul had moved into a room at the Ashers' home at 57 Wimpole Street in London's West End.

It was a significant change for Paul because, within a year of leaving his council house in Allerton, he was living in one of the most expensive areas of London's West End with a family which had a number of important social connections. Jane's father was a medical consultant and her mother a professor at the Guildhall School of Music. They had a study filled with paintings and scattered with scientific journals, where talk could range from pop music and theatre to some new

ALL MY LOVING
Written: Lennon/McCartney
Length: 2' 09"
UK release: *With The Beatles* album, November 22, 1963
US release: *Meet The Beatles* album, January 20, 1964

The Beatles appeared on BBC pop show *Juke Box Jury*, presented by the suave David Jacobs.

development in psychology. It all helped to broaden Paul's horizons and this in turn would affect his songwriting.

'All My Loving' was conceived as a poem by Paul one day as he was shaving. It wasn't until he'd finished his day's work that he put music to it, initially imagining it as a country and western song as he worked on the tune backstage at a British theatre while on tour. "It was the first song I ever wrote where I had the words before the music," he said. Like so many Beatle songs now that they were almost permanently on tour, it was about being separated, but whereas John would have been filled with apprehension, Paul is confident that things will work out. John, who was often grudging in his praise for Paul's songs, called it "a damn good piece of work".

LITTLE CHILD

As the lyrics to 'Little Child' are about a 'sad and lonely' boy wanting a girl to take a chance on him, the initial idea probably came from John. Asked about 'Little Child' in 1980, all John would say was that it was another effort to write a song for somebody, "probably Ringo". Paul later remembered that part of the song's melody was inspired by 'Whistle My Love', a 1950s song recorded by the British folk singer Elton Hayes and used in the Walt Disney film *Robin Hood*.

The earliest extant draft of the lyric is in Paul's hand and is substantially the same as the later record with the exception of the opening line to the first verse. On the record it is, 'Now if you want someone to make you feel so fine' but it was originally, 'If you want someone to have a ravin' time'.

The Beatles were now entering a period where they were being asked to provide songs for other artists. In April 1963, John had gone on holiday to Spain with Brian Epstein who used the opportunity to try to persuade him to write original material for the other acts he managed. The Beatles duly complied, writing 'I'll Be On My Way' and 'Bad To Me' for Billy J Kramer and the Dakotas, 'Tip Of My Tongue' for Tommy Quickly, 'Love Of The Loved' for Cilla Black, and 'Hello Little Girl' for the Fourmost.

Paul has since admitted they "knocked them out" in the belief that it was the job of a songwriting team to keep writing songs, reserving the best ones for themselves and giving the rest away.

Despite being a fairly melancholic song, 'Little Child' was probably written with the band's joker, Ringo, in mind.

LITTLE CHILD
Written: Lennon/McCartney
Length: 1' 48"
UK release: *With The Beatles* album, November 22, 1963
US release: *Meet The Beatles* album, January 20, 1964

DON'T BOTHER ME

'Don't Bother Me' was the first song by George Harrison ever to be recorded by the Beatles and indeed the first lyrical composition that he had ever come up with. He wrote it in August 1963 while staying at the Palace Court Hotel in Bournemouth. The Beatles were playing six nights at the seaside town's Gaumont Cinema and it was during this week that the photographer Robert Freeman came down to take the celebrated album cover photographs.

"I wrote the song as an exercise to see if I could write a song," George said. "I was sick in bed. Maybe that's why it turned out to be 'Don't Bother Me'." Bill Harry, the founder of the Liverpool music paper *Mersey Beat*, has suggested the title had another origin. Apparently, Harry used to pester George whenever he saw him to find out if he'd written anything since his first instrumental composition 'Cry For A Shadow' which was included on an album by Tony Sheridan in 1962. "When George was about to go out one night, he thought he might bump into me," Harry wrote, "so he started writing a number which he called 'Don't Bother Me'."

DON'T BOTHER ME

Written:	Harrison
Length:	2' 29"
UK release:	*With The Beatles* album, November 22, 1963
US release:	*Meet The Beatles* album, January 20, 1964

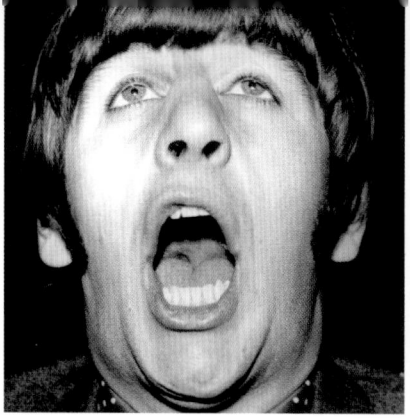

HOLD ME TIGHT

A version of 'Hold Me Tight' was recorded for the Beatles' first album but not used and rather than go back to the old tape they re-cut it for *With The Beatles*. Written by Paul, who considered it a "work song", John's only comment was that he "was never really interested in it either way".

It was influenced by the Shirelles, the New Jersey group who in 1961 had become the first all-girl group to make the Number 1 spot in the American charts. The Beatles were consistent champions of girl groups and girl singers, citing acts such as the Chiffons, Mary Wells, the Ronettes, the Donays and the Crystals as influences on their close harmony vocals. Even before they arrived in London, they were including Shirelles' songs in their act and on their debut album they featured two of them – 'Baby It's You' and 'Boys'.

The Shirelles – Shirley Owens, Micki Harris, Doris Coley and Beverly Lee – had seven Top 20 hits in America and three in Britain but 1963 proved to be their last year of chart glory as they were pushed aside by the invasion of British beat.

Although to most listeners at the time it sounded like a song about a quick 'kiss and cuddle' it was about a full sexual encounter. The narrator is alone with the girl at night and 'making love'.

Most pop songs at the time tended not to be so bold. The original lyric sheet, complete with doodles of a man's head, was reproduced in Mike McCartney's book *Thank U Very Much* (1981).

Ringo-sung songs such as 'I Wanna Be Your Man' (right) functioned as light relief.

HOLD ME TIGHT
Written: Lennon/McCartney
Length: 2' 32"
UK release: *With The Beatles* album, November 22, 1963
US release: *Meet The Beatles* album, January 20, 1964

I WANNA BE YOUR MAN

Although Ringo didn't have much of a singing voice he sang one number in each show that was within his limited vocal range and this tradition was carried on with the albums, with a doleful Ringo spot slotted in almost as light relief. It was with Ringo in mind that Paul started writing 'I Wanna Be Your Man', a basic four-chord number the lyric of which didn't progress much beyond the five words in the title but the song has become best known for the version recorded by the Rolling Stones.

The Beatles had known the group's manager Andrew Oldham since they first arrived in London because Brian Epstein had briefly hired him as the group's publicist. In April 1963, he had been tipped off about the Rolling Stones who were playing at the Station Hotel in Richmond. Soon afterwards he became their manager. He was a born hustler who created the Stones' bad boy image by getting the group to look mean when photographed, playing up any signs of anti-social behaviour and suggesting controversial headlines to newspapers and magazines.

Five months after taking the Stones on, he was anxious to find them good material for singles. Mick Jagger and Keith Richard were not yet writing and the group's first single, which had sold 100,000 copies, had been a cover of the Chuck Berry song 'Come On'.

On September 10th 1963 when John and Paul were leaving the Charing Cross Road offices of their publisher Dick James they bumped into Oldham in the street. He shared this concern about finding new material with the two Beatles who had already seen the Stones perform twice in London clubs and Paul immediately mentioned 'I Wanna Be Your Man'. They all then walked along to

I WANNA BE YOUR MAN
Written: Lennon/McCartney
Length: 1' 58"
UK release: *With The Beatles* album, November 22, 1963
US release: *Meet The Beatles* album, January 20, 1964

Studio 51 in Great Newport Street, a club run by jazz man Ken Colyer, where the Stones were rehearsing.

The song was played to the group and Brian Jones, then their acknowledged leader, said that he liked it and Decca was pressurizing them for a single. John and Paul talked it over and then John said, "Listen, if you guys really like the main part of the song, we'll finish it for you right now." They went off to a separate room and a few minutes later emerged with the completed song.

It was meant to emulate the feel of the Shirelles' song 'Boys' which Ringo sang in concert. It was the sound of the song rather than the lyrics that mattered for him. The dragged out 'maaaan' of the chorus was inspired by Benny Spellman's song 'Fortune Teller', the B side to his 1962 hit 'Lipstick Traces'.

'I Wanna Be Your Man', which the Stones recorded on October 7th 1963, went to Number 12 in Britain and helped to turn the group into a major act. The press liked to portray the Beatles and the Stones as the deadliest of enemies but in fact they were always close friends, turning up at each other's sessions and socializing in clubs. John later commented that, as far as the Beatles were concerned, 'I Wanna Be Your Man' was a 'throwaway' song, which is why they were happy to give it away before they had even recorded it themselves (which they did the next day with Ringo as vocalist). "We weren't going to give them anything great, right?" John said.

Prince Philip presents the band with a single award at the Carl-Alan Awards in the Empire Ballroom, Leicester Square, in March 1964.

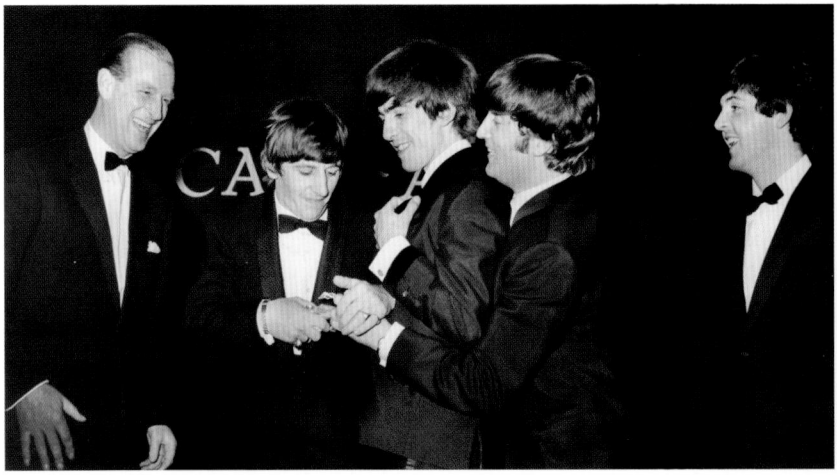

NOT A SECOND TIME

Paul has said that the musical inspiration behind 'Not A Second Time' was again Smokey Robinson and the Miracles, whereas the main writing honours were claimed by John. It was another example of John allowing his feelings, in this case of being wounded, to wash all over his work. After having been let down and made to cry the writer's response is to shut down his emotions because he can't face the possibility of being hurt all over again.

It was one of the first of the Beatles' songs to be subjected to critical analysis by a quality newspaper. William Mann, then music critic of the *Times* (London), compared part of it to Gustav Mahler's 'Song Of The Earth'. John would later say that this review was responsible for "starting the whole intellectual bit about the Beatles".

"Harmonic interest is typical of their quicker songs too," Mann wrote, "and one gets the impression that they think simultaneously of harmony and melody, so firmly are the major tonic sevenths and ninths built into their tunes, and the flat-submediant key-switches, so natural is the Aeolian cadence at the end of 'Not A Second Time'" John's comment on this was, "I didn't know what the hell it was all about". Another time he said that he thought Aeolian cadences sounded like exotic birds. He wasn't the only one to be confused by Mann's terminology. An 'Aeolian cadence' is not a recognised musical description and generations of music critics have puzzled over exactly what Mann was referring to. The review itself however has been credited with initiating serious musical criticism of the Beatles' work.

NOT A SECOND TIME
Written: Lennon/McCartney
Length: 2' 08"
UK release: *With The Beatles* album, November 22, 1963
US release: *Meet The Beatles* album, January 20, 1964

I WANT TO HOLD YOUR HAND

There was a piano in the basement den of the Ashers' home in Wimpole Street where John and Paul would sometimes work. It was here on October 16th 1963 that they created 'I Want To Hold Your Hand', the song that was to finally break them in America when it reached the Number 1 spot in January 1964.

It was a remarkable achievement because no British pop artists had ever really cracked America. In 1956 Lonnie Donegan, the 'king of skiffle', had reached the Top 10 with 'Rock Island Line' but only after four months of touring. Cliff Richard had toured, released a movie and appeared on the *Ed Sullivan Show* but had only a minor hit with 'Living Doll'. The only British records ever to make the Number 1 position had been Vera Lynn with 'Auf Wiedersehen' in 1952, Acker Bilk with 'Stranger On The Shore' in 1961 and the Tornadoes with 'Telstar' in 1962. After disappointing sales on the Vee

I WANT TO HOLD YOUR HAND

Written:	Lennon/McCartney
Length:	2' 24"
UK single release:	November 29, 1963
UK chart position:	1
US single release:	December 26, 1963
US chart position:	1

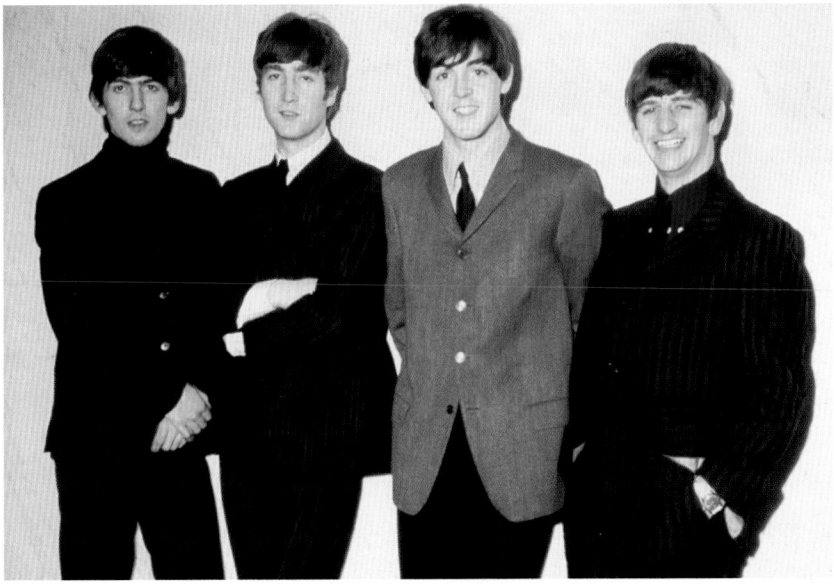

The Beatles wrote 'I Want To Hold Your Hand' with 'an American sound in mind' and it broke them in the US.

Jay and Swan labels, the Beatles were now with Capitol in America and Brian Epstein had promised that the first single for them would be designed with an 'American sound' in mind.

According to John, 'I Want To Hold Your Hand' sprang into being when, having come up with an opening line, Paul hit a chord on the piano. "I turned to him and said, 'That's it! Do that again!' In those days, we really used to absolutely write like that – both playing into each other's noses." Gordon Waller, schoolboy friend of Jane Asher's older brother Peter (with whom he had formed the singing duo Peter and Gordon), was also in the house that day. "As far as I can remember John was on a pedal organ and Paul was on a piano," he said. "The basement was the place where we all went to make our 'noise' and they called us down to hear this song they'd just written. It wasn't totally complete but the structure and the chorus were there."

The Beatles were, of course, still playing to their market, the teenage girls for whom hand holding and kissing was the ultimate in physical expression. 'I Want To Hold Your Hand' certainly wasn't an indication of their own sexual reticence.

Robert Freeman, the photographer who took the cover photo for *With The Beatles*, lived in a flat beneath John at 13 Emperor's

'This Boy' (right) saw the band mimicking the close harmonies of the Everly Brothers.

Gate in Kensington and tried to educate him in jazz and experimental music while John directed him towards rock'n'roll. "He (John) was intrigued by a contemporary French album of experimental music," Freeman recalled. "There was one track where a musical phrase repeated, as if the record had stuck. This effect was used in 'I Want To Hold Your Hand' – at my suggestion – 'that my love, I can't hide, I can't hide, I can't hide'."

The Beatles heard that 'I Want To Hold Your Hand' had made it to Number 1 in America when they were playing in Paris and it triggered plans for their first Stateside visit. It was because they knew that Cliff Richard had failed to set the charts alight there, despite having toured, that they determined only to make appearances when they could warrant top billing.

THIS BOY

'This Boy' was written by John and Paul in a hotel bedroom as an exercise in three-part harmony, which they had never attempted on record before, and was inspired, as so much else was at the time, by Smokey Robinson and the Miracles. "The middle eight," said George, "was John trying to do Smokey."

The lyrics, John said, amounted to nothing. All that was important was "sound and harmony". Harmony was integral to the early Beatles' work, and the influence of the Everly Brothers in particular is evident in this song. They'd become familiar with three-part harmonizing by singing Phil Spector's 'To Know Him Is To Love Him', a 1959 hit for the Teddy Bears.

Saying that the lyrics amounted to nothing was not the same as saying that they were without meaning, for again John was portraying himself here as a loser waiting for his loved one to return.

THIS BOY

Written:	Lennon/McCartney
Length:	2' 12"
UK single release:	November 29, 1963 as B-side of 'I Want To Hold Your Hand'
US release:	*Meet The Beatles* album, January 20, 1964

I CALL YOUR NAME

John reckoned that he wrote 'I Call Your Name' back when "there was no Beatles and no group". As the Quarry Men, his first group, was formed very shortly after the acquisition of his first guitar in March 1957, he must have either written it as he was learning to play

I CALL YOUR NAME

Written:	Lennon/McCartney
Length:	2' 09"
UK release:	On 'Long Tall Sally' EP, June 19, 1964
US release:	*The Beatles' Second Album*, April 10, 1964

or even earlier when he could only play banjo, although Paul can remember working on it in John's bedroom at Menlove Avenue. The Quarry Men was initially a skiffle group made up of friends from Quarry Bank High School for Boys. Rod Davis, who played banjo with them, can't recall John writing songs in those days. "What we did was to listen to the latest singles when they were played on the radio and try to copy the words down," he says. "The trouble was, if you couldn't make them out, or couldn't write quickly enough, you were stuck. So what John used to do was to add his own words to these tunes. No one ever seemed to notice because they didn't know the words either. There was a song called 'Streamline Train' which John rewrote as 'Long Black Train'. He also put new words to the Del Vikings' hit 'Come Go With Me' and I didn't realize what he'd done until I heard the original version many years later."

If the song was written as long ago as John thought, it's interesting that even in his schooldays he was writing about despair. The lines 'I never weep at night, I call your name' are close to his 1971 lines 'In the middle of the night, I call your name' in 'Oh Yoko' on the *Imagine* album.

John added the Jamaican blue beat instrumental break in 1964. Blue beat and ska music, brought to Britain by immigrants from the West Indies, were becoming popular with British mods and the Blue Beat label, founded by Ziggy Jackson in 1961, had released 213 singles in the previous three years. Two weeks after the recording of 'I Call Your Name', the *New Musical Express* asked whether ska and blue beat were going to be the major new talking point in pop music. With the Beatles around, there was no chance of that.

John had only just graduated from the banjo to guitar when he wrote 'I Call Your Name' in the Fifties.

A HARD DAY'S NIGHT

A Hard Day's Night marked a breakthrough as it was the first of their albums where every track was written by the Beatles. It was also a personal *tour de force* for John, who was the major contributor to ten of the album's 13 tracks. Being the oldest in the group and the founder member of the Quarry Men, John was the unacknowledged leader in those days. Although Paul was more musically accomplished – he had mastered guitar and piano ahead of John – they still maintained the same junior to senior pupil relationship established when they met in 1957.

John later recognized that this was his dominant period in the Beatles and it was only when, in his own words, he became "self-conscious and inhibited" that Paul began to take over. The majority of the group's singles up to this point, John claimed, had either been written by him, or featured him as lead vocalist. The only reason Paul sang on the track of 'A Hard Day's Night' was because John couldn't reach the high notes.

Seven of the songs were written for *A Hard Day's Night* although one of these, 'I'll Cry Instead', was eventually dropped in favour of 'Can't Buy Me Love', a single which Paul had written under pressure. The Beatles were still writing pop songs to deadlines but putting more of their personal concerns into the lyrics. For example, 'If I Fell' revealed a lot about John's troubled psyche. Equally, 'And I Love Her' was one of Paul's most personal songs yet – a declaration of his feelings for Jane Asher. At the time, few people knew how or why the songs had been written. It wouldn't be until the Beatles broke up that the authorship of individual songs became widely known and details, such as those behind the breakdown of John and Cynthia's marriage, would be revealed.

This one will sleigh you: the band pile on top of a sledge for the shooting of the *A Hard Day's Night* film.

Initially, the film of *A Hard Day's Night* was conceived as a vehicle to sell an album but, as with everything the Beatles touched in 1964, it turned into a great commercial success, recouping its production costs almost 30 times over. The initial premise was to capture the delirium of Beatlemania, in the style of a black and white television documentary. Designed to display their musical rather than acting abilities the Beatles were given undemanding acting roles with short lines and a strong supporting cast of character actors to cover any weaknesses.

"I was with the Beatles in Paris when they played there in January 1964," says screenwriter Alun Owen. "I was also around them in an unofficial capacity on a lot of other occasions. The biggest nonsense that has been written about the film is that it was ad-libbed. It wasn't. At the time they were 22 or 23 years old. They had never acted before. If you go through the script, you'll see that no sentence is longer than six words, because they couldn't have handled any more. The only ad-libs were made by John."

The Beatles were pleased with the final result. Although they knew it only showed one side of their personalities and wasn't as realistic as it could have been, they recognized that *A Hard Day's Night* avoided the clichés of most pop movies.

The album was released in America in June 1964 and a month later in Britain, making the Number 1 spot in both countries. The American version was substantially different, featuring only the seven soundtrack songs and 'I'll Cry Instead'. It was made up to a 12-track album by including several of George Martin's orchestral versions of Lennon and McCartney's songs.

A HARD DAY'S NIGHT

In the early Sixties, it was customary for pop stars to make a movie after a decent string of hits, just as Elvis Presley had done in the Fifties. The assumption was that movie stardom was longer lasting and more substantial than pop stardom. The *Young Ones* (1961) and *Summer Holiday* (1962) were big box-office hits in the UK for Cliff Richard, and even lesser British names such as Adam Faith, Tommy Steele, Billy Fury and Terry Dene had made it on to the silver screen.

The Beatles wanted to do something from a different angle and were fortunate in being introduced to director Dick Lester, whose fast cuts and imaginative camera work perfectly suited the excitement and freshness of pop. Negotiations over the film had begun in October 1963 and, in November, Liverpool-born writer Alun Owen, who had an ear for the Beatles' natural speech patterns, accompanied the group to Dublin and Belfast to observe them at work and catch the flavour of Beatlemania.

The Beatles had to write the songs for the film without having seen Owen's screenplay. Three were written in Paris during January 1964, three the next month in Miami during one two-hour session and the title track back home in in London. "All of the songs, except for 'A Hard Day's Night', were written independently of what I was writing," says Alun Owen. "Paul and John wrote them and they were woven into the script as things came up. None of them bear any relation to the story. They were just numbers."

The Beatles didn't have a title for the film, having already rejected *On The Move*, *Let's Go* and *Beatlemania*. 'A Hard Day's Night' was the last song written and it eventually became the title to both the album and the film. The phrase was attributed to Ringo Starr, who

The band have their moptops tended by Pattie Boyd, Tina Williams, Pru Berry and Susan Whiteman.

said in 1964: "I came up with the phrase 'a hard day's night'. It just came out. We went to do a job and we worked all day and then we happened to work all night. I came out, still thinking it was day and said, 'It's been a hard day…looked around, saw that it was dark and added…'s night.'"

If Ringo did invent the phrase it must have been in 1963, and not on the set of the film as has been reported, because John included it in his book *In His Own Write* which was written that year. In the story 'Sad Michael' John had the line, "He'd had a hard days [sic] night that day…" However it came about, Dick Lester liked it as a title because it summed up the frenetic pace of the film as well as the humour of the Beatles and, as he was driving him home one night, he told John that he planned to use it. The next morning John brought along a song to go with it.

The *Evening Standard* journalist Maureen Cleave, who had been one of the first London journalists to write about the Beatles

A HARD DAY'S NIGHT

Written:	Lennon/McCartney
Length:	2' 32"
UK single release:	July 10, 1964
UK chart position:	1
US release:	*A Hard Day's Night* album, June 26, 1964

(*Evening Standard,* February 2, 1963), can recall John coming into the studio on April 16, 1964, with the lyrics written on the back of a card to his son Julian, who had just had his first birthday. Initially the song ran: 'But when I get home to you, I find my tiredness is through, And I feel all right'. Cleave told him that she thought 'my tiredness is through' was a weak line. John took out a pen, crossed through the line, and wrote; 'I find the things that you do, They make me feel all right'. Maureen said that "The song seemed to materialize as if by magic. It consisted of John humming to the others, then they would all put their heads together and hum and three hours later they had this record."

Although Paul hadn't written the lyric, when promoting the film in America, he was asked to explain how it was put together: "It seemed a bit ridiculous writing a song called 'A Hard Day's Night'," he said, "because it sounded a funny phrase at the time but the idea came of saying that it had been a hard day's night and we'd been working all day and you get back to a girl and everything's fine. So it was turned into one of those songs."

'A Hard Day's Night' was featured over the opening and closing credits of the film. It was the first cut on the soundtrack album and became a Number 1 single in Britain and America. The comic actor Peter Sellers, once a member of John's favourite radio comedy group the Goons, recorded 'A Hard Day's Night' by speaking the lyric as if he was Laurence Olivier delivering a Shakespearean monologue. It made the British Top 20 in December 1965.

I SHOULD HAVE KNOWN BETTER

I SHOULD HAVE KNOWN BETTER
Written: Lennon/McCartney
Length: 2' 44"
UK release: *A Hard Day's Night* album, July 10, 1964
US release: *A Hard Day's Night* album, June 26, 1964

Released as the flip side of 'A Hard Day's Night' in America, 'I Should Have Known Better' was the first song in the film and was performed in a sequence where the Beatles and Paul's 'grandfather' (played by Wilfred Brambell) are on a train and banished to the mail van. They start playing cards and, several cuts later, appear with guitars, harmonica and drums. "It just seemed the natural place to have the first number," says Alun Owen.

Although much of the filming took place on trains travelling between London and the West Country, 'I Should Have Known Better' was actually filmed on a set at Twickenham Film Studios.

Surprisingly for a song by John it is very optimistic: he loves her, she loves him and everything is fine.

The Beatles sang 'I Should Have Known Better' in *A Hard Day's Night* as they emerged from a train's mail van.

IF I FELL

In *A Hard Day's Night* John had to sing 'If I Fell' to Ringo because there was no obvious place for it in the already-written script and no love interest. "We're in the television studio and Ringo is supposed to be sulking a bit," Paul explained in 1964. "John starts joking with him and then sings the song as though we're singing it to him. We got fits of the giggles just doing it."

The recording started on February 27, 1964 and, as the earliest draft of the song was written on a Valentine's Day card, it can be assumed that it was written somewhere in the two weeks between February 14 and 27.

'If I Fell' is one of John's most beautiful songs and is about an illicit relationship. He is asking the woman in question for an assurance that if he leaves his wife for her that she'll love him more than he's ever been loved. It is about someone eager to avoid confrontation.

In the early draft he had written 'I hope that she will cry/ When she hears we are two' rather than the final, softer 'And that she will cry…' This suggests that his first thought was a cruel sense of pleasure from his partner discovering his unfaithfulness. The cruelty is still there but it's harder to detect.

John said that the song was 'semi-autobiographical' and it is known that he was unfaithful to his wife Cynthia although she was oblivious to what was going on. "I'm a coward," he later said in 1968. "I wasn't going to go off and leave Cynthia and be by myself."

John saw this as his first proper ballad and a precursor to 'In My Life', his song about growing up, which was to use the same chord sequence.

John' had to use 'If I Fell, one of his most beautiful love songs, to serenade.Ringo.

IF I FELL
Written: Lennon/ McCartney
Length: 2' 22"
UK release: *A Hard Day's Night* album, July 10, 1964
US release: *A Hard Day's Night* album, June 26, 1964

AND I LOVE HER

Paul's love of rock'n'roll didn't mean that he despised the popular music that had preceded it. He loved the big band music of the Twenties and Thirties which his father played, the Victorian music-hall songs which his relatives sang round the piano and the show tunes of the Forties and Fifties.

Even in the days of Hamburg and the Cavern Club in Liverpool, Paul had sung 'Till There Was You', a song from the 1957 Broadway musical *The Music Man*, later popularized by Peggy Lee, and this was included on *With The Beatles*. Its success must have made him realize that ballads enriched the show, and wrote 'And I Love Her' to fill this space. John said it was Paul's first 'Yesterday'. Paul said it was, "the first song that I impressed myself with".

The initial idea was to write a song with a title that began mid-sentence. Paul then wrote the verses and came to John for help with the middle eight. It didn't escape Paul's notice that almost a decade later Perry Como recorded a song titled 'And I Love You So'.

Recording on the song began in February 1964 and it was the first Beatle track to feature just acoustic instruments (Ringo played bongos). In the film *A Hard Day's Night,* they are shown recording it for a television show.

Only the month before recording, Jane Asher commented to American writer Michael Braun: "The trouble (with Paul) is that he wants the fans' adulation and mine too. He's so selfish. That's his biggest fault. He can't see that my feelings for him are real and that the fans' (feelings for him) are fantasy." Paul has since said that it wasn't written with anyone in mind but it's hard to believe that in his first flush of love with Jane Asher he was writing such tender songs to an imaginary girl.

AND I LOVE HER
Written: Lennon/McCartney
Length: 2' 31"
UK release: *A Hard Day's Night* album, July 10, 1964
US release: *A Hard Day's Night* album, June 26, 1964

I'M HAPPY JUST TO DANCE WITH YOU

John and Paul wrote 'I'm Happy Just To Dance With You' for George to sing in the film "to give him a piece of the action" and it was filmed on stage at the Scala Theatre in Charlotte Street, London. As the youngest member of the Beatles, George was living in the shadow of Paul and John. When he started writing his own songs, he was resentful that more of them weren't considered for the albums.

John was equally hurt in 1980 when George published his biography *I Me Mine* and made no mention of John's influence on his songwriting. Paul has admitted that 'I'm Happy Just To Dance With You' was a 'formula song'.

I'M HAPPY JUST TO DANCE WITH YOU
Written: Lennon/McCartney
Length: 1' 58"
UK release: *A Hard Day's Night* album, July 10, 1964
US release: *A Hard Day's Night* album, June 26, 1964

George opens fan mail as he celebrates his 21st birthday, on February 25, 1964, with the help of a Beatles' management company employee.

TELL ME WHY

'Tell Me Why' was written to provide an 'upbeat' number for the concert sequence in *A Hard Day's Night*. John thought of something the Chiffons or the Shirelles might do and "knocked it off".

It's a typical John scenario. He has been lied to and deserted. He's crying. He appeals to his girl to let him know what he's done wrong so that he can put it right. Children whose parents either leave them or die suddenly are often left with a feeling that they must in some way be responsible. 'If there's something I have said or done, Tell me what and I'll apologize', John sang.

It was only when he underwent primal therapy in 1970 that he came to terms with these subconscious fears. Therapist Arthur Janov set him the exercise of looking back through all his Beatles' songs to see what they revealed of his anxieties. On his first post-therapy album, *John Lennon/Plastic Ono Band*, he was able to sing about these traumas in their original context in songs such as 'Mother', 'Hold On', 'Isolation' and 'My Mummy's Dead'.

TELL ME WHY

Written:	Lennon/McCartney
Length:	2' 10"
UK release:	*A Hard Day's Night* album, July 10, 1964
US release:	*A Hard Day's Night* album, June 26, 1964

CAN'T BUY ME LOVE

In January 1964, the Beatles went to Paris for 18 days of concerts at the Olympia Theatre. They stayed at the five-star George V hotel, just off the Champs Élysées, and an upright piano was moved into one of their suites so that songwriting could continue. It was here that John and Paul wrote 'One And One Is Two' for fellow Liverpool group the Strangers and Paul came up with 'Can't Buy Me Love'.

With a new single due in March and the news that 'I Want To Hold Your Hand' had rocketed to the top of the American charts, there was no time to waste. George Martin, who had come to the Pathé Marconi Studios in Paris to record the newly-written song along with German language versions of 'She Loves You' ('Sie Liebt Dich') and 'I Want To Hold Your Hand' ('Komm, Gib Mir Deine Hand'), made the suggestion of starting it with the chorus. Although 'She Loves You', 'I Wanna Be Your Man', 'Don't Bother Me' and 'All My Loving' were all used in *A Hard Day's Night*, 'Can't Buy Me Love' was the only previously-released song to be included on the soundtrack album. This was because it was pulled into the film at a late stage to replace 'I'll Cry Instead', which director Dick Lester didn't think was right for the scene where the Beatles break out.

'Can't Buy Me Love' was used in the film as the group ran down a fire escape at the back of the theatre (actually the Odeon in Hammersmith, London) and fooled around on some open ground (playing fields in Isleworth). It was the group's first experience of freedom in the film after having been locked for days in cars, trains, dressing rooms and hotels. Screenwriter Alun Owen remembers: "My stage direction at this point was very simple. It read: 'The boys come down the fire escape. It is the first time they have been free. They run about and play silly buggers'."

CAN'T BUY ME LOVE
Written: Lennon/McCartney
Length: 2' 14"
UK single release: March 20, 1964
UK chart position: 1
US single release: March 16, 1964
US chart position: 1

Paul examines his own waxwork at Madame Tussaud's in London in April 1964.

The lyric suggests it's partly an answer song to Berry Gordy and Janie Bradford's 'Money', a number the Beatles had started performing in 1960 and had recorded on *With The Beatles*. The Gordy/Bradford line was that money could get you anything. The Lennon/McCartney response was that it could get you anything but love. Paul has cited Little Richard as a musical influence and Dominic Pedler (*The Beatles as Musicians*) suggests that it was 'Lucille' that supplied the template for the verses.

American journalists asked Paul in 1966 whether 'Can't Buy Me Love' was a song about prostitution. He replied that all the songs were open to interpretation but that that particular suggestion was taking things too far.

ANY TIME AT ALL

Having written the songs which would be used in the film, the race was on to come up with a number for what would be the second side of the soundtrack album.

John was obviously the more prolific songwriter at the time, having written five of the seven songs in the film and going on to write all but one of the tracks on the other side. This had not been achieved without some difficulty. 'Any Time At All', he later admitted, was a rewriting of his earlier song 'It Won't Be Long', using the same chord progression from C to A minor and back and, when it came to recording, employing the same bawling vocal style.

His original draft of the song was two verses longer, the third verse starting; 'I'll be waiting here all alone/ Just like I've always done…' but there were already enough words in the song and neither of the additional verses advanced the story.

In January 1964 he spoke about some of the changes in his songwriting techniques. "If I found a new chord (I used to) write a song around it," he said. "I thought that if there were a million chords I'd never run out. Sometimes the chords got to be an obsession and we started to put unnecessary ones in. We then decided to keep the songs simple and it's the best way. It might have sounded okay for us but the extra chords wouldn't make other people like them any better. That's the way we've kept it all along."

There were only three other occasions when he claimed Beatles' songs had been recycled. 'Yes It Is' he said was a rewrite of 'This Boy', 'Paperback Writer' was "Son of 'Day Tripper'" and 'Get Back' was a "potboiler rewrite" of 'Lady Madonna'.

Despite the Beatles' stellar productivity, John confessed that the band occasionally recycled song ideas.

ANY TIME AT ALL
Written: Lennon/ McCartney
Length: 2' 13"
UK release: *A Hard Day's Night* album, July 10, 1964
US release: *Something New* album, July 20, 1964

I'LL CRY INSTEAD

I'll Cry Instead' was the song originally set to be used over the fire escape sequence in *A Hard Day's Night* but then dropped in favour of the already-released 'Can't Buy Me Love'. However, when the film was re-mastered for video release in 1986, the song was put back in by running it over a collage sequence preceding the opening credits.

John had written about crying in many of his songs to date but 'I'll Cry Instead' was different in that he was saying that once he'd finished crying he would return to seek vengeance. He imagined coming back and breaking girls' hearts around the world, as if by causing people to fall for him and then spurning them, he would be able to punish everyone who had ever rejected him. He would later admit having been violent at times and in 'Getting Better' he was able to write about his cruelty to women as something he had overcome.

This was also the first song in which John admitted having a chip on his shoulder, a sign that he was entering a period of intense self-examination, that was to continue until his first solo albums, after the break-up of the Beatles.

I'LL CRY INSTEAD

Written:	Lennon/McCartney
Length:	1' 47"
UK release:	*A Hard Day's Night* album, July 10, 1964
US release:	*A Hard Day's Night* album, June 26, 1964

THINGS WE SAID TODAY

In May 1964, having completed the filming of *A Hard Day's Night* and after fulfilling some performing commitments in England and Scotland, the Beatles and their partners took off for a holiday break. John and George made a round-the-world trip with stop-offs in Holland, Polynesia, Hawaii and Canada, while Paul and Ringo went to France and Portugal before taking off for the Virgin Islands.

While in the Caribbean, Paul hired a yacht called *Happy Days* and it was while on board with Ringo, Maureen and Jane that he wrote 'Things We Said Today' on his acoustic guitar. He started the song in one of the cabins but found the smell of engine oil too nauseating so he came up and finished sitting out on the back deck.

The song was a reflection on his relationship with Jane in light of the fact that he knew, by the nature of their work, that times together would be few. When they were separated, he said, he would take comfort from the memory of the things they'd said that day.

Ringo turned 24 on July 7, 1964, and the next day the Beatles obligingly gave him the bumps at a BBC studio.

THINGS WE SAID TODAY

Written:	Lennon/McCartney
Length:	2' 38"
UK single release:	July 10, 1964 as B-side of 'A Hard Day's Night'
US release:	*Something New* album, July 20, 1964

WHEN I GET HOME

Too innovative to be satisfied with a mere guitar/bass/drums set-up, the Beatles made frequent use of more exotic instrumentation.

'When I Get Home' was described by John as a "four-in-the-bar cowbell song", influenced by his love of Motown and American soul music. Around the time it was recorded, he was asked what song he wished he had written and he said his first choice would be Marvin Gaye's 'Can I Get A Witness'. "Then there's other stuff on Tamla Motown that we like," he went on. "It's harder to write good 12-bar numbers because so much has been done before with them. I'd rather write a song with chords all over the place."

An unusually optimistic song for John, the lyric revealed his thoughts about what he was going to say and do to his 'girl', when he got home. Slightly close in subject matter to the single 'A Hard Day's Night' ('when I get home to you...') it shows that he still thought of home as the place where true love would be waiting. Despite his image as the 'lad' in the group, John was really a 'homebody' who liked nothing more than to curl up in front of a television with a supply of books and magazines. It's fitting that he spent much of his final decade as a 'house husband', happy to be confined to his rooms in the Dakota Buildings in New York.

WHEN I GET HOME

Written:	Lennon/McCartney
Length:	2' 18"
UK release:	*A Hard Day's Night* album, July 10, 1964
US release:	*Something New* album, July 20, 1964

YOU CAN'T DO THAT

In both Britain and America 'You Can't Do That' became the B side of 'Can't Buy Me Love'. In this song, instead of weeping, John tries threatening. He tells his girl that if he catches her talking to another boy he's going to leave her immediately. He knows what it feels like to be spurned and he's determined that it won't happen again.

The musical influence, John later said, was Wilson Pickett, the former gospel singer from Alabama who at the time had only released three singles under his own name in America, only one of which had been a minor hit. It wasn't until 1965, his contract then having been acquired by Atlantic Records, that Pickett became known as one of the great soul singers of the Sixties with hits such as 'Mustang Sally', '634-5789' and 'In The Midnight Hour'. It was at the suggestion of guitarist Duane Allman that Pickett recorded 'Hey Jude' in 1969 and managed to have a hit with it at the same time that the Beatles' version was in the charts.

On the recording of 'You Can't Do That', John played lead on his newly-acquired Rickenbacker while George played 12-string guitar for the first time on a Beatles' record. "I find it a drag to play rhythm guitar all the time," John told *Melody Maker.* "I like to work out something interesting to play. The best example is what I did on 'You Can't Do That'. There wasn't really a lead guitarist and a rhythm guitarist on that because...rhythm guitar is too thin for records."

Recorded at Abbey Road after returning from their first visit to America it was used in the TV show sequence of *A Hard Day's Night* but didn't make the final cut.

Perennial magpies, the Beatles were inspired by musicians as diverse as Wilson Pickett and Del Shannon.

YOU CAN'T DO THAT
Written: Lennon/McCartney
Length: 2' 37"
UK single release: March 20, 1964 as B-side of 'Can't Buy Me Love'
US single release: March 16, 1964 as B-side of 'Can't Buy Me Love'

I'LL BE BACK

John found the chords for 'I'll Be Back' while playing a Del Shannon song. This was probably 'Runaway', which the Beatles had played in their early shows and which also starts with a minor chord and has a descending bass line.

Shannon had hits in 1961 and 1962 with 'Runaway', 'Hats Off To Larry', 'So Long Baby' and 'Hey Little Girl'. In 1963, after a hit with 'Little Town Flirt', he played London's Royal Albert Hall (April 18) with the Beatles and suggested to them that he could help expose their work in America by covering one of their songs as a single.

The Beatles agreed and Shannon went back home and recorded a version of 'From Me To You' which, although it only reached Number 77, was the first Lennon and McCartney composition to feature in the American charts.

The song was originally recorded in 3/4 waltz time but John found it too difficult to sing so he altered it to 4/4 time.

I'LL BE BACK

Written:	Lennon/McCartney
Length:	2' 20"
UK release:	*A Hard Day's Night* album, July 10, 1964
US release:	*Beatles '65* album, December 15, 1964

BEATLES FOR SALE

The *Beatles For Sale* sleeve revealed the flip side of Beatlemania – the exhaustion, bewilderment and loneliness of life at the top. John, Paul, George and Ringo look frazzled and world-weary in Robert Freeman's cover photographs and, the same pressurized feeling coloured their new songs. They only had time to write eight of the album's 14 tracks. Covers of their early rock'n'roll favourites were used to fill out the quota.

The songs they did write showed all the signs of having been written in the hothouse of fame. Although 'Eight Days a Week' was a love song, its title was inspired by a comment on overwork. John's songs were bleaker than anything he'd written before, with 'I'm A Loser' offering a foretaste of his confessional style of songwriting. For 'I'll Follow The Sun', Paul had to go back through his old school notebooks to polish up a song he'd last played in the Cavern days.

Bob Dylan, who Paul and John both heard and met for the first time during 1964, was beginning to be an influence. In the early days, the Beatles had concentrated mainly on mastering the musical side of the songs – chord changes, arrangements, harmonies and delivery. Dylan was the first recording artist to affect them primarily as lyricists. Initially, Paul was the big Dylan fan, but John soon caught up with him.

John had been writing poems and short stories for years, mostly for the amusement of friends. Some of these were published in his book *In His Own Write* in 1964, when he was hailed by the press as 'the literary Beatle' and comparisons of his work were made with that of Lewis Carroll, Edward Lear and the James Joyce of *Finnegan's Wake*. Dylan, and later the British journalist Kenneth Allsop, impressed

The rushed *Beatles For Sale* album saw the band stressed by the pressures of their fame and feral Beatlemania.

upon him the need to close the gap between his 'literary' outpourings and lyric writing. John interpreted this to mean that, "Instead of projecting myself into a situation, I would try to express what I felt about myself (as I had done) in my book."

The group's press officer Derek Taylor was surely right when he wrote in the sleeve notes; "The kids of AD 2000 will draw from the music much the same sense of wellbeing and warmth as we do today. For the magic of the Beatles is, I suspect, timeless and ageless… it is adored by the world."

Beatles For Sale took two and a half months to record and was released in December 1964, reaching Number 1 in Britain. The American equivalent, *Beatles '65*, also hit the top spot and sold a million copies in the first week.

I FEEL FINE

The Beatles completed the album *A Hard Day's Night* in June 1964 and by mid-August were back in the studio to start work on *Beatles For Sale*. On August 19, they left Britain to tour America and returned a month later to work on *Beatles For Sale*. *A Hard Day's Night* had been the first album to consist solely of Lennon and McCartney songs but, with so little time between projects, they found it impossible to come up with enough original material for *Beatles For Sale*.

On October 6, while recording 'Eight Days A Week', John was working out the guitar riff that would become the basis of 'I Feel Fine', a song they recorded only 12 days later. It was obviously inspired by Bobby Parker's riff on his 1961 track 'Watch Your Step'. "I actually wrote 'I Feel Fine' around the riff which is going on in the background," John said in December 1964. "I tried to get that effect into every song on the LP, but the others wouldn't have it.

"I told them that I'd write a song specially for this riff so they said, 'Yes. You go away and do that,' knowing that we'd almost finished the album. Anyway, going into the studio one morning I said to Ringo, 'I've written this song but it's lousy', but we tried it, complete with riff, and it sounded like an A side, so we decided to release it just like that."

Apart from the riff, the distinctive feature of 'I Feel Fine' is the sound of feedback from John's guitar that blends into the opening chords. It was one of those discoveries that they made in the studio and decided to use on a track because they liked it. John's semi-acoustic Gibson guitar was leaning against an amplifier after a take of a song and an electronic whine was set up. This along with other innovations on *Beatles For Sale* was a significant development in their approach to recording. Having mastered the studio basics, they were now encouraging George

I FEEL FINE

Written:	Lennon/McCartney
Length:	2' 20"
UK single release:	November 27, 1964
UK chart position:	1
US single release:	November 23, 1964
US chart position:	1

Martin to take risks and were finding fresh sources of inspiration in noises that would previously have been eliminated as mistakes (electronic goofs, twisted tapes, talkback). Feedback was to become a familiar part of recording – used by artists such as Jimi Hendrix and the Who – and John remained proud of the fact that the Beatles were the first group to purposefully put it on a record.

'I Feel Fine', John's most optimistic song to date, became a Number 1 single in both Britain and America.

As the Beatles topped charts in Britain and the US, transatlantic flights became part of a wearying routine.

SHE'S A WOMAN

'She's A Woman' was conceived by Paul on the streets of St John's Wood on October 8, 1964 and was finished the same day in the studio, Paul performing it in the high-pitched scream which he adopted to emulate Little Richard. It was a conscious decision to bring a more bluesy sound to the Beatles. Some lines and the middle eight were added by John. "We needed a real screaming rocker for the live act," said Paul. "It was always good if you were stuck for something to close with or if there was a dull moment."

On the early takes Paul improvised extensively. Take 7, for example, lasted almost six and a half minutes, and contained lots of ad libs and screams. At the end Paul can be heard saying, "We've got a song and an instrumental there!" Unfortunately the song also contained one of the most strained rhymes in the Beatles songbook when 'present' was matched with 'she's no peasant'.

'She's A Woman' was also the first Beatles' song to contain a veiled drug reference. John later confessed that they were quite proud to have inserted the line 'turns me on when I get lonely' and for it to have escaped the attention of the broadcast censors. When they used the phrase 'turn you on' three years later (in 'A Day In The Life'), it led to a radio ban: by then, the authorities had become aware of the growing drug culture and its terminology.

Significantly, it was just five weeks before recording 'She's A Woman' that the Beatles had smoked marijuana for the first time. Until then, their only experience of drugs had been Drinamyl and Preludin tablets that they'd discovered in Hamburg and the strips from Benzedrine inhalers that they'd been shown in Liverpool. They were introduced to marijuana in the company of Bob Dylan, who met them for the first time in their suite at the Delmonico

SHE'S A WOMAN
Written: Lennon/McCartney
Length: 2' 57"
UK single release: November 27, 1964 as B-side of 'I Feel Fine'
US single release: November 23, 1964 as B-side of 'I Feel Fine'

'She's A Woman' saw the Beatles make their first hidden reference to drugs in a song after they were initated in the joys of marijuana by Bob Dylan.

Hotel in New York City. The Beatles were happy to drink cheap wine into the small hours, but Dylan wanted to smoke a joint and assumed that they were all dope smokers because he mistakenly thought they had sung 'I get high', instead of 'I can't hide' in 'I Want To Hold Your Hand'.

The Beatles were apprehensive about joining in at first, but before long the lights were lowered, candles and incense were lit and towels were stuffed along the bottoms of the doors. For the next few hours, the musicians were "legless with laughing" as George Harrison later put it. Paul thought that he'd suddenly been blessed with amazing insights and even went to the trouble of recording his insights on a notepad.

'She's A Woman' was released as the B side of 'I Feel Fine' in Britain and America. "At first, it wasn't so well received," said Paul in 1965. "A lot of people thought that I was just singing too high and that I'd picked the wrong key. It sounded as though I was screeching, but it was on purpose. It wasn't a mistake."

EIGHT DAYS A WEEK

John always claimed that 'Eight Days A Week' was written by Paul as a potential title track for the Beatles' follow-up film to *A Hard Day's Night.*

Director Dick Lester denied this, pointing out that 'Eight Days A Week' was recorded in October 1964, whereas filming on *Help!* didn't begin until late February 1965. It's unlikely that they were considering film music this far in advance. "The film was always supposed to be called *Help* but there was a copyright problem in that someone else had registered this title," says Lester. "So we originally called it *Beatles II* and then *Eight Arms To Hold You,* but the possibility of having to write a song called 'Eight Arms to Hold You' had everyone throwing their hands in the air and saying that it was impossible. It was because of this that we thought, sod it, we'll take the chance, because the laws of registration were so vague. We decided to stick in an exclamation mark because the one that was registered didn't have one."

EIGHT DAYS A WEEK

Written:	Lennon/McCartney
Length:	2' 45"
UK release:	*Beatles For Sale* album, December 4, 1964
US single release:	February 15, 1965
US chart position:	1

Paul heard the phrase 'eight days a week' from a chauffeur who drove him to John's home in Weybridge one day for a writing session. Asked by Paul if he had been busy lately the chauffeur replied, "Busy? I've been working eight days a week." When they arrived in Weybridge Paul went straight in and told John that he had the title for the song they were going to write that day. American radio DJ Larry Kane, who accompanied the Beatles on their 1964 US tour, claims in his book that he heard the group running through the tune on a flight between Dallas and New York on September 20.

'Eight Days A Week', the first track to be recorded with a fade-in, was under consideration as a single in Britain until John came up with 'I Feel Fine'. In America, it was released as the follow-up to 'I Feel Fine' and made the Number 1 spot.

The Beatles managed to maintain standards of prodigious creativity despite being at the heart of relentless media attention and their fans' adulation.

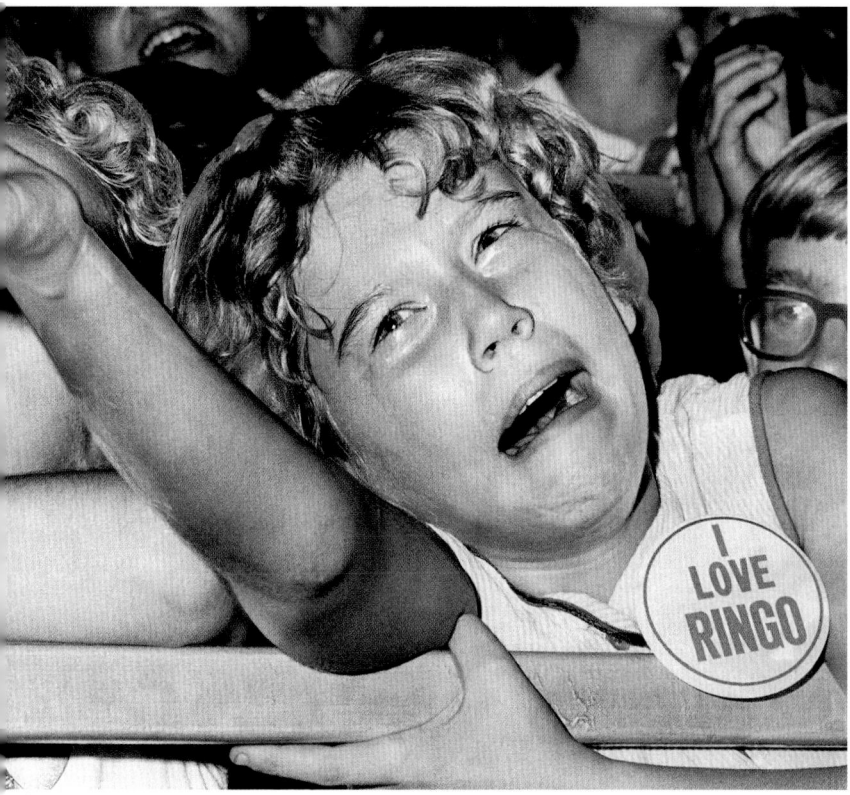

I'M A LOSER

Two events during 1964 were to have a profound effect on John's writing. The first was hearing Bob Dylan's music in Paris during January, when Paul acquired *The Freewheelin' Bob Dylan* from an interviewer at a local radio station.

Paul had heard Dylan's music before through his student friends in Liverpool but it was the first time John had heard it. After hearing *Freewheelin'*, which was Dylan's second album, they went out and bought his debut album *Bob Dylan* and, according to John, "for the rest of our three weeks we didn't stop playing them. We all went potty on Dylan."

The second event to affect John in a big way was meeting the journalist Kenneth Allsop, a writer for the *Daily Mail* and a regular interviewer on BBC Television's news magazine programme *Tonight*. John first met him on March 23, and then again at a Foyles Literary Luncheon at the Dorchester Hotel in London's Park Lane and later that day was interviewed for four minutes on *Tonight* about his book *In His Own Write*. Allsop, a handsome craggy Yorkshireman, was 44 years old at the time and about to become one of the best-known faces on British television. He had been in journalism since 1938, with a brief interruption caused by the war, during which he served in the Royal Air Force.

It was in the 'green room', the hospitality suite, at the BBC's Lime Grove Studios on March 23 that Allsop first spoke to John about his songwriting, encouraging him not to hide his true feelings behind the conventions of the pop song. It was obvious to Allsop from reading *In His Own Write* that John had much more to give if he was prepared to explore his deeper feelings.

Years later, John told his confidant Elliot Mintz that this meeting marked a significant turning point in his songwriting. "He told me

After John and Paul were exposed to the music of Bob Dylan in 1964, they 'went potty on Dylan' for weeks.

that he was very nervous that day and, because of this, became very talkative and engaged Allsop in conversation," says Mintz.

"Allsop had in essence said to him that he wasn't terribly enamoured with Beatles' songs because they all tended to be 'she loves him', 'he loves her', 'they love her' and 'I love her'. He suggested to John that he try to write something more autobiographical, based on personal experience rather than these abstract images. That struck a chord with him."

Although recorded five months later, 'I'm A Loser' was the first fruit of this meeting with Allsop. It would be wrong to say it was a complete change of direction, because from the beginning John had written songs in which he exposed himself as lonely, sad and abandoned, but in 'I'm A Loser' he let a little more of his true self show. On the surface, it's another song about having lost a girl but the lines that announce that beneath his mask he is 'wearing a frown', suggest that he considers himself a loser in more ways than one. He's not just a loser in love; he feels that he's a loser in life.

All this would be idle speculation if not for the fact that 'I'm A Loser' can now be seen as an early stage in John's tortuous journey towards candid self-revelation in his songwriting. At the time, he was quick to credit the effect Bob Dylan had on 'I'm A Loser'. "Anyone who is one of the best in his field – as Dylan is – is bound to

The incessant demands of superstardom took their toll on the band's equanimity: 'Sometimes I wonder how the hell we keep it up,' admitted John.

influence people," he said at the time. "I wouldn't be surprised if we influenced him in some way."

Kenneth Allsop went on to present the television news programme *24 Hours* and then, in May 1973, he was found dead at his home. The cause of his death was an overdose of painkillers but the lack of a suicide note meant that the inquest recorded an open verdict.

Hard Travellin', Allsop's account of the life of the American hobo which was first published in 1967, has become a classic of its kind and is still in print.

'I'm a Loser' was recorded in August 1964. The honesty of the song's confession can be proved by a comment John made to Ray Coleman of *Melody Maker* two months later while backstage before a concert. "I wish I could paint a smile on too," he said as he applied stage make-up. "Don't you think I'll manage one tonight? Sometimes, I wonder how the hell we keep it up."

I'M A LOSER

Written:	Lennon/McCartney
Length:	2' 33"
UK release:	*Beatles For Sale* album, December 4, 1964
US release:	*Beatles '65* album, December 15, 1964

NO REPLY

'No Reply' was a typical John song of betrayal and jealousy; a story of a girl taking off with another guy. It was based, he once said, not on his own experience but on 'Silhouettes', a big hit in 1957 for the Rays on Philadelphia's independent Cameo label. Written by Bob Crewe and Frank Slaye, who went on to write hits for Freddy Cannon, 'Silhouettes' put a new twist on the old love cheat story: the boy discovers he is being two-timed when he notices the silhouettes on the curtains of his lover's house.

In John's version, the boy becomes suspicious when his girl doesn't answer the door and, when he calls her on the phone, her parents tell him she's not at home. As in 'Silhouettes', he returns to her house and, watching from the shadows, sees her go in 'with another man'. His repetition of the line 'I saw the light', referring to the light behind the curtain but also to the revelation that he was being two-timed, could possibly be an allusion to Hank Williams' well-known song of personal salvation 'I Saw The Light' (1948).

Ever since 'Please Please Me', the Beatles' compositions had been published by Northern Songs, a company set up by John, Paul, Brian Epstein and music publisher Dick James, who was a friend of George Martin. James had experience both as singer and songwriter before getting into publishing and, when he heard 'No Reply', he said to John: "That's the first complete song you've written, the first song which resolves itself. It's a complete story."

NO REPLY
Written: Lennon/McCartney
Length: 2' 17"
UK release: *Beatles For Sale* album, December 4, 1964
US release: *Beatles '65* album, December 15, 1964

I DON'T WANT TO SPOIL THE PARTY

The Beatles briefly visited America in February 1964, playing in Washington DC and New York City to promote 'I Want To Hold Your Hand' and doing live TV shows for Ed Sullivan in New York and Miami. It wasn't until August 1964 that they arrived for their first full-fledged tour, a month-long trek that would take them to 20 US cities plus three in Canada. Playing 12 songs per show, they were supported by four American acts – the Bill Black Combo, the Exciters, Jackie DeShannon and the Righteous Brothers.

It is highly likely that John wrote 'I Don't Want To Spoil The Party' in Los Angeles the night of August 24th 1964. Of the eight self-written songs on the album two had already been written before the tour ('Baby's In Black' and 'I'm A Loser') and two were written in Britain on their return ('Eight Days A Week' and 'She's A Woman'). That leaves four songs that must have been written on the tour. Paul told an interviewer that he had written two songs when staying at the La Fayette Motor Inn in Atlantic City. That leaves two songs for which John would have been the primary writer and the best guess is 'No Reply' and 'I Don't Want To Spoil The Party'.

I DON'T WANT TO SPOIL THE PARTY

Written:	Lennon/McCartney
Length:	2' 36"
US single release:	February 15, 1965, as B-side of 'Eight Days A Week'

The Beatles played the *Ed Sullivan Show* on US TV in February 1964 before playing a full tour later that year.

The evidence for 'I Don't Want To Spoil The Party' being written in LA is that we know from contemporary accounts that John stayed in on the night of the 24th to write a song. We also know that in order to do so he turned down an invitation to a party at Burt Lancaster's house that George, Paul and Ringo went to. It would make sense that John's mind would turn to the subject of being a party pooper.

The two days in LA had been particularly stressful for the Beatles. They had arrived the day before at 03:55, flown in from Vancouver, and had been housed in a mansion at 356 St Pierre Road owned by British actor Reginald Owens. They gave a press conference for over 200 journalists the first day and then in the evening played at the Hollywood Bowl. Later there had been a party at the mansion where John had been locked in conversation with Joan Baez.

The next day the Beatles had to pump flesh for an hour at a charity garden party for the Haemophilia Foundation. Adults could only attend if they brought a child. It was just the sort of event that John hated because he had to play the role of the cheerful Beatle.

This might have put him in just the mood to write a song about his inability to pretend that he's enjoying himself. Significantly when discussing the song later he said it was "deeply personal" to him.

I'LL FOLLOW THE SUN

The contrast between John and Paul's outlook on life and love could hardly have been greater. Whereas John usually saw himself as a victim, Paul felt himself to be in charge of life. In 'If I Fell', John demanded a promise that love would last. In 'I'll Follow The Sun', Paul accepts that no such guarantee is possible. He knows that stormy weather may hit his relationship and so he makes plans to follow the sun. A selfish song in a way because it doesn't consider how the abandoned girl might find her own sunshine, it was nonetheless an accurate reflection of Paul's romantic life.

Polished up for use when the pressure was on for the Beatles to come up with their own material, the song was originally written in 1959 at Forthlin Road. There was a wave of interest in Buddy Holly following his death that gave him four hit singles in Britain before the year was out. In 'I'll Follow The Sun', it's easy to detect the effect that he had on the young Paul McCartney. Holly was a significant influence on the Beatles because, unlike Elvis, he wrote all his own songs and had a permanent, identifiable backing group. John (who was short-sighted) was encouraged

I'LL FOLLOW THE SUN

Written:	Lennon/McCartney
Length:	1'51"
UK release:	*Beatles For Sale* album, December 4, 1964
US release:	*Beatles '65* album, December 15, 1964

Paul shows Ed Sullivan a few basic chords before the Beatles play his TV show, 1964.

that a bespectacled singer could become a rock'n'roll star and the initial naming of the group 'Beetles' was inspired by Buddy's Crickets.

Beatles For Sale included a Chuck Berry track ('Rock And Roll Music'), a Leiber and Stoller ('Kansas City'), a Little Richard ('Hey, Hey, Hey'), a Buddy Holly ('Words Of Love') and two songs by Carl Perkins ('Honey Don't' and 'Everybody's Trying To Be My Baby'), all of them recorded hurriedly towards the end of the sessions. "There are still one or two of our very early numbers which are worth recording," Paul explained to *Mersey Beat* at the time. "Every now and then we remember one of the good ones we wrote in the early days and one of them, 'I'll Follow The Sun', is on the LP."

In the Seventies, Paul's company MPL Communications bought Holly's publishing catalogue and has since been responsible for organizing an annual Buddy Holly Day.

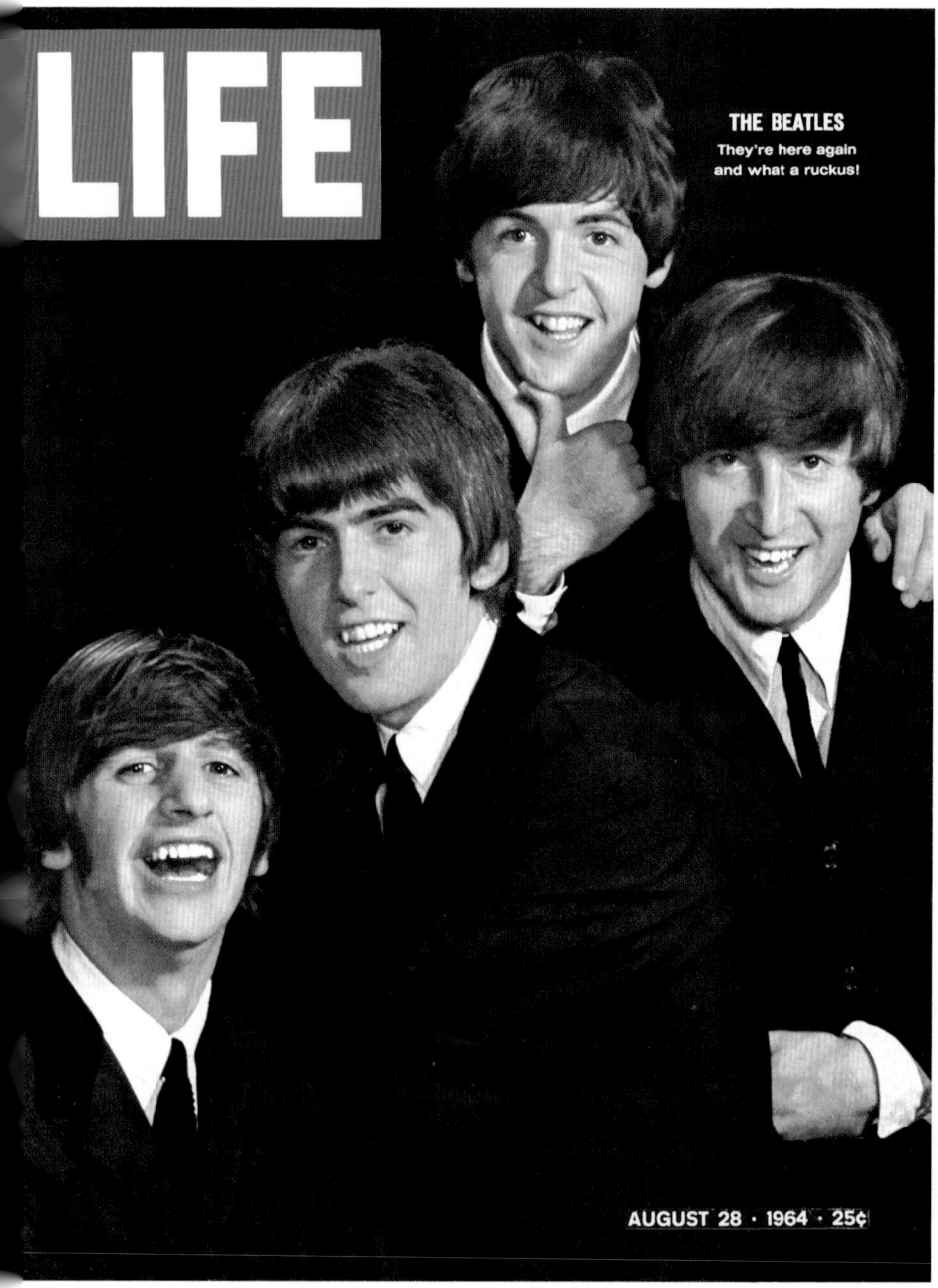
LIFE
THE BEATLES
They're here again
and what a ruckus!
AUGUST 28 · 1964 · 25¢

BABY'S IN BLACK

"They're here again and what a ruckus!" proclaimed *Time* as the Beatles began their US tour in August 1964.

BABY'S IN BLACK
Written: Lennon/McCartney
Length: 2' 07"
UK release: *Beatles For Sale* album, December 4, 1964
US release: *Beatles '65* album, December 15, 1964

A simple song with a simple story. Boy loves girl, girl loves other boy, other boy doesn't love girl. Girl is sad and therefore dresses in black.

By 1964, Lennon and McCartney seldom sat together and wrote a song from start to finish as they had done so often in the past. Even though some songs were still collaborations, this now usually meant that an unfinished song was given a middle eight by the other partner or awkward lines were improved. The nose-to-nose writing that had happened in Liverpool and during the early days in London was coming to an end. "It would be daft to sit around waiting for a partner to finish your song off with you," explained Paul at the time. "If you happen to be on your own, you might as well get it finished yourself. If I get stuck on the middle eight of a new number, I give up, knowing that when I see John he will finish it off for me. He'll bring a new approach to it and that particular song will finish up half and half, Lennon and McCartney."

'Baby's In Black' was a genuine joint effort, the first since 'I Want To Hold Your Hand' almost a year before, with John and Paul writing the song together in the same room at Kenwood. According to Paul it was another attempt to write something "a little bit darker, bluesy…" It became the first song to be recorded for *Beatles For Sale*.

EVERY LITTLE THING

'Every Little Thing', was written by Paul for Jane Asher and had much the same theme as 'Things We Said Today'. Reflecting the values of the era it tells the tale of a lucky guy whose girl loves him so much she does everything for him.

It's another song which wouldn't go down so well in the Nineties because the girl's needs are not even considered, the assumption being that she should find her fulfilment in serving her man. Ironically, it was the attitudes expressed in this song that Jane Asher later challenged when she told Paul she need to find fulfilment in her acting career. It wasn't enough for her to be simply the girlfriend of one of the world's most desirable pop stars; she wanted to make her own mark in the world of the arts.

Although this song was credited solely to Paul who had come up with the basis for the track in his room at the Asher family home in Wimpole Street, John remembered that he might have "thrown something in" too. It was an attempt at writing a single, but became an album track.

Paul wrote 'Every Little Thing' for his girlfriend, Jane Asher, while living at the Asher family home in London.

EVERY LITTLE THING

Written:	Lennon/McCartney
Length:	2' 04"
UK release:	*Beatles For Sale* album, December 4, 1964
US release:	*Beatles '65* album, December 15, 1964

WHAT YOU'RE DOING

Although 'What You're Doing' tells a fairly straightforward story of a boy being given the runaround by his girl, the lyric contains some inventive rhyming in 'doing' and 'blue an', 'running' and 'fun in'. The most memorable part of the arrangement was the Beatles shouting the first word of each verse, with Paul completing the phrases. It was possibly one of two songs that Paul started while staying at the La Fayette Motor Inn in Atlantic City on August 31st 1964.

Tim Riley, author of a book about the Beatles' music entitled *Tell Me Why,* praised the track for its pop ingenuity, saying that the addition of piano for just the guitar solo and the final fade-out suggested a love of detail that they were later to develop more fully: "The Beatles' conception of what the studio allowed them to do in altering textures and changing musical colours is emerging as a stylistic trait, not just a gimmick."

'What You're Doing' was another song written by Paul specifically for *Beatles For Sale* with additions from John. The recording was quite painstaking, beginning in September 1964 and picking up again in late October, at which time the track was completely re-made. Paul's final verdict was that it was a better recording than it was a song.

WHAT YOU'RE DOING
Written: Lennon/McCartney
Length: 2' 34"
UK release: *Beatles For Sale* album, December 4, 1964
US release: *Beatles VI* album, June 14, 1965

HELP!

The Beatles' second feature film was shot between February and May 1965 at a number of locations including New Providence Island in the Bahamas, the Austrian Alps, London's Cliveden House and Twickenham Film Studios.

The original script was by American Marc Behm who wanted Ringo to play a man who mistakenly signs his own death warrant and is pursued by a homicidal maniac played by Peter Sellers.

"We were just about to begin shooting when I learned that Philip de Brocca was filming the very same story – *The Troubles of a Chinaman in China* starring Jean-Paul Belmondo," says Behm. "I rushed to my pads and pencils and in a day or so wrote another script, *The Indian Giver*. It was this script that Richard Lester asked Charles Wood to do an 'English draft' of because he considered mine too American!"

Ringo was still the main protagonist in the rewrite where he was cast as the inheritor of a magic ring pursued by members of an evil cult. Again, all the songs, apart from the title track, were written with no knowledge of the script and dropped into the film at appropriate points. Dick Lester was given a tape of the songs and chose the six that he considered would best fit.

The Beatles later expressed dissatisfaction with *Help!*, saying that they'd been no more than extras in their own film. However, it was to mark the beginning of undoubtedly their most fertile period of songwriting.

John wrote the film's title track, using the word 'help' to explore his insecurity: it was to remain one of his favourite Beatles' songs. Paul's 'Yesterday', which was used on the non-soundtrack side of the

The Beatles were to express dissatisfaction with 1965 movie *Help!*, saying they had been 'no more than extras in their own film'.

album, went on to become the most covered of all the Beatles' songs and the first to be regarded as a classic.

Having discovered pot during the previous year, the Beatles were now smoking the drug regularly and John remembered this as their 'pot period', describing how reels of film had to be scrapped because all they featured were the Beatles in fits of uncontrollable laughter.

Help!, the album, was released in August 1965 and topped the charts in Britain and America. As with *A Hard Day's Night*, the American version consisted only of the songs in the film plus a few tracks by George Martin and an orchestra.

Posing with a piano (and a mysterious 'third leg' behind George) while shooting *Help!* in the Swiss Alps in 1965.

YES IT IS

John spoke about having once written love songs purely for 'the meat market' and yet it's hard to find the songs he was referring to. 'Yes It Is', though, was one song he felt particularly embarrassed about in later years, scoffing at the line 'for red is the colour that will make me blue'. John claimed that it was nothing more than an attempt to rewrite 'This Boy' as it had the same chords, harmonies and "double-Dutch words".

The lyric is a warning to a girl not to wear red because this is the colour that the singer's 'baby' always wore. John's final verdict on the song was that "it didn't work".

It was released as the B side to 'Ticket To Ride' in both Britain and America during April 1965.

YES IT IS

Written:	Lennon/McCartney
Length:	2' 42"
UK single release:	April 9, 1965 as B-side of 'Ticket To Ride'
US chart release:	April 19, 1965 as B-side of 'Ticket To Ride'

I'M DOWN

The B side of the single 'Help!', 'I'm Down' is an unashamed attempt by Paul to write a Little Richard song with which to replace 'Long Tall Sally' in the Beatles' set. "We spent a lot of time trying to write a real corker – something like 'Long Tall Sally'", Paul said in October 1964. "It's very difficult. 'I Saw Her Standing There' was the nearest we got to it. We're still trying to compose a Little Richard sort of song. I'd liken it to abstract painting. People think of 'Long Tall Sally' and say it sounds so easy to write. But it's the most difficult thing we've attempted. Writing a three-chord song that's clever is not easy."

'She's A Woman', although not as frenetic, was a similar attempt to get into the Little Richard mode but Paul always felt culturally disadvantaged because he hadn't been exposed to gospel music during his formative years. Church of England choirs and Salvation Army bands didn't quite provide the same sort of education for writing barn-storming rock'n'roll.

Little Richard, who'd had his first British hit with 'Rip It Up' in 1956,met the Beatles when they shared a bill at the Tower Ballroom,

I'M DOWN

Written:	Lennon/McCartney
Length:	2' 31"
UK single release:	July 23, 1965 as B-side of 'I'm Down'
US single release:	July 19, 1965 as B-side of 'I'm Down'

New Brighton, on October 12, 1962, one week after the release of 'Love Me Do'. It was a great moment for the group, who had featured 'Rip It Up', 'Good Golly Miss Molly', 'Tutti Frutti', 'Lucille' among several Little Richard numbers in their shows.

"I met them in Liverpool before the world ever knew about them," says Little Richard. "Paul especially was into my music and had been playing it since he was in high school. He was impressed with my hollerin' and, when I was on stage in Liverpool and later in Hamburg (at the Star Club the following month), he used to stay in the wings and watch me sing. I felt honoured that they liked my music. My style is very dynamic. It's full of joy, it's full of fun and it's alive. There is nothing dead about it. There's never a dull moment. It keeps you on your toes, it keeps you movin' and I think that's what everybody gets from my music. People know that if they sing one of my songs on stage, they're gonna light up the house."

Fittingly, the Beatles used 'I'm Down' to close the show during their 1965 and 1966 tours. The last song they ever played live in concert, though, at San Francisco's Candlestick Park on August 29, 1966, was Little Richard's 'Long Tall Sally'.

The band tread water in the swimming pool at the Nassau Beach Hotel while filming *Help!* in the Bahamas.

HELP!

As soon as he had embarked on his solo career in the Seventies, John would often refer to 'Help!' as one of his favourite Beatles' songs. He liked it, he said, because it was "real". His sole regret was that, for commercial reasons, they had changed it from a slow Dylanesque number into a jolly Beatles' tune.

'Help!' was written with Paul at John's Weybridge home, Kenwood, in April 1965. The lyric was a candid insight into John's dissatisfaction with himself. He was eating and drinking too much, had put on weight and felt trapped by fame. The song, he would later admit, really was a cry for help, despite being written to order for the film. "I needed the help," he said. "The song was about me."

Putting his feelings at the centre of a song, wasn't so much a departure as it was a consolidation of the self-examination that had always lurked beneath even the most innocent-sounding of his songs. The only difference was that now he seemed to be admitting that fame, wealth and success had heightened rather than relieved his anxiety.

At the pinnacle of pop stardom, John had started to look back with longing to what he now saw as those relatively uncomplicated days at Menlove Avenue. The idealization of his boyhood and adolescence was a theme that was to grow in significance in his songwriting.

Maureen Cleave, the London journalist who had helped out on the lyrics for A Hard Day's Night, felt that John should start to use words of more than one syllable. 'Help!' was his first serious attempt to do this, and he managed to incorporate 'self-assured', 'appreciate', 'independence' and 'insecure' within the song. (Maureen Cleave was actually at Weybridge, visiting Cynthia, when the song was being written.)

Despite being the main protagonist of *Help!*, Ringo looks less than enamoured of his lot as filming continues on Salisbury Plain.

In the film *Help!*, again directed by Dick Lester, the song was used in the title sequence, where black and white footage of the Beatles was projected on to a screen set up in the temple of the religious cult.

HELP!

Written:	Lennon/McCartney
Length:	2' 21"
UK single release:	July 23, 1965
UK chart position:	1
US single release:	July 19, 1965
US chart position:	1

THE NIGHT BEFORE

As with *A Hard Day's Night*, the songs used in *Help!* owed nothing to the script. "I think all the songs in *Help!* were written before the screenplay was even completed," confirms Dick Lester. "I was given a demo tape with about eleven songs and I chose six of them in a rather arbitrary way, thinking that they were ones which I could do something with. It was as casual as that and I fitted the songs into the film in places where I thought I could do something with them."

Composed as a song of regret over a love lost, Paul was filmed singing 'The Night Before' while surrounded by troops and tanks on Salisbury Plain. The track was recorded in February 1965 and filmed three months later.

THE NIGHT BEFORE

Written:	Lennon/McCartney
Length:	2' 36"
UK release:	*Help!* album, August 6, 1965
US release:	*Help!* album, August 13, 1965

YOU'VE GOT TO HIDE YOUR LOVE AWAY

Bob Dylan's music – (the acoustic *Another Side Of Bob Dylan* was his most recent album) – directed John towards a more intense and personal style of writing. He began to write songs in which his state of mind became the immediate starting point. In the first lines of 'You've Got To Hide Your Love Away', the image of John standing facing a wall with his head in his hands was probably a perfect description of how he felt when he was writing.

The song is about a relationship that has gone wrong and John's hidden feelings for a girl he has lost. Tony Bramwell suggests that it was written for Brian Epstein, warning him to keep his homosexual relationships (which, at the time, were illegal in Britain) from public view. It was also rumoured that it referred to a secret affair John was having.

Written by John at Kenwood, it was used in the film during a scene in which British actress Eleanor Bron visited the group in their terraced house to retrieve the missing ring.

John's childhood friend, Pete Shotton, was with him at Kenwood and remembered that in the original version he had sung that he felt 'two foot tall'. However, when he sang it to Paul, he mistakenly sang 'two foot small', which Paul liked better and so it was kept. Shotton went to the recording on February 18, 1965, and added some 'heys' to the chorus.

YOU'VE GOT TO HIDE YOUR LOVE AWAY
Written: Lennon/McCartney
Length: 2' 11"
UK release: *Help!* album, August 6, 1965
US release: *Help!* album, August 13, 1965

I NEED YOU

I NEED YOU
Written: Harrison
Length: 2' 31"
UK release: *Help!* album, August 6, 1965
US release: *Help!* album, August 13, 1965

A formulaic love song, 'I Need You' was written by George for his girlfriend Pattie Boyd, and was one of two of his Beatles' songs which he didn't comment on in his 1980 book *I Me Mine* (the other was 'You Like Me Too Much').

It was also the only George song to be featured in the film *Help!* (in the Salisbury Plain sequence) and the first to use a wah-wah pedal to distort the guitar sound.

Some Beatles' books have claimed that George wrote it in the Bahamas while separated from Pattie, but this can't be true as recording began on February 15, 1965, and these Bahamian scenes weren't shot until the following week.

George wrote 'I Need You' for Pattie Boyd but it is one of the less distinguished numbers in the Beatles' canon.

ANOTHER GIRL

'Another Girl' was written by Paul during a ten-day holiday in Tunisia and used in a scene filmed on Balmoral Island in the Bahamas.

In this song, Paul talks about being under pressure to commit long-term to his girlfriend but how he's not going to do this, mainly because he's already got himself another girl. This may have been a reference to the fact that although he was still firmly linked to Jane Asher in the public mind he was also seeing other women.

Speaking to Barry Miles for his authorised biography *Many Years From Now* Paul wrongly identified the villa as British Embassy property. It was actually Sebastian's Villa built in the coastal resort of Hammanet in the 1920s by George Sebastian. The Moorish-style building was later described by the great American architect Frank Lloyd Wright as "the most beautiful house I know." It was visited by Ernest Hemingway, F. Scott Fitzgerald and King Edward VII. During the war is was requisitioned by Rommell and then Churchill stayed there. It was gifted to the Tunisian state in 1959 and in 1964 an amphitheatre was added in the grounds. It was in the villa's huge sunken bath surrounded by colonnades that Paul wrote the song. Sebastian's Villa is now Hammanet's International Cultural Centre.

John once said that the Beatles' songs were like signatures; even when they weren't trying to give anything away they would betray their most fund-amental attitudes. "It was always apparent – if you looked below the surface – what was being said. Resentfulness or love or hate, it's apparent in all our work."

'Another Girl' was recorded the day after Paul returned from his holiday.

ANOTHER GIRL
Written: Lennon/McCartney
Length: 2' 08"
UK release: *Help!* album, August 6, 1965
US release: *Help!* album, August 13, 1965

YOU'RE GOING TO LOSE THAT GIRL

YOU'RE GOING TO LOSE THAT GIRL
Written: Lennon/McCartney
Length: 2' 20"
UK release: *Help!* album, August 6, 1965
US release: *Help!* album, August 13, 1965

The Beatles sang 'You're Going To Lose That Girl' in a scene in *Help!* set in the recording studio, which was actually filmed at Twickenham Film Studios. The song is interrupted when the gang chasing Ringo cut a hole around his drum kit from the ceiling of the room below.

Written mainly by John but completed with Paul at Weybridge, it is a warning to an unidentified male that if he doesn't start treating his girlfriend right, he (John) is going to move in on her, developing a theme he first outlined in 'She Loves You'.

Despite its comedic use in *Help!*, 'That Girl' developed a menacing lyrical theme John had first explored in 'She Loves You'.

Ringo, complete with the tools of his trade, peers from a carriage window during the filming of the promo for 'Ticket To Ride'.

TICKET TO RIDE

'Ticket To Ride' was written by John and Paul as a single and was described by John as "one of the earliest heavy metal records made". Although they were pipped at the post in the heavy metal stakes by the Kinks' 'You Really Got Me', this was the first Beatles' track to feature an insistent, clanking riff underpinned by a heavy drum beat and it used a fade-out with an altered melody.

Used in *Help!*, during the Austrian snow scenes, it was released as a single in April 1965 and had already topped the charts in Britain and America by the time the film came out. Paul confessed to his biographer Barry Miles that the apparently loopy suggestion made by some American Beatles' fans at the time that the song was referring to a British Railways ticket to the town of Ryde on the Isle of Wight was partly right. Paul's cousin Betty Robbins and her husband Mike ran the Bow Bars in Union Street, Ryde, and Paul and John had visited them there. Although the song was primarily about a girl riding out of the life of the narrator, they were conscious of the potential for a double meaning.

Don Short, a show business journalist who travelled extensively with the Beatles in the Sixties, was told by John that the phrase had yet another meaning. "The girls who worked the streets in Hamburg had to have a clean bill of health and so the medical authorities would give them a card saying that they didn't have a dose of anything," says Short. "I was with the Beatles when they went back to Hamburg in June 1966 and it was then that John told me that he had coined the phrase 'a ticket to ride' to describe these cards. He could have been joking – you always had to be careful with John like that – but I certainly remember him telling me that."

TICKET TO RIDE
Written: Lennon/McCartney
Length: 3' 12"
UK single release: April 9, 1965
UK chart position: 1
US chart release: April 19, 1965
US chart position: 1

TELL ME WHAT YOU SEE

'Tell Me What You See' was another 'work song' by Paul who asks his girl to give her heart to him because he's utterly trustworthy and will brighten up her life. If she doesn't believe him, he suggests that she take a look in his eyes and tell him what she sees.

The track was recorded before the filming of *Help!* and offered to Dick Lester for the soundtrack, but was rejected. Obviously, he was not too keen on what he heard. Tim Riley, in his book about the Beatles' music, notes that it is one of the album's weaker songs, suggesting that it became a working draft for the altogether stronger track 'I'm Looking Through You'.

TELL ME WHAT YOU SEE

Written:	Lennon/McCartney
Length:	2' 39"
UK release:	*Help!* album, August 6, 1965
US release:	*Beatles VI* album, June 14, 1965

YOU LIKE ME TOO MUCH

'You Like Me Too Much' was written and recorded by George for the soundtrack and recorded before filming started on *Help!* It was eventually relegated to the B side of the album.

George chose not to discuss 'You Like Me Too Much' in his otherwise comprehensive account of his songwriting, *I Me Mine*, presumably because there was nothing much to say. A standard love story, the song describes how having been jilted, the lover feels everything will turn out all right in the end, as the girl simply loves him too much. If it had been written by John, he would undoubtedly have dismissed it as one of his throwaways.

YOU LIKE ME TOO MUCH
Written: Harrison
Length: 2' 38"
UK release: *Help!* album, August 6, 1965
US release: *Beatles VI* album, June 14, 1965

George's 'You Like Me Too Much' was one of the lesser tracks on the *Help!* soundtrack.

IT'S ONLY LOVE

John wrote 'It's Only Love' as an upbeat number, chock-full of the most clichéd rhymes and images, so it is little wonder people think this song is completely out of character. In the lyric, he describes how his girl lights up the night for him and yet he's suffering from butterflies in his stomach. The real problem is that he is in love.

It was one of the few Beatles' songs that John really hated. "I was always ashamed of that because of the abominable lyrics," he admitted in 1969. All the songs that John regretted having written were condemned on the grounds of their lyrics rather than their melodies, because he felt that he had produced platitudes rather than expressed any real feeling.

In this case, the song's shortcomings could have been a result of the pressure to come up with a further side of songs to complete the soundtrack album or simply that John was feeling at a low ebb.

George Martin and his orchestra recorded the composition as an instrumental using John's original working title of 'That's A Nice Hat'.

IT'S ONLY LOVE

Written:	Lennon/McCartney
Length:	1' 58"
UK release:	*Help!* album, August 6, 1965
US release:	*Rubber Soul* album, December 6, 1965

I'VE JUST SEEN A FACE

'I've Just Seen A Face' was a tune which Paul had been playing on piano for some time. He played it at family get-togethers back in Liverpool and his Auntie Gin loved it so much that it was dubbed 'Auntie Gin's Theme'. The George Martin Orchestra went on to record an instrumental version under this title.

Auntie Gin was the youngest sister of Paul's father Jim and would later get a mention in 'Let 'Em In' recorded by Wings, Paul's post-Beatle band.

I'VE JUST SEEN A FACE
Written: Lennon/McCartney
Length: 2' 07"
UK release: *Help!* album, August 6, 1965
US release: *Rubber Soul* album, December 6, 1965

A definite tonic to Paul's Auntie Gin, 'I've Just Seen A Face' was aired at McCartney family parties.

YESTERDAY

Paul woke up one morning in his top floor bedroom at the Ashers' home in Wimpole Street with the tune for 'Yesterday' in his head. There was a piano by the bed and he went straight to it and started playing. "It was just all there," he said. "A complete thing. I couldn't believe it."

Although at that point it had no lyric, Paul was worried that the tune itself might have been unconsciously plagiarized, and that what had seemed like a flash of inspiration may only have been a surge of recollection. "For about a month, I went round to people in the music business and asked them whether they had ever heard it before," he said. "Eventually it became like handing something in to the police. I thought that if no one claimed it after a few weeks then I would have it."

He then came up with the provisional title 'Scrambled Eggs' and began singing 'Scrambled eggs, Oh you've got such lovely legs', simply to get a feel for the vocal. This was a common practice and sometimes gave rise to interesting lines that were kept in the final version.

"We were shooting *Help!* in the studio for about four weeks," remembers Dick Lester. "At some time during that period, we had a piano on one of the stages and he was playing this 'Scrambled Eggs' all the time. It got to the point where I said to him, 'If you play that bloody song any longer I'll have the piano taken off stage. Either finish it or give it up!' "

Paul must have conceived the tune early in 1965, but it wasn't until June when he took a brief holiday in Portugal at the villa of Shadows' guitarist Bruce Welch that he'd completed the lyric. He then hit on the idea of using a one-word title – 'Yesterday'.

YESTERDAY

Written:	Lennon/McCartney
Length:	2' 07"
UK release:	*Help!* album, August 6, 1965
US single release:	September 13, 1966
US chart position:	1

"I was packing to leave and Paul asked me if I had a guitar," says Welch. "He'd apparently been working on the lyrics as he drove to Albufeira from the airport at Lisbon. He borrowed my guitar and started playing the song we all now know as 'Yesterday'."

Two days after returning from Portugal, Paul recorded it at Abbey Road. The song startled pop fans at the time because it featured a string quartet with Paul as the only Beatle on the session. In America, it became a single and reached the Number 1 spot but, in Britain, it was never released as either an A or a B side during the group's career.

It rapidly became a pop standard, covered by everyone from Frank Sinatra to Marianne Faithfull. Nowadays, some 30 years on, it is still one of the most played tracks on American radio.

Although John claimed that he never wished that he had written it, he did admit that it was a "beautiful" song with "good" lyrics but argued that the lyrics were never resolved.

However, others have felt that its strength lies in its vagueness. All the listener needs to know is that it's about someone wanting to turn back the clock, to retreat to a time before a tragic event. The application is universal.

There has been speculation that in Paul's case the tragedy referred to was the death of his mother and the regret was over his inability to express his grief at the time.

Iris Caldwell remembered an interesting incident in connection with the song. She had broken up with Paul in March 1963 after a silly argument over her dogs (Paul wasn't too keen on dogs at the time) and, when he later called up to speak to Iris, her mother told Paul that her daughter didn't want to speak to him because he had no feelings.

Two and a half years later, on Sunday August 1, 1965, Paul was scheduled to sing 'Yesterday' on a live television programme, *Blackpool*

"Have you come far? And what do you do?" The Beatles encounter Princess Margaret at the London premiere of *Help!*, July 1965.

Night Out. During that week, he phoned Mrs Caldwell and said; "You know that you said that I had no feelings? Watch the telly on Sunday and then tell me that I've got no feelings."

In July 2003 the Liverpool writer Spencer Leigh made the discovery that there were both musical and lyrical similarities between 'Yesterday' and the Nat King Cole song 'Answer Me' (1953). The Cole song even has the lines 'Yesterday I believed that love was here to stay/ Won't you tell me that I've gone astray?' The response from Paul's office when the news broke was that the two songs were as alike as 'Get Back' and 'God Save The Queen'.

RUBBER SOUL

Although there had been hints of a new direction on the preceding albums, *Rubber Soul* marked a major period of transition. John would later call it the beginning of the group's 'self-conscious' period; the end of the Beatles' 'tribal child-like' stage.

Despite the cover, with its deliberately distorted photograph of the Beatles suggesting the perception shifts of LSD and marijuana, this wasn't a psychedelic album. Musically, however, it was an exploration of new sounds and new subject matter, introducing Paul on fuzz bass and George on sitar.

When producer George Martin played the piano solo back at double-speed to create a baroque sound, it was the first time that they'd tampered with tapes to create an effect.

There was a playfulness to *Rubber Soul* that extended from the wordplay of the title down to the 'beep beeps' and 'tit tits' of the backing vocals. Paul was quoted at the time as saying that they were now into humorous songs and both 'Drive My Car', with its role reversal, and 'Norwegian Wood', with its naive seduction scene, fitted into this category.

For a group that had only ever sung about love, 'Nowhere Man', a song about lack of belief, was a breakthrough: other songs like 'The Word' and 'In My Life' were only tangentially about boy-girl relationships.

The love songs of this evidenced a new maturity. Paul's 'We Can Work It Out', stemming from his own increasingly troubled relationship with Jane Asher, was a long way from the simple hope expressed in 'She Loves You' or 'I Want To Hold Your Hand'. John's 'The Word' pointed in the direction of the universal love that would

Although *Rubber Soul* saw the band getting more experimental, John and Paul were into 'humorous songs".

later be the basis of songs like 'Within You Without You' and 'All You Need Is Love'.

Recorded over a four-week period in the autumn of 1965, *Rubber Soul* was released in December and became a chart-topping album in Britain and America. Four of the British tracks were left off the American album and these were replaced by two tracks from *Help!*

DAY TRIPPER

'Day Tripper' was written under pressure when the Beatles needed a new single for the Christmas market. John wrote most of the lyric and the basic guitar break, coming up with a riff that he later admitted was derived from 'I Feel Fine'. Paul helped on the verses and his bass riff owed something to the bass riff on Roy Orbison's 'Oh Pretty Woman' (1964).

In the summer of 1965, John and George had been introduced to LSD by a London dentist who slipped it into their coffee after an evening meal. In August, while in America, they took a trip of their own free will and from then on John confessed that he "just ate it all the time". 'Day Tripper' was a typical play on words by John, who wanted to reflect the influence of the growing drug culture within a Beatles' song. It was his way of referring to those who couldn't, like him, afford the luxury of being almost permanently tripped out. "It's just a rock'n'roll song," commented John. "Day trippers are people who go on a day trip, right? Usually on a ferryboat or something. But (the song) was kind of…you're just a weekend hippie. Get it?"

The song is about a girl who leads the singer on. His oblique description of the girl as a 'big teaser', was a knowing reference to the term 'prick teaser', a phrase used by British men about women who encouraged sexual arousal with no intention of having sex.

'Day Tripper' was released in both Britain and America as a double A-side single with 'We Can Work It Out'. It was the more popular song in Britain, reaching Number 1, but in America it peaked at five. The Beatles later said that 'We Can Work It Out' was their choice for the A side.

DAY TRIPPER
Written: Lennon/McCartney
Length: 2' 49"
UK single release: December 3, 1965 as double A-side with 'We Can Work It Out'
UK chart position: 1
US single release: December 6, 1965 as double A-side with 'We Can Work It Out'
US chart position: 5
** Although 'Day Tripper'/'We Can Work It Out' was a double A-side single, US chart compilers calculated their sales separately*

WE CAN WORK IT OUT

Despite its references to drugs, 'Day Tripper' (left) was aimed at the Christmas market.

WE CAN WORK IT OUT
Written: Lennon/McCartney
Length: 2' 15"
UK single release: December 3, 1965 as double A-side with 'Day Tripper'
UK chart position: 1
US single release: December 6, 1965 as double A-side with 'Day Tripper'
US chart position: 1

In October 1965, Jane Asher decided to join the Bristol Old Vic Company, which meant that she moved away from London to the west of England just at the time the Beatles were recording tracks for *Rubber Soul.* Her departure upset Paul and caused the first major rift in their relationship. As had been suggested in his songs, Paul's notion of a good woman then was someone who would be happy just to be around him. Jane's outlook was unusual at that time. She was not content to be a rock star's 'chick'. She was well-educated, independently minded and wanted, above all, to establish her own career.

In 'We Can Work It Out', Paul doesn't try to argue the merits of his case, but simply pleads with his woman to see things his way because he believes he is right and she is wrong. It was typical of Paul that, faced with what could be the end of a relationship, he didn't retreat sobbing to his room, but emerged with the positive slogan 'we can work it out'. The slightly downbeat middle eight, with its intimations of mortality, was added by John.

"You've got Paul writing 'we can work it out'," said John. "Real optimistic, and me, impatient, (with) 'Life is very short, And there's no time, For fussing and fighting my friend.'" The song was written at Paul's father's house in Heswall, Cheshire. The harmonium 'wash' was added in the studio as an afterthought and George Harrison suggested changing the middle-eight to waltz time.

DRIVE MY CAR

A first hearing of 'Drive My Car' might suggest that the Beatles are telling some 'baby' to drive their car, but closer inspection of the lyric reveals that it's the male narrator who is being asked to do the driving. He's trying to chat someone up, using that well-worn line, 'Well, what do you want to be?' – suggesting sexual favours in return for promises of career advancement.

The woman tells him that she wants to be a movie star – but then reverses the roles by saying that she might (and it is only might) agree to give him some love if he agrees to be her chauffeur. By the second verse it's the man who is pleading his case, arguing that his 'prospects are good'.

Paul remembered this song as the only one he got stuck on, the storyline being pulled together at the last minute with some help from John. When he arrived at Abbey Road on October 20, 1965, to record the song, the chorus was 'I can give you golden rings, I can give you anything, Baby I love you'. John dismissed this as "crap" and so the two of them huddled together to create an alternative and came up with 'Baby, you can drive my car', a tougher, more sexually-charged image

DRIVE MY CAR

Written:	Lennon/McCartney
Length:	2' 30"
UK release:	*Rubber Soul* album, December 3, 1965
US release:	*Yesterday And Today* album, June 20, 1966

"We've written some funny songs – songs with jokes in," said Paul, shortly after the band had finished recording 'Drive My Car'.

which in turn gave rise to the 'Beep beep beep beep yeah' background vocal. This was of course a playful reference to the 'yeah, yeah, yeah' that had become their signature shout and a gift to headline writers but it may also have been a nod to 'Beep Beep' by the Playmates (1958), a song that was a fixture on BBC's radio programming for children at the time that the Beatles started out.

John always agreed it was Paul's song with a bit of last-minute tuning and Paul said: "The idea of the girl being a bitch was the same but (the change) made the key line better." Two days after recording 'Drive My Car', Paul told a music magazine, "We've written some funny songs – songs with jokes in. We think that comedy numbers are the next thing after protest songs."

The bass line was patterned after Donald 'Duck' Dunn's playing on Otis Redding's 'Respect' (1965), which had been released the month before 'Drive My Car' was recorded.

NORWEGIAN WOOD

Although John was famous as the married Beatle he was not happily married. Nor was he faithful. He took advantage of backstage groupies, admitted to having been photographed on his hands and knees outside a Dutch brothel, and confessed to Cynthia in 1968 that he had had affairs. 'Norwegian Wood' was about one such entanglement. In language John later described as 'gobbledygook', the song details a seduction scene where again the woman appears to be the one in control.

The lyrics open with a boast about a girl John has 'had', but he quickly corrects himself by saying that it was she who 'had' him. She takes him back to her apartment and asks him to admire the furnishings that are made out of cheap Norwegian pine. After talking and drinking until two in the morning, she says it's time for bed. In the song, he makes his excuses and leaves for a night in the bathroom, but in reality the story obviously had a different ending because he said it had been written about an act of unfaithfulness, "without letting my wife know I was writing about an affair". John's friend Pete Shotton has said that it was about a female journalist that John was close to.

John began 'Norwegian Wood' in February 1965 while on a skiing holiday in St Moritz, Switzerland, with Cynthia, George Martin and George's future wife, Judy, but only came up with the basic tune and an opening couplet. He later asked Paul for help and Paul suggested that he should develop a story about a girl who leads a man on and ends with the man setting the apartment on fire as an act of revenge. Pete Shotton thought this could have referred to John's habit of burning furniture in the fireplace at Gambier Terrace

NORWEGIAN WOOD
Written: Lennon/McCartney
Length: 2' 05"
UK release: *Rubber Soul* album, December 3, 1965
US release: *Rubber Soul* album, December 6, 1965

in Liverpool when there was no money for coal. While he was there, John would sometimes ask guests to sleep in the bath, the memory of which may have prompted the line in 'Norwegian Wood' about sleeping in the bath.

Paul saw the song as a complete fantasy. The Norwegian wood of the title was suggested by the decoration of Peter Asher's room in Wimpole Street but to John it was definitely about a secret affair.

The track stood out on *Rubber Soul* for its use of sitar – it was the first time the Indian instrument had been used on a pop record. George Harrison had become fascinated with the sitar after coming across one while filming *Help!* in the Bahamas, and would later study under the Indian master Ravi Shankar.

John, Cynthia and Julian Lennon pose for a Goons-style slapstick photo, but the Beatle was unfaithful to his wife on a regular basis..

YOU WON'T SEE ME

As his relationship with Jane Asher turned sour, Paul's songs for her grew increasingly pained and vulnerable.

'You Won't See Me' was another song written by Paul during the crisis in his relationship with Jane Asher. By now, he was suffering the indignity of unanswered phone calls and other rejections. The dip in his romantic fortunes raised his writing to new heights because he now found he was the one in the vulnerable position. Paul had never seen life from this perspective. Throughout *Beatles For Sale* and *Help!*, he'd been dreaming up situations for his love songs but now, perhaps for the first time, he was writing from the heart.

It was written as a two-note progression and Paul had the Motown sound in mind, particularly the melodic bass playing of James Jamerson, the legendary studio musician. Ian MacDonald in *Revolution In The Head* suggests that the specific model he might have had in mind might have been 'It's The Same Old Song' by The Four Tops.

'You Won't See Me' was recorded during the last session for *Rubber Soul*, by which time Jane was playing in *Great Expectations* at the Theatre Royal, Bristol.

YOU WON'T SEE ME

Written:	Lennon/McCartney
Length:	3' 22"
UK release:	*Rubber Soul* album, December 3, 1965
US release:	*Rubber Soul* album, December 6, 1965

NOWHERE MAN

Recorded on October 21 and 22, 'Nowhere Man' has the distinction of being the first Beatles' song not to be about love. John wrote it early one morning after a night out and it marked the beginning of his overtly philosophical musings.

'Nowhere Man' was always assumed to be either about a specific person (in her Hollywood exposé *You'll Never Eat Lunch In This Town Again*, Julia Phillips speculated that it was written about an entrepreneur called Michael Brown) or about an archetypal member of 'straight' society whose life had no purpose.

John said that he was the 'Nowhere Man' in question, and that desperation had driven him to it after he'd been writing solidly for over five hours, feeling that he wouldn't be able to complete another song for the album. "I'd actually stopped trying to think of something," he told Beatles' biographer Hunter Davies. "Nothing would come. I was cheesed off and went for a lie-down, having given up. Then I thought of myself as Nowhere Man – sitting in his nowhere land."

Like 'Help' it was about John's lack of self-worth and probably also about the fact that he felt both trapped in his marriage and trapped in the suburbs.

NOWHERE MAN
Written: Lennon/McCartney
Length: 2' 44"
UK release: *Rubber Soul* album, December 3, 1965
US single release: February 21, 1966
US chart position: 3

THINK FOR YOURSELF

Think For Yourself', a song written by George Harrison, is an admonition against listening to lies. Recorded just a few months before his engagement to Pattie Boyd, it was presumably not about his wife-to-be. "It must be about 'somebody' from the sound of it," he wrote in his book *I Me Mine*. "But all this time later, I don't quite recall who inspired that tune. Probably the government."

THINK FOR YOURSELF
Written: Harrison
Length: 2' 19"
UK release: *Rubber Soul* album, December 3, 1965
US release: *Rubber Soul* album, December 6, 1965

George and Pattie Boyd on their wedding day, January 21, 1966.

THE WORD

THE WORD
Written: Lennon/McCartney
Length: 2' 43"
UK release: *Rubber Soul* album, December 3, 1965
US release: *Rubber Soul* album, December 6, 1965

Recorded two years after 'She Loves You' and two years before 'All You Need Is Love', 'The Word' marks the transition between the boy-meets-girl love of Beatlemania and the peace-and-harmony love of the hippy era.

Understood at the time as just another Beatles' love song, it was actually sprinkled with clues pointing to a song of a different kind. The love that John was now singing about offered 'freedom' and 'light'. It even offered 'the way'. He may even have been thinking of 'the word' in the evangelistic sense of 'preaching the word'.

In their classic study, *The Varieties Of Psychedelic Experience*, Masters and Houston found that not only did LSD often produce experiences of a religious nature, but it could provide people with the idea that "a universal or brotherly love is possible and constitutes man's best if not only hope". It was for this reason that 'love' became such a buzz word within the drug culture of the mid-to-late Sixties, John being one of the first songwriters to catch the mood. He later recalled the song as one of the Beatles' first 'message songs' and the beginnings of the group's role as cultural leaders expected to supply answers to social and spiritual questions.

John told *Playboy* that it was a song about "getting smart", meaning the state of realization which users of marijuana and LSD were claiming as theirs. "It's love," he said. "It's the marijuana period. It's the love and peace thing. The word is 'love', right?"

Appropriately, when John and Paul had finished writing it at Kenwood they rolled joints and wrote out a psychedically decorated lyric sheet which John later gave to composer John Cage for his 50th birthday. A reproduction can be seen in Cage's book *Notations*.

MICHELLE

Nina Simone's phrasing on her hit 'I Put A Spell On You" helped to shape 'Michelle'.

'Michelle' dates back to Liverpool days when Paul went to parties thrown by one of John's art tutors, Austin Mitchell. This was at a time when the intellectual life of the Parisian Left Bank was fashionable among art students and bohemianism was signalled by berets, beards and Gitanes. "Back in those days people would point at you in the street in Liverpool if you had a beard," remembers Rod Murray, who shared the Gambier Terrace flat with John and Stuart Sutcliffe. "If you had a beret, they would call you a beatnik. We liked Juliette Greco and everyone fancied getting in with Brigitte Bardot."

At one of these parties, a student with a goatee beard and a striped T-shirt was hunched over his guitar singing what sounded like a French song. Soon after, Paul began to work a comical imitation to amuse his friends.

It remained a party piece with nothing more than Charles Aznavour-style Gallic groanings as accompaniment until, in 1965, John suggested that Paul should write proper words for it and include it on the album.

Radio presenter Muriel Young, then working for Radio Luxembourg, can remember Paul visiting her at her holiday home in Portugal while he was working on it. This was probably during September 1965 when the Beatles took a month off between the American tour, which had finished on August 31, and the new album which was due to begin recording on October 12.

"He sat on our sofa with Jane Asher and he was trying to find the words," Muriel says. "It wasn't 'Michelle, ma belle' then. He was singing 'Goodnight sweetheart' and then 'Hello my dear', just looking for something that would fit the rhythm."

Eventually, Paul chose to go with the French feel and to incorporate a French name and some French words. He spoke to Jan Vaughan, the wife of his old school friend Ivan Vaughan (the person responsible for introducing Paul to John), who was a French language teacher. "I asked her what sort of things I could say that were French and which would go together well," said Paul. "It was because I'd always thought that the song sounded French that I stuck with it. I can't speak French properly so that's why I needed help in sorting out the actual words."

Jan remembers that Paul first spoke to her about it when she and Ivan were visiting him at the Ashers' London home. "He asked me if I could think of a French girl's first name, with two syllables, and then a description of the girl which would rhyme. He played me the rhythm on his guitar and that's when I came up with 'Michelle, ma belle', which wasn't actually that hard to think of! I think it was some days later that he phoned me up and asked if I could translate the phrase 'these are words that go together well' and I told him that it should be 'sont les mots qui vont très bien ensemble'."

When Paul played the song to John he suggested the 'I love you' in the middle section, specifying that the emphasis should fall on the word 'love' each time. He was inspired by Nina Simone's recording of 'I Put A Spell On You', a hit in Britain during August 1965, where she had used the same phrase but placed the emphasis on the 'you'. "My contribution to Paul's songs was always to add a little bluesy edge to them," John said. "Otherwise, 'Michelle' is a straight ballad."

Instrumentally, Paul was inspired by the finger picking style of Chet Atkins as exemplified on 'Trambone' (1961) and was proud to have introduced the new chord of F7 #9 that he had been taught by Jim Gretty, the regular musical demonstrator at Frank Hessy's Musical Store in Liverpool.

"I remember George and I were in the shop when Gretty played it," said Paul. "We said 'wow! What was that, man?' And he answered, 'It's just basically an F, but you barre the top two strings at the fourth fret with your little finger. We immediately learned that and for a while it was the only jazz chord we knew."

MICHELLE
Written: Lennon/McCartney
Length: 2' 42"
UK release: *Rubber Soul* album, December 3, 1965
US release: *Rubber Soul* album, December 6, 1965

WHAT GOES ON

'What Goes On' was actually one of the four songs which the Beatles played to George Martin on March 5, 1963, as possible follow-ups to 'Please Please Me'. (The other three were 'From Me To You', 'Thank You Girl' and 'The One After 909').

Written by John some time previously, it was the only song Martin chose not to record on that day and it was forgotten until November 4, 1965, when it was taken out and dusted down for Ringo's vocal number. A new middle eight was added by Paul and Ringo; giving Ringo his first-ever credit as a composer. Asked in 1966 what exactly his contribution to the song had been, Ringo said: "About five words".

In America, it was released as the B side of 'Nowhere Man' in February 1966.

The Beatles revisited their achive of unused songs for 'What Goes On', which Ringo sang.

WHAT GOES ON

Written:	Lennon/McCartney
Length:	2' 50"
UK release:	*Rubber Soul* album, December 3, 1965
US single release:	February 21, 1966 as B-side to 'Nowhere Man'
US chart position:	3

GIRL

Asked who the girl was in 'Girl', John said that she was a figure from a dream, the ideal woman who had not yet appeared in his life. "I always had this dream of this particular woman coming into my life," he said. "I knew it wouldn't be someone buying Beatles' records. I was hoping for a woman who could give me what I get from a man intellectually. I wanted someone I could be myself with."

However, the girl in the song seems far from his ideal. She's heartless, she's conceited and she humiliates him. Perhaps there are two girls in the song: the dream girl in the first half, whom he appears almost addicted to, and the nightmare girl in the second half who holds him up to ridicule.

The most John ever said about the song, though, was not to do with his images of women but his image of the Christian church.

In 1970, he revealed to *Rolling Stone* that the verse which asks whether she had been taught that pain would lead to pleasure, and that a man must break his back to earn leisure, was a reference to, "the Catholic/Christian concept – be tortured and then it'll be all

GIRL

Written:	Lennon/McCartney
Length:	2' 33"
UK release:	*Rubber Soul* album, December 3, 1965
US release:	*Rubber Soul* album, December 6, 1965

The bouzouki guitar of 'Girl" is likely to have been influenced by a hit taken from the soundtrack of movie *Zorba the Greek*..

right." He added, "I was...trying to say something or other about Christianity, which I was opposed to at the time."

He could have been thinking of the Genesis account of the effects of Adam and Eve's disobedience, where Eve is told that "with pain you will give birth to children" and Adam is told that "cursed is the ground because of you; through painful toil you will eat of it all the days of your life."

Christianity, and in particular Jesus Christ, seemed to bother John. At the time of writing 'Girl', he was devouring books about religion, a subject that preoccupied him until his death, and four months later he gave the interview to Maureen Cleave containing his infamous comment that the Beatles were"more popular than Jesus".

The bouzouki style of guitar playing could have been influenced by the recent hit single 'Zorba's Dance' by Marcello Minerbi taken from the soundtrack of *Zorba The Greek*. The background vocals emulated the 'la la la la' chorus the Beach Boys used on 'You're So Good To me' (July 1965) but for a joke they sang 'tit tit tit tit' in the studio rather than the scheduled 'dit dit dit dit'. These borrowings show that the Beatles were as influenced by current chart music as they were by rare B sides and fifties r & b hits.

I'M LOOKING THROUGH YOU

Jane Asher's move to Bristol continued to preoccupy Paul. It meant that she was no longer readily at hand even though he was still living in her family home in Wimpole Street. As a young working-class man from Liverpool, he found it hard to come to terms with a girl who put her career before romance.

He later admitted to Hunter Davies that his whole existence so far revolved around living a carefree bachelor's life. He hadn't treated women as most people did. He'd always had a lot around him, even when he had steady girlfriends. "I knew I was selfish," he said. "It caused a few rows. Jane went off and I said, 'OK then. Leave. I'll find someone else.' It was shattering to be without her. That was when I wrote 'I'm Looking Through You'."

This was Paul's most bitter song so far. Rather than question his own attitudes, Paul accuses his woman of changing and holds out the thinly veiled threat of withdrawing his affection. Love has a habit, he warns, of disappearing overnight. He would later remember the song as having served to get rid of "some emotional baggage".

I'M LOOKING THROUGH YOU

Written:	Lennon/McCartney
Length:	2' 27"
UK release:	*Rubber Soul* album, December 3, 1965
US release:	*Rubber Soul* album, December 6, 1965

IN MY LIFE

Although John had been writing more obviously autobiographical songs for over a year now, it was with 'In My Life' that he felt he'd made the breakthrough that Kenneth Allsop had encouraged him to make in March 1964, when he suggested focusing on his own interior life.

Recorded in October 1965, the song was a long time in gestation. It started, John said, as a long poem in which he reflected on favourite childhood haunts by tracing a journey from his home on Menlove Avenue down to the 'Docker's Umbrella', the overhead railway which ran along Liverpool's dockside until 1958 and beneath which dockers would shelter from the rain.

Elliot Mintz, who was hired by Yoko Ono to carry out an inventory of all John's personal possessions after his death, remembers seeing the first handwritten draft of the song. "It was part of a large book in which he kept all his original Beatles' compositions," says Mintz. "He had already told me about how the song was written and that he considered it a significant turning point in his writing and, just as he had described to me, the song went on at great length and included lots of place names including Penny Lane."

In a later single-page draft of this rambling lyric, John listed Penny Lane, Church Road, the clock tower, the Abbey Cinema, the tram sheds, the Dutch cafe, St Columbus Church, the Docker's Umbrella and Calderstones Park. Although this fulfiled the requirement of being autobiographical, John realized that it was no more than a series of snapshots held loosely together by his feeling that once familiar landmarks were fast disappearing. The tramsheds were now 'without trams' and the Docker's Umbrella had been 'pulled down'. "It was the most boring sort of 'what I did on my holidays' bus trip

John felt that 'In My Life' represented a major leap in his bid to become a more raw, confessional writer.

IN MY LIFE

Written:	Lennon/McCartney
Length:	2' 27"
UK release:	*Rubber Soul* album, December 3, 1965
US release:	*Rubber Soul* album, December 6, 1965

song and it wasn't working at all..." he said. "Then I lay back and these lyrics started coming to me about the places I remember."

John jettisoned all the specific place names, and worked up the sense of mourning for a disappeared childhood and youth, turning what would otherwise have been a song about the changing face of Liverpool into a universal song about confronting death and decay. Here was a tough guy, who had been known to laugh at cripples and who poured scorn on the middle-class nature of his upbringing, but who was also a sentimentalist. Throughout his life, he kept a box of childhood mementos in his apartment and once wrote to his Aunt Mimi asking her to send him his Quarry Bank school tie.

He later told Pete Shotton that when he wrote the line about friends in 'In My Life', some of whom were dead and some of whom were living, he was thinking specifically of Shotton and former Beatle Stuart Sutcliffe, who had died of a brain tumour in April 1962.

The lyric bears a surprising resemblance to Charles Lamb's 18th-century poem 'The old Familiar Faces' which John could well have come across in the popular poetry anthology *Palgrave's Treasury*. The poem starts:

I have had playmates, I have had companions,
In my days of childhood, in my joyful schooldays:
All, all are gone, the old familiar faces.

Six verses later it concludes with:

How some they have died,
and some they have left me,
And some are taken from me; all are departed;
All, all are gone, the old familiar faces.

The source of the melody to 'In My Life' remains in dispute. John has said that Paul helped out with a section on which he was stuck. Paul still believes he wrote it all. "I remember that he had the words written out like a long poem and I went off and worked something out on the Mellotron," he said. "The tune, if I remember rightly, was inspired by the Miracles." He was almost certainly referring to 'You Really Got A Hold On Me'.

On the track itself, the instrumental break was played by George Martin who recorded himself on piano and then played it back at double speed to create a baroque effect. John's opinion on the finished result was that it was his "first real major piece of work".

WAIT

WAIT
Written: Lennon/McCartney
Length: 2' 16"
UK release: *Rubber Soul* album, December 3, 1965
US release: *Rubber Soul* album, December 6, 1965

The Beatles don't appear to have had any great affection for 'Wait'. It was first recorded for *Help!* in June 1965, but not used, and was taken up again as the *Rubber Soul* sessions finished – but only because the album was a song short.

Written mostly by Paul, it's an all-purpose song about a couple who have been separated and now that they're back together everything's going to be all right. Paul's recollection is that it was written in the Bahamas during filming and that the late Brandon de Wilde, the child star of *Shane*, had watched as he wrote it.

Written in Nassau as the band filmed *Help!*, the unloved 'Wait' was a makeweight on the *Rubber Soul* album.

IF I NEEDED SOMEONE

'If I Needed Someone' was written by George for girlfriend Pattie, and grew out of a musical exercise using the D chord. "That guitar line, or variations on it, is found in many a song and it amazes me that people still find new permutations of the same notes," he said.

When Beatles' press officer Derek Taylor moved to Los Angeles and began to represent the Byrds, George asked him to pass a message to Byrds' guitarist Roger McGuinn saying that the tune to 'If I Needed Someone' had been inspired by two Byrds' tracks – 'The Bells Of Rhymney' and 'She Don't Care About Time'.

'The Bells of Rhymney' had been a track on the Byrds' first album *Mr Tambourine Man* that had come out in August 1965. 'She Don't Care About Time', written by vocalist Gene Clark, was the B side of the single 'Turn! Turn! Turn!' released in October 1965, the same month that 'If I Needed Someone' was recorded.

George admitted that his inspiration for 'If I Needed Someone' was two tracks by West Coast band the Byrds.

IF I NEEDED SOMEONE

Written:	Harrison
Length:	2' 23"
UK release:	*Rubber Soul* album, December 3, 1965
US release:	*Yesterday And Today* album, June 20, 1966

RUN FOR YOUR LIFE

John developed 'Run For Your Life' from the line 'I'd rather see you dead little girl than see you with another man', which occurred towards the end of Elvis Presley's 1955 Sun single 'Baby, Let's Play House'. Indeed, John referred to this as "an old blues song that Presley did once" but in fact it only dates back to 1954 and was written by a 28-year-old preacher's son from Nashville named Arthur Gunter.

Gunter in turn had based his song on a 1951 country hit by Eddy Arnold, 'I Want To Play House With You', and had recorded it for the Excello label in late 1954. It wasn't a national hit but it was heard by Elvis who took it into the studios with him on February 5, 1955. When 'Baby, Let's Play House' reached Number 10 in Billboard's country chart in July 1955, it became the first Elvis record to chart nationally in America. Gunter's song was one of devotion. He wanted the girl to move in with him and the line which took John's attention was an indication of the depths of his feelings for her, not a threat.

However, in John's mouth the lines become threatening. If he sees his girl with anyone else she'd better run because he's going to bump her off. It was another revenge fantasy in the mould of 'I'll Cry Instead'. The singer explains his behaviour by saying that he's 'wicked' and that he was born with 'a jealous mind'; lines which contain intimations of later songs such as 'Jealous Guy' and 'Crippled Inside'.

Although it was the first track recorded for *Rubber Soul*, John always cited 'Run For Your Life' as an example of his worst work. It was written under pressure, he said and, as such, was a "throwaway song".

RUN FOR YOUR LIFE
Written: Lennon/McCartney
Length: 2' 18"
UK release: *Rubber Soul* album, December 3, 1965
US release: *Rubber Soul* album, December 6, 1965

REVOLVER

Revolver marked a significant development in the Beatles' sound, as well as the end of an era. After it, all their music was developed in the studio, unconstrained by considerations of whether the songs could be reproduced in concert. Now showing the obvious influence of contact with the emerging counter-culture and developments in avant garde art their work was appealing to a hipper audience. Encounters with the underground scene, along with the effect of psychedelic drugs, were to alter their perceptions both of themselves and of their music.

In a March 1966 interview with British teenage magazine *Rave*, Paul enthused about George's interest in Indian music and his own explorations of theatre, painting, film-making and electronic music. "We've all got interested in things that never used to occur to us," he said. "I've got thousands, millions, of new ideas myself."

Revolver was certainly an album brimming with new ideas. Eclecticism has since become common in rock'n'roll, but this was where it started. Not only did it involve musical styles ranging from a children's singalong to a psychedelic mélange of backward tape loops, it also presented a broad mix of lyrical concerns – death, taxation, pill doctors, lonely spinsters, sleep, ocean adventures and sunshine.

Yet, despite its experimental nature, *Revolver* was not inaccessible. 'Eleanor Rigby', 'For No One' and 'Here, There And Everywhere' were three of the most beautiful and popular songs Paul ever wrote. 'Taxman' and 'I Want To Tell You' were George's best compositions so far and John's dream-like 'I'm Only Sleeping' and 'She Said She Said' perfectly captured the mood of the times.

George's new interest in Indian music was a major influence on the groundbreaking sound of the *Revolver* album..

Released during what turned out to be their final tour, none of the 14 songs would ever be played on stage by the Beatles. They had become recording artists rather than performers, and were now happy to concentrate on the art of making records rather than having to squeeze their songwriting between touring and frequent appearances on film and television.

Revolver was released in August 1966 and made the top spot in both America and Britain. This was the last time that the British and American versions of a Beatles' album were to differ. Three of John's songs – 'I'm Only Sleeping', 'And Your Bird Can Sing' and 'Doctor Robert' – had already appeared in the US on the album *Yesterday And Today*.

PAPERBACK WRITER

The Beach Boys' *Pet Sounds* influenced the background harmonies of 'Paperback Writer'.

The Beatles' first single not to have a love theme ('Nowhere Man' had been the first song), 'Paperback Writer' was the story of a novelist begging a publisher's editor to take on his thousand-page book. Written by Paul in the form of a letter, it was startling at the time to hear a pop single on such an unusual subject.

British disc jockey Jimmy Savile, who then worked for Radio Luxembourg as well as BBC Television's *Top Of The Pops*, claims he was backstage after a show when Paul first conceived the idea for the song. John had been principal writer of the Beatles' last five singles and so it was generally agreed that it was Paul's turn to come up with something.

Savile recalled John asking Paul what he was going to do because there were only a few days left before they were due to record. "Paul told him that one of his aunts had just asked if he could ever write a single that wasn't about love," remembers Savile. "With that thought obviously still in his mind, he walked around the room and noticed that Ringo was reading a book. He took one look and announced that he would write a song about a book."

Paul has said that he had always liked the sound of the words 'paperback writer' and decided to build his story round them. The epistolary style of the song came to him as he drove down to Weybridge for a day's writing with John. "As soon as I arrived I told him that I wanted us to write it as if it was a letter," he said. Tony Bramwell recalls that the inspiration for much of the lyric came from an actual letter written to Paul by an aspiring novelist.

Paperbacks had caused a publishing revolution, making books available to people who would have found hardbacks too expensive to buy. Poet Royston Ellis, the first published author the Beatles had ever met when they played music backing his poetry in 1960, is convinced that Paul latched on to the phrase 'paperback writer' from his conversations with them. "Although I was writing poetry books then, if they asked me what I wanted to be I would always say 'a paperback writer' because that's what you had to be if you wanted to reach a mass market," says Ellis, who went on to become a writer of travel books and plantation novels. "My ambition was to be a writer who sold his books and made money out of it. It was my equivalent of their ambition of making a million-selling single."

As with many of Paul's songs, the lyric was driven more by the sound of the words than the logic of the story. Taken literally, it's about a writer who has composed a book based on a novel about a paperback writer. In other words, it's a novel based on a novel about a man writing a novel – which is in turn presumably based on a novel about a man writing a novel. The 'man named Lear' is probably a reference to Edward Lear, the Victorian painter who, although he never wrote a novel, did write nonsense poems and songs which John began to read when reviewers of *In His Own Write* suggested that he must have been an influence. The *Daily Mail* gets a mention because it was John's regular newspaper and copies would often be around the Weybridge house when they were writing. Stories from the *Daily Mail* would later be used as inspiration for two songs on *Sgt Pepper*.

PAPERBACK WRITER
Written: Lennon/McCartney
Length: 2' 18"
UK single release: June 10, 1966
UK chart position: 1
US single release: May 30, 1966
US chart position: 1

The main musical innovation in 'Paperback Writer' was the boosted bass sound that allowed it to be used as a lead instrument for the first time. Paul was now playing a Rickenbacker and, through some studio innovations made by engineer Ken Townsend, the bass became the most prominent instrument on the track, bringing it into line with recent American recordings by Otis Redding and Wilson Pickett. The background harmonies were inspired by the Beach Boys' album *Pet Sounds* that had been completed by the end of March 1966 and an advance pressing brought to London by Kim Fowley in order to get it 'talked up' by influential people like the Beatles. John and Paul were given a preview at the Waldorf Hotel in the Aldwych. On part of the harmonies for 'Paperback Writer' the Beatles can be heard singing 'Frère Jacques' as a subliminal exercise in evoking childhood memories.

'Paperback Writer' was a Number 1 single in many countries including Britain, America, Germany and Australia.

RAIN

In 'There's A Place' on the Beatles' first album, John had voiced the opinion that state of mind matters more than events 'out there'. In 'Rain', he returned to the theme but this time with the experience of psychedelic drugs as a subtext. On one level, it was a simple song about "people moaning because...they don't like the weather" as he once said. But on another level it was a song that recommended transcending the conventional categories of good and evil. In the same way that we should be indifferent to the weather, he feels that there is a need for people to rise above their circumstances. The use of 'I can show you' and 'Can you hear me?' indicated that John was starting to adopt the role of a leader.

'Rain' was the first Beatles' release that suggested new altered states of consciousness, not just in its lyric but in the music. The mournfully dragged-out vocal, the slowed-down instruments and the backward tape at the end were intimations of experiments to come.

Backward taping became a controversial issue in the rock industry during the Seventies and Eighties when some artists were accused

RAIN

Written:	Lennon/McCartney
Length:	3' 02"
UK single release:	June 10, 1966 as B-side to 'Paperback Writer'
US single release:	May 30, 1966 as B-side to 'Paperback Writer'

'Rain' was the first song that saw the Beatles experiment with tape delay and effects,

of concealing hidden messages within their recordings. The Beatles had not done it to conceal messages but simply to suggest a mind free from conventional logic.

George Martin said that he came up with the idea experimenting on his own after the Beatles had left the studio. He played back his new effects to them the next day. John, who wrote 'Rain' at Kenwood, always claimed that he'd discovered the process trying to thread a demo tape of the song on his home recorder while high on marijuana. He was in such a disoriented state that he got the tape twisted and when he heard what sounded like an eastern religious chant coming from his headphones, he knew he had found a sound which accurately reflected his stoned consciousness.

TAXMAN

'Taxman' was written by George Harrison after he found himself in the British 'super-tax' bracket, which then meant paying 19 shillings and three pence (96p) out of every twenty shillings (£1) in tax. It has been suggested that the theme music to the TV series *Batman* may have been an influence – the 'taxman' chorus at the end of the song bears a resemblance to the 'Batman' chorus. This is possible because the first series starring Adam West as Batman started in January 1966 although it wasn't shown in Britain until May 1966, the month after 'Taxman' was recorded.

Until 1966, the Beatles' touring schedule had been so hectic that there had been no time to examine their accounts in detail. When they did get round to it, they discovered that they didn't have as much money as they had imagined. "We were actually giving most (of our money) away in taxes," said George. "It was, and still is, typical. Why should this be so? Are we being punished for something we have forgotten to do?" Ironically, in light of his later conversion to a religious view that stressed the futility of material things, George had always been the Beatle to mention money when asked about his ambitions.

John later said that he had a hand in the writing of 'Taxman' and he was bitter that George had neglected to mention this in the account of the song's composition in his autobiography, *I Me Mine*. John claimed that George phoned him up as he was writing it. "I threw in a few one-liners to help the song along, because that's what he asked for," he said "I didn't want to do it…but because I loved him...I just sort of bit my tongue and said OK."

Certainly the recorded version improved on George's rough draft, in which 'get some bread' was rhymed with 'before you're dead'. On

TAXMAN
Written: Harrison
Length: 2' 39"
UK release: *Revolver* album, August 5, 1966
US release: *Revolver* album, August 8, 1966

George wrote 'Taxman' after discovering he was liable for 'supertax' and had to pay a 96% rate of income tax.

the first takes the background chorus was 'Anybody gotta lotta money/ anybody gotta lotta money/ anybody gotta lotta money?' sung at break-neck speed, but this was later changed to mention Prime Minister Harold Wilson and Leader of the Opposition Edward Heath. These two politicians shared the distinction of being the first living people to be named in a Beatles' song. Although they had never met Heath, they had met Wilson (a fellow Northerner) on several occasions and had each received MBEs in the honours list that Wilson approved after leading Britain's Labour Party to victory in 1964.

The Beatles – four enterprising young people with regional accents who came from mainly working class backgrounds – were just the sort of people Wilson wanted to encourage as part of his vision for a new classless Great Britain.

When the Trappist monk, poet and spiritual writer Thomas Merton (*Seven Storey Mountain*) heard 'Taxman' he wrote in his diary (June 10th 1967): "The Beatles' 'Taxman' is running through my head. They are good. Good beat. Independence, wit, insight, voice, originality. They take pleasure in being Beatles and I do not resent the fact that they are multi-millionaires, for that is part of it. They have to contend with that sneaky tax man."

ELEANOR RIGBY

As was the case with many of Paul's songs, the melody and the first words of 'Eleanor Rigby' came to him as he sat playing his piano. By asking himself what type of person would be picking up rice in a church where a wedding had been he was eventually led to his protagonist. She was originally going to be named Miss Daisy Hawkins as this fitted the rhythm.

'Eleanor Rigby' was called Daisy Hawkins, Eleanor Bygraves and even Ola Na Tungee before Paul finally settled on the title.

Paul started by imagining Daisy as a young girl but soon realised that anyone who cleaned churches after weddings was likely to be older. If she was older, she might he a spinster and the church cleaning became a metaphor of her missed opportunities for marriage. He then based her on what he remembered of old people he'd known when he was running errands as a Boy Scout in Liverpool. "I couldn't think of any more so I put it away," he remarked.

Paul continued to mull over the song but wasn't comfortable with the name of Miss Daisy Hawkins. It didn't sound 'real' enough. Sixties folksinger Donovan remembered Paul playing him a version of the song where the protagonist was called Ola Na Tungee. "The words hadn't yet come out right for him," says Donovan."

He has always said that he settled on the name Eleanor because of Eleanor Bron, the leading actress in *Help!* Songwriter Lionel Bart, however, was convinced that the choice was inspired by a gravestone he saw in Putney Vale Cemetery in London as they sauntered through it together one day. "The name on the gravestone was Eleanor Bygraves," said Bart, "and Paul thought that would fit his song. He came back to my office and began playing it on my clavichord."

The surname originated when Paul came across the name Rigby in January 1966, while in Bristol visiting Jane Asher who was playing

ELEANOR RIGBY

Written:	Lennon/McCartney
Length:	2' 07"
UK release:	*Revolver* album, August 5, 1966
US release:	*Revolver* album, August 8, 1966

the role of Barbara Cahoun in John Dighton's *The Happiest Days Of Your Life*. The Theatre Royal, home of the Bristol Old Vic, is at 35 King Street and, as Paul was waiting for Jane to finish, he strolled past Rigby & Evens Ltd, Wine & Spirit Shippers, which was then on the opposite side of the road at number 22. It had the two-syllable surname he was looking for to go with Eleanor.

The song was completed at Kenwood when John, George, Ringo and John's boyhood friend Pete Shotton crowded into the music room where Paul played it through. They each contributed ideas to flesh out the story. One of them suggested an old man rifling through garbage cans whom Eleanor Rigby could have a romance with, but it was decided that would complicate the story. A priest called Father McCartney was introduced. Ringo suggested that he could be darning his socks, an idea that Paul liked. George came up with a line about 'lonely people'. Paul reckoned that he should change the priest's name from Father McCartney because people would think it was a reference to his dad. A look through the phone directory produced Father McKenzie as an alternative.

Paul was then stuck for an ending to his story and Shotton suggested that he bring the two lonely people together in the final verse as Father McKenzie takes Eleanor Rigby's funeral and stands beside her grave. At the time, the idea was knocked down by John who thought that Shotton had missed the point but Paul, who didn't say anything at the time, used the scene to finish off the song, and later acknowledged the help he'd received.

Extraordinarily, sometime in the Eighties the gravestone of an Eleanor Rigby was discovered in the churchyard of St Peter's, Woolton, within yards of the spot where John and Paul had met at the church's annual summer fete in 1957. It's clear that Paul didn't get his idea directly from this gravestone, but it's possible that he saw it as a teenager and the pleasing sound of the name lay buried in his subconscious until called up by the requirements of this song. At the time he said: "I was looking for a name that was natural. Eleanor Rigby sounded natural."

In a further coincidence, the firm of Rigby and Evens Ltd, whose sign had inspired Paul in Bristol in 1966, was owned by a Liverpudlian, Frank Rigby, who established his company in Dale Street, Liverpool, in the 19th century.

As a single 'Eleanor Rigby' reached the top of the British hit parade but peaked at Number 11 in America.

Although the Beatles enjoyed unparalleled levels of success in 1966, John admitted that he was becoming increasingly lazy.

I'M ONLY SLEEPING

The first draft of John's lyric for 'I'm Only Sleeping', then called 'I'm Sleeping', was scratched on to the back of a letter from the Post Office, dated April 25, 1966, reminding him that he owed them 12 pounds and three shillings for an outstanding radiophone bill. Two days later the Beatles started to record it. It is clear from this first draft that he was writing about the joys of staying in bed rather than about a drug-induced dream state. His first opening line was 'Try to sleep again, got to get to sleep'.

John loved his bed. When he wasn't sleeping in it, he would be lying on it propped up by pillows writing or watching television. 'I'm Only Sleeping' celebrated the bed and its value as a place for contemplation. It also prefigured 'Watching The Wheels' on the *Double Fantasy* album. The more worrying truth, however, was that John was losing his grip on the Beatles, spending too much time either in bed or lazing around Kenwood. This indolent behaviour allowed Paul to grab the reins, something that was easier for him to do anyway because of his lack of family ties and the proximity to Abbey Road of his newly purchased London home.

It was the month before this recording that the *Evening Standard* ran Maureen Cleave's famous interview with John where he declared that "We're more popular than Jesus now; I don't know which will go first – rock'n'roll or Christianity." In the story Cleave noted: "He can sleep almost indefinitely, is probably the laziest person in England. 'Physically lazy,' he said. 'I don't mind writing or reading or watching or speaking, but sex is the only physical thing I can be bothered with any more'."

I'M ONLY SLEEPING
Written: Lennon/McCartney
Length: 3' 01"
UK release: *Revolver* album, August 5, 1966
US release: *Yesterday And Today* album, June 20, 1966

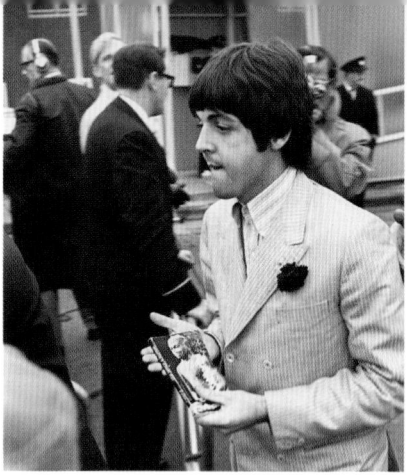

LOVE YOU TO

Although 'Norwegian Wood' had featured sitar, it had been added as an afterthought. 'Love You To' was the first song written by George with the instrument specifically in mind. On this recording, he also featured tabla player Anil Bhagwat.

In his biography, *I Me Mine*, George recollected that he had used tabla and sitar on the basic track, overdubbing vocals and guitar at a later stage. However Mark Lewisohn, author of *The Complete Beatles Recording Sessions*, gained access to the original tapes and discovered that the sitar didn't appear until the third take and the tabla wasn't added until the sixth.

The song's working title was 'Granny Smith' – after the apple variety – simply because George couldn't think of anything better. As the words 'love you to' don't appear in the song, the eventual title is rather puzzling: perhaps 'love me while you can' might have been more appropriate as this sums up what the song is saying.

Despite writing 'Here There and Everywhere' (right) for Jane Asher, Paul denied they were to marry in 1966.

LOVE YOU TO

Written:	Harrison
Length:	3' 01"
UK release:	*Revolver* album, August 5, 1966
US release:	*Revolver* album, August 8, 1966

HERE, THERE AND EVERYWHERE

With things starting to look up again in his romance with Jane Asher, Paul wrote what is widely regarded as his greatest love song. Both John and Paul declared that it was one of their favourite Beatles' songs; Paul eventually re-recording it for use in his film *Give My Regards To Broad Street*.

Paul wrote 'Here, There And Everywhere' in June 1966 while sitting by John's outdoor pool. He'd arrived early for a writing session only to find John still in bed so he began to write alone. Wanting to set himself a structural challenge he built each verse of the song around the three adverbs in the title. When he recorded it he imagined the ethereal voice of Marianne Faithfull.

This song was the one of the album most obviously influenced by *Pet Sounds*. Paul had been particularly taken with the shimmering quality of 'God Only Knows' and wanted to write a number that captured the same mood.

HERE, THERE AND EVERYWHERE

Written:	Lennon/McCartney
Length:	2' 25"
UK release:	*Revolver* album, August 5, 1966
US release:	*Revolver* album, August 8, 1966

YELLOW SUBMARINE

The idea of writing a children's song about different coloured submarines came into Paul's head as he was drifting into sleep at the Asher home one night. This was to develop into 'Yellow Submarine', the tale of a boy who listens to the tall stories of an old sailor about his exploits in the 'land of submarines' and decides to go sailing and see for himself.

Between 1962 and 1965, the Beatles had obeyed the unwritten rules for writing pop singles: they should have love at the centre, last less than three minutes and be easily reproducible in concert. They were now enjoying seeing how many of these rules could be broken while still retaining the immediacy and excitement of commercial pop. 'Paperback Writer' had been their first non-love single; 'Eleanor Rigby' and 'Rain' were the first of their singles never to be played at a Beatles' concert and 'Yellow Submarine' was their first singalong song.

Paul used only short words in the lyric because he wanted it to be learned quickly and sung by children. While writing it, he visited Donovan at his flat in Maida Vale. "We were in the habit of just dropping in on each other," remembers Donovan. "I was just waiting for the release of my album *Sunshine Superman* and so we played each other our latest songs. One of the songs Paul played me was about a yellow submarine but he said he was missing a line or two. He asked me if I'd like to make a contribution. I left the room for a bit and came back with 'Sky of blue and sea of green, In our yellow submarine'. It wasn't an earth-shattering creation but Paul liked it enough to use it on the eventual recording."

The earliest takes of the song include the sound of marching feet before the song proper begins and Ringo intoning a spoken introduction.

Paul claimed 'Yellow Submarine' was "just a children's song" despite critics detecting druggy references – and Stanley Unwin.

The Stanley Unwin-inspired wordplay in the stanza suggests that this was written by John. 'And we will march 'til three the day/ To see them gathered there/ From Land O'Groats to John O'Greer with Stepney do we tread/ To see us yellow submarine/ We love it.' (Unwin may have had an effect on the album title itself. His first spoken-word recording, released in 1960, was called (Rotatey Diskers.)

Released as the flip side of 'Eleanor Rigby' in August 1966, the same month that *Revolver* came out, the rumour quickly spread that the yellow submarine was a veiled reference to drugs. In New York, Nembutal capsules started to be known as 'yellow submarines'. Paul denied the allegations and said that the only submarine he knew that you could eat was a sugary sweet he'd come across in Greece while on holiday. These had to be dropped in water and were known as 'submarines'. "I knew 'Yellow Submarine' would get connotations," said Paul, "but it really was a children's song."

YELLOW SUBMARINE

Written:	Lennon/McCartney
Length:	2' 40"
UK release:	*Revolver* album, August 5, 1966
US release:	*Revolver* album, August 8, 1966

SHE SAID SHE SAID

Peter Fonda fell foul of an LSD-tripping John Lennon when the band threw a party at their Hollywood base.

When the Beatles visited Los Angeles in August 1965, they rented a house at 2850 Benedict Canyon for a week while they played dates in Portland, San Diego, the Hollywood Bowl and San Francisco.

One afternoon they threw a party, and Neil Aspinall, Roger McGuinn and David Crosby from the Byrds, the actor Peter Fonda and the *Daily Mirror* show business correspondent Don Short were among the guests. "Neil Aspinall was sent to escort me downstairs to the pool room," remembers Short, "because I was the only journalist on the premises. His job was to divert my attention from the fact that everyone else was taking acid."

Upstairs, out of Short's sight, everyone (except for Paul), was indeed tripping out on LSD. It was the first time John and George had deliberately taken the drug and they were anxious to have a good experience after the disturbing visions of their first, unintentional trip. Fonda had tripped out many times and saw his role as that of a guide. "I remember sitting out on the deck of the house with George, who was telling me that he thought he was dying," says Fonda. "I told

SHE SAID, SHE SAID

Written:	Lennon/McCartney
Length:	2' 37"
UK release:	*Revolver* album, August 5, 1966
US release:	*Revolver* album, August 8, 1966

him that there was nothing to be afraid of and that all he needed to do was to relax. I said that I knew what it was like to be dead because when I was 10 years old I'd accidentally shot myself in the stomach and my heart stopped beating three times while I was on the operating table because I'd lost so much blood.

John was passing by at the time and heard me saying 'I know what it's like to be dead.' He looked at me and said, 'You're making me feel I've never been born. Who put all that shit in your head?'"

Roger McGuinn felt that the idea had upset John because he was feeling insecure. "We were all on acid and John couldn't take it," McGuinn says. "John said, 'Get this guy out of here'. It was morbid and bizarre. We'd just finished watching *Cat Ballou* with Jane Fonda in it and John didn't want anything to do with any of the Fondas. He was holding the movie against Peter and then what he said just added to it."

Indeed, the earliest demo of the song (where it was called 'He Said, He Said') is far more aggressive than the final recording: 'I said, "Who put all that crap in your head?/ I know what it's like to be mad/ And it's making me feel like my trousers are torn'". But John felt that as a song this was leading nowhere and abandoned it.

Although it came out of a real experience it meant nothing, he said. It was just a sound. But days later he picked it up again and tried to find a middle eight. "I wrote the first thing that came into my head," said John, "and it was 'when I was a boy', in a different beat. But it was real, because it had just happened."

Peter Fonda has no doubt about the origins of the song. "When I heard *Revolver* for the first time I knew exactly where the song had come from, although John never acknowledged it to me and I never mentioned it to anyone."

GOOD DAY SUNSHINE

'Good Day Sunshine' was written by Paul at John's house on a particularly sunny day. Paul admitted in 1984 that it had been influenced by the Lovin' Spoonful, the New York-based folk-rock group that had scored two American hits with 'Do You Believe In Magic?' and 'You Didn't Have To Be So Nice'. The group was distinguished by the lyrical, folksy tunes of founder member John Sebastian who later, as a solo artist, turned in a memorable performance in the *Woodstock* movie with 'The Younger Generation'.

The specific song that inspired Paul that day was 'Daydream', the Lovin' Spoonful's first British hit, which was in the Top 20 as the Beatles recorded *Revolver* in May 1966. Like 'Good Day Sunshine', 'Daydream' starts off with a choppy guitar beat before launching into a story of love-induced bliss heightened by beautiful weather: 'I'm blowin' the day to take a walk in the sun, And fall on my face on somebody's new-mown lawn'.

"One of the wonderful things the Beatles had going for them," says Sebastian, "is that they were so original that when they did cop an idea from somebody else it never occurred to you. I thought there were one or two of their songs which were Spoonful-oid but it wasn't until Paul mentioned it in a *Playboy* interview that I specifically realized we'd inspired 'Good Day Sunshine'."

'Daydream' itself was inspired by the Tamla beat on songs such as 'Where Did Our Love Go?' and 'Baby Love' that the Lovin' Spoonful heard while touring America with the Supremes. "I said, we gotta have a tune like 'Baby Love'," Sebastian remembers. "I wrote the song while trying to approximate the 'Baby Love' feel on one guitar.

GOOD DAY SUNSHINE
Written: Lennon/McCartney
Length: 2' 09"
UK release: *Revolver* album, August 5, 1966
US release: *Revolver* album, August 8, 1966

New York folk rockers the Lovin' Spoonful were flattered to learn they had influenced 'Good Day Sunshine'.

Sometimes you attempt to cop something and what you come up with is something very much your own."

The Lovin' Spoonful owed its foundation to a meeting between Sebastian and fellow guitarist Zal Yanovsky which took place at (Mama) Cass Elliot's house where the two men had been invited independently to see the Beatles debut on the *Ed Sullivan Show* in February 1964. "Seeing the Beatles that night crystallized the idea for us both of wanting to be part of a self-contained unit which wrote its own music," remarks Sebastian. "I eventually got to meet them in April 1966 (April 18th). John, Paul and George came to see us at the Marquee Club in London's Soho and it was that night that George had his first proper meeting with Eric Clapton. Unfortunately, we never got to play together because everyone was just so busy in those days. We had other meetings but we always seemed to be together because we were waiting for something else to happen.

"When they played Shea Stadium in New York in August 1966 I went backstage and had a few laughs with John who was beginning to look a lot like me. He was getting a lot of ribbing from the other Beatles about copying me. I always wished I could have spent more time with them."

AND YOUR BIRD CAN SING

John dismissed this song of his as "a horror" (1971) and "a throwaway" (1980) although it's hard to figure out what caused his dissatisfaction. The lyric was one of his most enigmatic and was probably a dig at Paul cloaked in the garments of poetry. After all, there had only been one previous Beatles' song title beginning with the word 'and' – Paul's 'And I Love Her'. Was John mocking this innovation and at the same time giving us a clue as to the target of his put-down?

The song is about someone who doesn't 'get' John, someone who does all the things that hip people do but isn't hip by nature. This was a gripe that he often made about Paul. The line 'You say you've seen seven wonders' could therefore be a reference to the first time the Beatles smoked pot in New York when Paul thought he had discovered the answer to all of life's big questions and wrote his insight on a piece of paper. When he read it the next morning all it said was 'There are seven levels'.

The period during which *Revolver* was recorded coincided with a time when Paul had a ravenous appetite for new cultural experiences

AND YOUR BIRD CAN SING

Written:	Lennon/McCartney
Length:	2' 01"
UK release:	*Revolver* album, August 5, 1966
US release:	*Yesterday And Today* album, June 20, 1966

and this made John feel uneasy because he felt that, as an ex-art student, this was his territory. In April 1966 Paul was in print enthusing about the different forms of music he was getting into – Indian, classical, electronic – and bemoaning the fact that there simply wasn't time to listen to everything he wanted to. "The only thing to do is to listen to everything and then make your mind up about it." Could talk like this have led John to write, 'Tell me that you've heard every sound there is.'?

If this was a put-down, it 's unlikely that Paul was aware of it. During a session to add vocal overdubs he breaks up in hysterics when John deliberately mis-quotes his own lines and sings,'When your bike is broken' instead of 'When your bird is broken' and then whistles the tune instead of singing.

'And Your Bird Can Sing' shows signs of having been a typically sardonic put-down of Paul by the jealous and insecure John.

FOR NO ONE

With its haunting melody and horn section, this was one of Paul's most beautiful songs. 'For No One' was written in a rented chalet half a mile outside the Swiss ski resort of Klosters, where he and Jane Asher spent a brief holiday in March 1966. He returned from Switzerland to work on *Revolver* and Jane began rehearsals for her role as the young Ellen Terry in *Sixty Thousand Nights* at the Royal Theatre, Bristol.

Through a series of flashbacks of their life together, the song captures the dawning realization that someone's feelings of love have disappeared. In an early interview, Paul said that it was all about his own experience of living with a woman when he was fresh from leaving home. The working title was 'Why Did It Die?' and he later admitted that it was probably written "about another argument" with Jane.

Paul and John worked on 'For No One' after Paul composed it on holiday before starting the *Revolver* sessions.

FOR NO ONE

Written:	Lennon/McCartney
Length:	2' 01"
UK release:	*Revolver* album, August 5, 1966
US release:	*Revolver* album, August 8, 1966

DOCTOR ROBERT

On their American visits the Beatles heard about a chic New York doctor who gave mysterious 'vitamin' injections. "We'd hear people say, 'You can get anything off him, any pills you want'," said Paul. "It was a big racket. The song was a joke about this fellow who cured everyone of everything with all these pills and tranquillizers. He just kept New York high."

Dr Robert was almost certainly Dr Robert Freymann, a 60-year-old German-born physician with a practice on East 78th Street. (The Dr Charles Roberts cited in some Beatles' books didn't exist. It was an alias used by the biographer of Warhol actress Edie Sedgwick, Jean Stein, to conceal the identity of another 'speed doctor'.) Known as Dr Robert or the Great White Father (he had a shock of white hair), Freymann was well connected to the city's vibrant arts scene. He had helped, among others, Theolonius Monk and Charlie Parker (whose death certificate he signed in 1955), and had a reputation for being generous with amphetamines. "I have a clientele that is remarkable, from every sphere of life," he once boasted. "I could tell you in ten minutes probably 100 famous names who come here." John, who wrote 'Dr Robert', was one of these famous names according to Freymann's daughter.

Initially prescribed as anti-depressants, amphetamines soon became a recreational drug for hip New Yorkers. One former patient of Dr Robert Freymann's, quoted in the *New York Times* in 1973, said: "If you want to make a big night of it you'd go over to Max's [Dr Max Jacobson] and then over to Freymann's and then down to Bishop's [Dr John Bishop]. It was just another kind of bar hopping." The film director Joel Schumacher, who used speed doctors in the Sixties,

Crammed with their luggage in a small car, the Beatles arrive at a rainy London airport in August 1966 on the way to a US tour. It was to be their last.

DOCTOR ROBERT

Written:	Lennon/McCartney
Length:	2' 15"
UK release:	*Revolver* album, August 5, 1966
US release:	*Yesterday And Today* album, June 20, 1966

agrees: "We thought of them as vitamin injections but then became speed freaks."

Administering amphetamines was not illegal at the time although regulations warned against prescribing 'excessive quantities' or giving the drug when it wasn't necessary. Dr Robert lost his licence to practise for six months in 1968 and, in 1975, was expelled from the New York State Medical Society for malpractice. Asked by the *New York Times* in March 1973 to defend his actions, he said: "the addicts killed a good drug". He died in 1987.

GOT TO GET YOU INTO MY LIFE

'Got To Get You Into My Life' was written by Paul who wanted to emulate the Motown sound recently developed by the writer-producer team of Holland-Dozier-Holland with The Supremes. It was the first Beatles' track to use brass.

John believed that by mentioning 'another kind of mind' in the lyrics, Paul was alluding to his drug experiences. He has since confirmed that he was. It was a hymn in praise of pot, disguised as a love song. It wasn't a woman that he needed every single day of his life but a joint.

On June 19, 1967, he was confronted by a British television news reporter who asked whether it wouldn't have been better if he'd kept his drug-taking private. "I was asked a question by a newspaper and the decision was whether to tell a lie or tell the truth," he said. "I decided to tell him the truth but...if I'd had my way, I wouldn't have told anyone because I'm not trying to spread the word about this...I'll keep it a personal thing if he does too. But he wanted to spread it, so it's his responsibility for spreading it. Not mine."

GOT TO GET YOU INTO MY LIFE

Written:	Lennon/McCartney
Length:	2' 30"
UK release:	*Revolver* album, August 5, 1966
US release:	*Revolver* album, August 8, 1966

I WANT TO TELL YOU

'I Want To Tell You', written by George, was about the frustrations of having things to say but being unable to articulate them. "It's about the avalanche of thoughts that are so hard to write down or say or transmit", he later said, adding that if he were to write the song again he would amend the bridge section which says: 'But if I seem to act unkind, It's only me, it's not my mind, That's confusing things' so that it was clear that his mind was responsible for the confusion. "The mind is the thing that hops about telling us to do this and do that. What we need is to lose the mind," explained George.

Appropriately for a song which was about not knowing what to say, 'I Want To Tell You' was recorded under the nonsensical title 'Laxton's Superb'; a name of an English apple, first suggested by engineer Geoff Emerick. It later became known as 'I Don't Know', after George Martin had asked George what he wanted to title it and had been given this answer.

I WANT TO TELL YOU
Written: Harrison
Length: 2' 29"
UK release: *Revolver* album, August 5, 1966
US release: *Revolver* album, August 8, 1966

The Beatles at a press conference at New York's Warwick Hotel at the start of the final US tour in 1966.

TOMORROW NEVER KNOWS

As the last track on the album, and the clearest signpost of things to come, it's often assumed that 'Tomorrow Never Knows' was the last track recorded. In fact, it was the first. Certainly the weirdest and most experimental piece of music to appear under the Beatles' name at the time, this was John's attempt to create in words and sounds a suitable guide track for the LSD experience.

The words were borrowed, adapted and embellished from Timothy Leary's 1964 book *The Psychedelic Experience*, which was itself a poetic reinterpretation of the ancient Tibetan *Book Of The Dead*.

John had been sent the book by Barry Miles, who ran Indica Books in Southampton Row and was an influential figure on the British underground scene in the Sixties. He had an arrangement with the Beatles to send them significant books, magazines and newspapers to keep them up-to-date.

Leary, known as the High Priest of LSD, had spent seven months in the Himalayas studying Tibetan Buddhism under Lama Govinda. *The Psychedelic Experience* was a direct result of this period of study.

"I would ask Lama Govinda questions," says Leary, "and then I tried to translate what he said into something useful for people. *Book Of The Dead* really means 'Book Of The Dying' but it's your ego rather than your body which is dying. The book is a classic. It's the bible of Tibetan Buddhism. The concept of Buddhism is of the void and of reaching the void – that is what John captured in the song."

The words of the Tibetan *Book Of The Dead* were written to be spoken to a dying person in order to guide them through the states of delusion that come with the approach of death. Many people experienced the death of their egos while on LSD and so the words

TOMORROW NEVER KNOWS

Written:	Lennon/McCartney
Length:	2' 57"
UK release:	*Revolver* album, August 5, 1966
US release:	*Revolver* album, August 8, 1966

could be employed to keep trippers on track and protect them from the horrors. John is believed to have made a tape of Leary's words to listen to on headphones while he was tripping at home.

The working title of the track was in fact 'The Void', taken from Leary's line "Beyond the restless flowing electricity of Life is the ultimate reality – the void." Its eventual title was a Ringoism that John adopted because it added levity to what otherwise might have sounded like a bleak journey into nothingness.

The actual sound of the piece, which consists of tape loops made by each of the Beatles fading in and out, grew out of Paul's home experimentation on his tape recorder. "He had this little Grundig," says George Martin. "He found by moving the erase head and putting a loop on he could actually saturate the tape with a single noise. It would go round and round and eventually the tape couldn't absorb any more and he'd bring it in and play it."

John wanted it to sound like a chorus of Tibetan monks chanting on a mountain top." He said he wanted to hear the words but he didn't want to hear him," says George Martin. The result, which sounds as if John is singing at the end of a long tunnel, was achieved by feeding his voice through a Leslie speaker.

The Beatles relax by a hotel swimming pool as their 1966 US tour gets underway.

SGT PEPPER'S LONELY HEARTS CLUB BAND

The fruitful period which produced the singles 'Penny Lane' and 'Strawberry Fields Forever' as well as the *Sgt Pepper* album was the first in which the Beatles could be totally devoted to the studio because they were free of touring commitments. They took an unprecedented 105 hours to record both sides of the single and then a further five months to complete the album.

Paul conceived the album as a show staged by a fictional Edwardian brass band transported through time into the psychedelic age and played, of course, by the electronically equipped Beatles. Released in June 1967, *Sgt Pepper* was the album of what became known as 'The Summer Of Love' – a brief season when the hippie ethic developed in San Francisco seemed to pervade the whole of the Western world. For anyone who was young at the time, the music automatically evokes the sight of beads and kaftans, the sound of tinkling bells and the aroma of marijuana masked by joss sticks. Despite this, there were only four songs on *Sgt Pepper* – 'Lucy In The Sky With Diamonds', 'She's Leaving Home', 'Within You Without You' and 'A Day In The Life' – that even alluded to the social upheaval caused by the changing youth culture.

The rest of the songs were very British pop songs, tackling a range of domestic subjects from neighbourliness ('A Little Help From My Friends') and self-improvement ('Getting Better'), through suburban living ('Good Morning, Good Morning') and home decoration ('Fixing A Hole'), to Victorian entertainment ('Being For The Benefit Of Mr Kite'). The language of the songs was often deliberately antiquated – 'guaranteed to raise a smile', 'may I inquire discreetly', 'meeting a man from the motor trade', 'a splendid time is guaranteed for all', 'indicate

The audacious *Sgt Pepper's Lonely Hearts Club Band* became synonymous with 1967's remarkable Summer of Love.

precisely what you mean to say' – as if this really was an Edwardian production staged by the good Sergeant Pepper and his men from the local Lonely Hearts club.

Yet, the spirit of 1967 suffused the album in significant ways. It was a fruit of the belief that limits to the imagination were culturally imposed and should therefore be challenged. Anything that seemed technically possible was worth an attempt from a climaxing orchestral frenzy on 'A Day In The Life' to a note of such a high frequency that only a dog could hear it on the play-out groove.

Sgt Pepper was one of the first records to have a gatefold sleeve, printed lyrics, decorated inner bag, free gift and a cover designed by a celebrated artist. Its reputation as the first 'concept album' though is undeserved. Merle Travis's *Folk Songs From the Hills* (1947) was a concept album as was Frank Sinatra's *In The Wee Small Hours* (1955) and, more recently, Johnny Cash's *Blood Sweat and Tears* (1963) and *Bitter Tears* (1965). Indeed, it's arguable whether *Sgt Pepper* was a concept album at all. The only unifying theme was the Pepper song and its reprise and the photographs on the sleeve. There was no theme holding the individual songs together. "Basically *Sgt Pepper* was McCartney's album, not Lennon's," says Barry Miles, who was the group's main contact on the London underground scene at the time. "People make the mistake of thinking it must have been Lennon's because he was so hip. Actually, he was taking so many drugs and trying to get rid of his ego that it was much more McCartney's idea."

PENNY LANE

The band ensured that Penny Lane in Liverpool has become one of Britain's most famous street names.

Penny Lane is a Liverpool street but also the name given to the area that surrounds its junction with Smithdown Road. None of the places mentioned in 'Penny Lane' exists in the lane itself. Anyone not raised in this area of Liverpool might find it , as musician and art critic George Melly once put it, a "dull suburban shopping centre". But to Paul and John, who had spent their early years in the area, it represented a time in their lives when everyone appeared to be friendly and the sun shone for ever in a clear blue sky. Living in the bubble of fame their memories of childhood were more gilded. As John had observed in 'She Said, She Said', 'When I was a boy, everything was right.'

John had incorporated Penny Lane into an early draft of 'In My Life', but it was Paul who made it work. He created a Liverpool street scene that could have been taken from a children's picture book with a pretty nurse, a jolly barber, an eccentric banker, a patriotic fireman and some friendly passers by. "It's part fact," he admitted. "It's part nostalgia." At first it sounds as though a summer scene is being described ('blue suburban skies') but then rain is mentioned as well as someone selling poppies (November 11). The point is that the song is a series of snapshots, not all of them necessarily taken on the same day.

There was a barber's shop in Penny Lane, run by a Mr Bioletti who claimed to have cut hair for John, Paul and George as children; there were two banks (Barclays and Lloyds), a fire station in Allerton Road and, in the middle of the roundabout, a shelter. The banker without a mac and fireman with a portrait of the Queen in his pocket were Paul's embellishments. "I wrote that the barber had photographs of every head he'd had the pleasure of knowing," said

Paul. "Actually he just had photos of different hairstyles. But all the people who come and go do stop and say hello."

Finger pie was a Liverpudlian sexual reference included in the song to amuse the locals. "It was just a nice little joke for the Liverpool lads who like a bit of smut," said Paul. "For months afterwards, girls serving in local chip shops had to put up with requests for 'fish and finger pie'."

Liverpool poet Roger McGough, who was in the music and satire group Scaffold with Paul's brother Mike, believes that 'Penny Lane' and 'Strawberry Fields' were significant because, for the first time, British rather than American landmarks were being celebrated in rock'n'roll.

"The Beatles were starting to write songs about home," McGough says. "They began to draw on things like the rhymes we used to sing in the streets and old songs our parents remembered from the days of the music halls. Liverpool didn't have a mythology until they created one."

Today, because of the song, Penny Lane is a Liverpool tourist attraction and this itself has altered the area. The original street signs were stolen years ago and their replacements have had to be screwed to walls and placed beyond easy reach. The barber's shop has become a unisex salon with a picture of the Beatles displayed in the window. The shelter on the roundabout has been renovated and re-opened as Sgt Pepper's Bistro. The Penny Lane Wine Bar has the song's lyrics painted above its windows.

PENNY LANE

Written:	Lennon/McCartney
Length:	3' 03"
UK single release:	February 17, 1967 as double A-side with 'Strawberry Fields Forever'
UK chart position:	2
US single release:	February 13, 1967 as double A-side with 'Strawberry Fields Forever'
US chart position:	1

STRAWBERRY FIELDS FOREVER

In the autumn of 1966, John went to Spain to film the role of Private Gripweed in Dick Lester's *How I Won The War*. While relaxing between shots on the beach at Almeira he began composing 'Strawberry Fields Forever', a song he conceived as a slow talking-blues. Further work on the song took place in a large house he was renting in nearby Santa Isabel.

The song began with what would become the second verse in the recorded version. It was a meditation on the conviction he'd had since he was a child that he was somehow different from everyone else; that he saw and felt things that other people didn't. In the earliest preserved version of his Spanish tapes he starts, "No one is on my wavelength", later changing the line to "No one I think is in my tree", presumably to disguise what could be seen as arrogance. He was saying that he believed that no one could tune in to his way of thinking, and that therefore he must either be a genius ('high') or insane ('low'). "I seem to see things in a different way from most people," he once said. It was only on take four of the songwriting tape that he introduced Strawberry Fields (but without the 'forever') and on take five he added the line 'nothing to get mad about' that was later altered to 'nothing to get hung about'. He was already using the deliberately hesitant mode – "er", "that is", "I mean", "I think" – to underline the truth that this was an attempt to articulate concepts that can't actually be put into words.

On his return to England he worked on the song at Kenwood where the final verse was added. It wasn't until he went into the studio that he finished the song by adding the opening verse, a fact that helps to explain why the sentiment of the introduction seems out of joint with the rest of the song.

STRAWBERRY FIELDS FOREVER
Written: Lennon/McCartney
Length: 4' 10"
UK single release: February 17, 1967 as double A-side with 'Penny Lane'
UK chart position: 2
US single release: February 13, 1967 as double A-side with 'Penny Lane'
US chart position: 8*
** Although 'Penny Lane'/'Strawberry Fields Forever was a double A-side single, US chart compilers calculated the two songs' sales separately*

In the completed version a place is made to represent a state of mind. Strawberry Fields (John added the 's') was a Salvation Army orphanage in Beaconsfield Road, Woolton, a five-minute walk from his home in Menlove Avenue. A huge Victorian building set in wooded grounds, it was a place where John would go with his Aunt Mimi for summer fêtes but also somewhere that he would sneak into during evenings and at weekends with friends such as Pete Shotton and Ivan Vaughan. It became their private adventure playground.

These illicit visits were, to John, like Alice's escapades down the rabbit hole and through the looking glass. He felt that he was entering another world, a world that more closely corresponded with his inner world, and as an adult he would associate these moments of bliss with his lost childhood and also with a feeling of drug-free psychedelia.

In his *Playboy* interview of 1980 he told David Sheff that he would 'trance out into alpha' as a child, seeing 'hallucinatory images' of his face when looking into a mirror. He said it was only when he later discovered the work of artists like the surrealists that he realised that he wasn't mad but a part of 'an exclusive club that sees the world in those terms'.

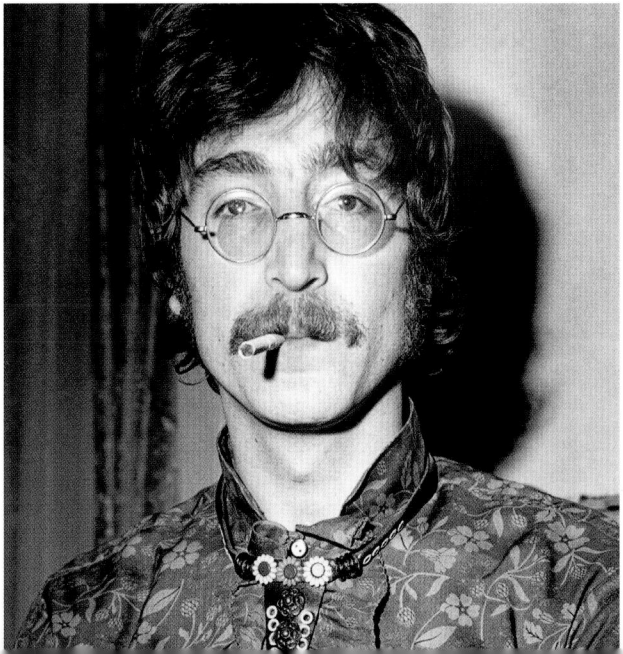

'Strawberry Fields Forever' was named after a Salvation Army orphanage in Woolton, a five-minute walk from John's home in Menlove Avenue.

SGT PEPPER'S LONELY HEARTS CLUB BAND

Success meant that the public expected the Beatles not only to deliver another artistic masterpiece but a prophetic vision. To relieve this pressure, Paul developed the personae of Sgt Pepper and his musicians, an identity that would give the band more creative freedom. They had become self-conscious as the Beatles but as the Lonely Hearts Club Band they would have nothing to live up to.

Paul conceived the idea on a flight back to London from Nairobi on November 19th 1966. During an earlier part of this holiday when he was in France he had used a facial disguise in order to travel incognito. This had led him to consider how free the Beatles would be if they could adopt a group disguise.

The conceit, however, wasn't sustained beyond the opening track and the reprise although it succeeded in giving the impression to many people that *Sgt Pepper's Lonely Hearts Club Band* was a 'concept album'. "The songs, if you listen to them, have no connection at all," George Martin admits. "Paul said, 'Why don't we make the band 'Pepper' and Ringo 'Billy Shears' because it gives a nice beginning to the thing? It wasn't really a concept album at all. It was just a question of me trying to make something coherent by doing segues as much as possible." Later on, Martin came up with the idea for the reprise, which helped to wrap it all up.

Sgt Pepper and his band achieved the feat of being very West Coast 1967 (you could picture their name on a psychedelic poster for the Avalon Ballroom in San Francisco) at the same time as remaining quintessentially English (you could imagine them playing on an Edwardian summer lawn). Paul had intended to play it both ways, writing old-fashioned lyrics delivered with a satirical psychedelic

SGT PEPPER'S LONELY HEARTS CLUB BAND
Written: Lennon/McCartney
Length: 2' 02"
UK release: *Sgt Pepper's Lonely Hearts Club Band* album, June 1, 1967
US release: *Sgt Pepper's Lonely Hearts Club Band* album, June 2, 1967

intensity, and using a title that appealed to the late Sixties vogue for long and surreal band names – Jefferson Airplane, Quicksilver Messenger Service, Incredible String Band, Big Brother and the Holding Company. "They're a bit of a brass band in a way," Paul said at the time, "but they're also a rock band because they've got that San Francisco thing."

The origin of the name Sgt Pepper is disputed. The Beatles' former road manager Mal Evans is sometimes cited as having created it as a jokey substitute for 'salt 'n' pepper'. Others suggest that the name was derived from the popular American soft drink 'Dr Pepper'.

Sgt Pepper's Lonely Hearts Club Band was both evocative of the West Coast 1967 sound of America and quintessentially English.

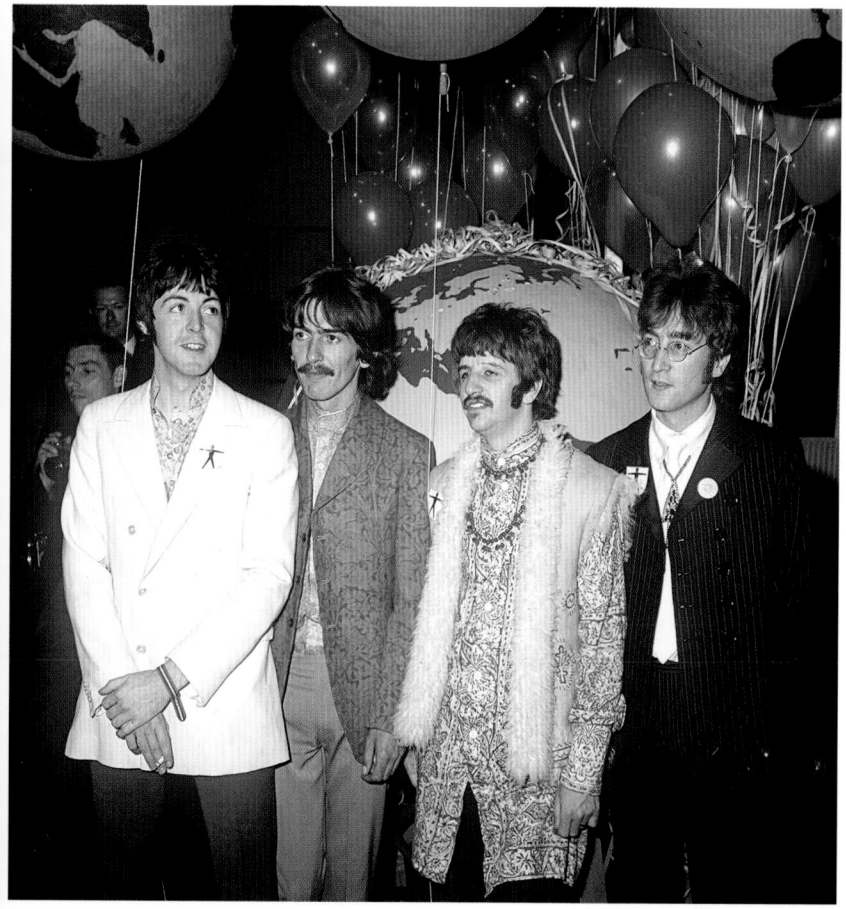

WITH A LITTLE HELP FROM MY FRIENDS

Journalist Hunter Davies was granted a unique insight into the Beatles' writing methods while working on their eponymous 1968 authorised biography. On the afternoon of March 29, 1967, Davies went to Paul's house in Cavendish Avenue and watched as Paul and John worked on 'With A Little Help From My Friends'. It was one of the first times a journalist had witnessed Lennon and McCartney composing. "They wanted to do a Ringo-type song," remembers Davies. "They knew it would have to be for the kids, a sing-along type of song. That was what they thought was missing on the album so far. I recorded them trying to get all the rhymes right and somewhere I've got a list of all the ones they didn't use."

At the beginning of the afternoon, all the writers had was a chorus line and a bit of a melody. For the first two hours, they thrashed away on guitars, neither of them getting very far. It was John who eventually suggested starting each verse with a question. The

WITH A LITTLE HELP FROM MY FRIENDS

Written:	Lennon/McCartney
Length:	2' 44"
UK release:	*Sgt Pepper's Lonely Hearts Club Band* album, June 1, 1967
US release:	*Sgt Pepper's Lonely Hearts Club Band* album, June 2, 1967

'With A Little Help From My Friends' began to take shape when John suggested beginning each verse with a question.

line, 'Do you believe in love at first sight?' didn't have the right number of syllables and so it became 'a love at first sight'. John answer to this was 'Yes, I'm certain that it happens all the time'. This was then followed by 'Are you afraid when you turn out the light?' but rephrased to 'What do you see when...'.

Cynthia Lennon then came in and suggested 'I'm just fine' as an answer, but John dismissed it saying that 'just' was either a filler or a meaningless word. Instead, he tried 'I know it's mine', eventually coming up with the more substantial 'I can't tell you, but I know it's mine'.

After a few hours of playing around with words, their minds began to wander. They began fooling around, singing 'Can't Buy Me Love' and playing 'Tequila' (a 1958 hit for the Champs) on the piano. "When they got stuck, they would go back and do a rock'n'roll song," remembers Davies. "Sometimes they would sing an Englebert Humperdinck song and just bugger around and then get back to the job in hand."

A recording session was due to begin at seven o'clock and they called Ringo to tell him that his song was ready, even though the lyrics weren't quite there yet. The lyrics were completed in the studio, where ten takes of the song were recorded that night. As John had an injured finger at the time it was initially known as 'Bad Finger Boogie' but was later changed to the rather apt 'With A Little Help From My Friends'.

LUCY IN THE SKY WITH DIAMONDS

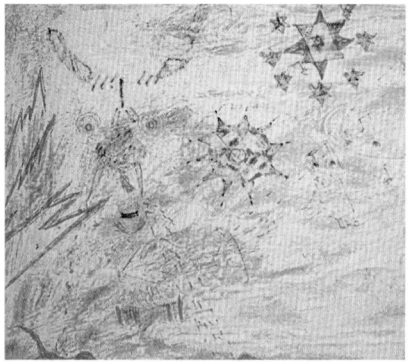

Julian Lennon told his dad that this drawing of a school classmate depicted "Lucy – in the sky with diamonds".

One afternoon early in 1967, Julian Lennon came home from his nursery school with a coloured drawing that he said was of his classmate, four-year-old Lucy O'Donnell. Explaining his artwork to his father, Julian said it was Lucy – 'in the sky with diamonds'.

This phrase struck John and triggered off the associations that led to the writing of the dream-like 'Lucy In The Sky With Diamonds', one of three tracks on the *Sgt Pepper* album that were supposed to be 'about drugs'. Although it's unlikely that John would have written such a piece of reverie without ever having experimented with hallucinogenics, this song was equally affected by his love of surrealism, word play and the works of Lewis Carroll.

That the song was a description of an LSD trip seemed to be proved when it was noted that the initials in the title spelt LSD. Yet John consistently denied this both in public and in private, although he was never hesitant to discuss songs that did refer to drugs. He insisted that the title was taken from what Julian had said about his painting. Julian himself recalls, "I don't know why I called it that or why it stood out from all my other drawings but I obviously had an affection for Lucy at that age. I used to show dad everything I'd built or painted at school and this one sparked off the idea for a song about Lucy in the sky with diamonds."

Lucy O'Donnell (who now works as a teacher with special needs' children) lived near the Lennon family in Weybridge and she and Julian were pupils at Heath House, a nursery school run by two old ladies in a rambling Edwardian house. "I can remember Julian at school," says Lucy, who didn't discover that she'd been immortalized in a Beatles' song until she was 13. "I can remember him very well. I can see his face clearly…

LUCY IN THE SKY WITH DIAMONDS
Written: Lennon/McCartney
Length: 3' 28"
UK release: *Sgt Pepper's Lonely Hearts Club Band* album, June 1, 1967
US release: *Sgt Pepper's Lonely Hearts Club Band* album, June 2, 1967

we used to sit alongside each other at proper old-fashioned desks. The house was enormous and they had heavy curtains to divide the classrooms. Julian and I were a couple of little menaces from what I've been told."

John claimed that the hallucinatory images in the song were inspired by the 'Wool And Water' chapter in Lewis Carroll's *Through The Looking Glass*, where Alice is taken down a river in a rowing boat by the Queen, who has suddenly changed into a sheep.

As a child, *Alice's Adventures In Wonderland* and *Through The Looking Glass* were two of John's favourite books. They'd been given to him as birthday presents and in a 1965 interview he claimed that he read both books once a year. In a later interview he claimed that it was partly through reading them that he realized the images in his own mind weren't indications of insanity. "Surrealism to me is reality," he said. "Psychedelic vision is reality to me and always was."

For similar reasons, John was attracted to *The Goon Show*, the British radio comedy show featuring Spike Milligan, Harry Secombe and Peter Sellers which was broadcast by the BBC between June 1952 and January 1960. *The Goon Show* scripts, principally written by Milligan, lampooned establishment figures, attacked post-war stuffiness and popularized surreal humour. The celebrated Beatle 'wackiness' owed a lot to the Goons, as did John's poetry and writing. He told Spike Milligan that 'Lucy In The Sky With Diamonds' and several other songs had been partly inspired by his love of Goon Show dialogue.

"We used to talk about 'plasticine ties' in *The Goon Show* and this crept up in Lucy as 'plasticine porters with looking glass ties'," says Milligan who, as a friend of George Martin, sat in on some of the *Sgt Pepper* sessions. "I knew Lennon quite well. He used to talk a lot about comedy. He was a *Goon Show* freak. It all stopped when he married Yoko Ono. Everything stopped. He never asked for me again."

When Paul arrived at Weybridge to work on the song John had only completed the first verse and the chorus. For the rest of the writing they traded lines and images; Paul coming up with 'newspaper taxis' and 'cellophane flowers', John with 'kaleidoscope eyes'.

GETTING BETTER

Much of *Sgt Pepper* was written as the album was being recorded, with John and Paul grabbing inspiration from whatever was happening around them. Hunter Davies was with Paul on one such occasion – when he was struck by the phrase which became the basis of 'Getting Better'. "I was walking around Primrose Hill with Paul and his dog Martha," he says. "It was bright and sunny – the first spring-like morning we'd had that year. Thinking about the weather Paul said, 'It's getting better'. He was meaning that spring was here but he started laughing and, when I asked him why, he told me that it reminded him of something."

The phrase took Paul's mind back to drummer Jimmy Nicol, who briefly became a Beatle in June 1964, substituting on tour for a sick Ringo. Nicol was an experienced musician who had worked with the Spotnicks and Georgie Fame's Blue Flames, but he had to learn to be a Beatle overnight. Called in by George Martin on June 3, he met John, Paul and George that afternoon and was on stage with them in Copenhagen the following night. A week later in Adelaide, after playing just five dates, Nicol was given his fee, together with a jokey 'retirement present', a gold watch. "After every concert, John and Paul would go up to Jimmy Nicol and ask him how he was getting on," says Hunter Davies. "All that Jimmy would ever say was, 'It's getting better'. That was the only comment they could get out of him. It ended up becoming a joke phrase and whenever the boys thought of Jimmy they'd think of 'it's getting better'."

After the walk on Primrose Hill, Paul drove back to his home in St John's Wood and sang the phrase over and over, while picking out a tune on his guitar. Then he worked it out on the piano in his music

GETTING BETTER
Written: Lennon/McCartney
Length: 2' 47"
UK release: *Sgt Pepper's Lonely Hearts Club Band* album, June 1, 1967
US release: *Sgt Pepper's Lonely Hearts Club Band* album, June 2, 1967

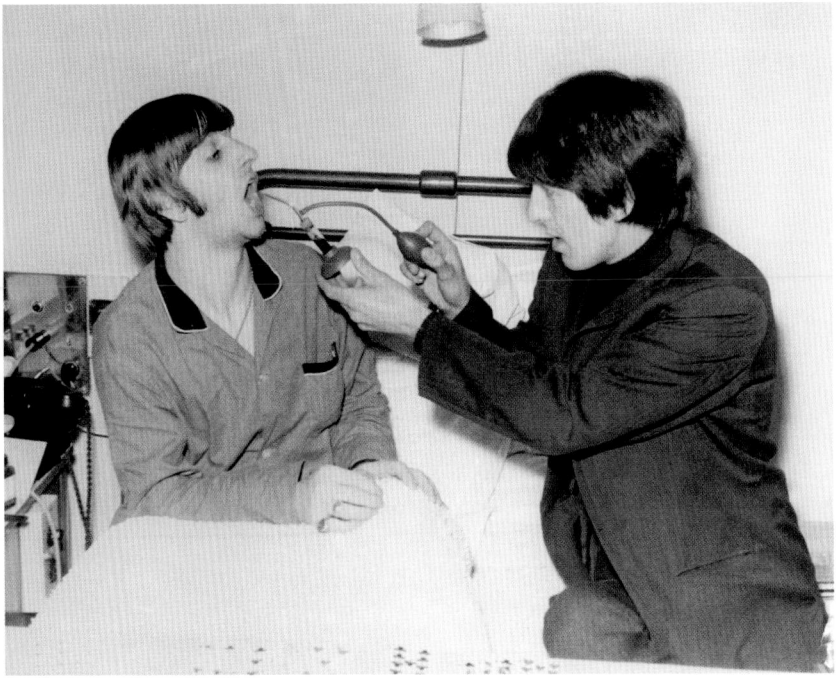

'Getting Better' was inspired by a comment made by replacement Beatles drummer Jimmy Nicol, who filled in in 1964 when Ringo was ill with tonsillitis.

room which had a strange tone that sounded almost out of tune. "That evening John came round," remembers Davies. "Paul suggested writing a song called 'It's Getting Better'. Now and again, they'd write whole songs individually, but mostly one of them had half a song and the other one would finish it off. That's how it was with this one. Paul played what he'd come up with to John and together they finished it."

'Getting Better' proved an interesting example of how they curbed each other's excesses when they worked together. The optimism of Paul's chorus, where everything is improving because of love, is counterbalanced by John's confession that he was once a schoolboy rebel, an angry young man and a wife beater. When Paul sings that things are getting better all the time, John chimes in with 'it couldn't get much worse'.

Asked about the song years later, John admitted it referred to his aggressive tendencies, "I sincerely believe in love and peace. I am a violent man who has learned not to be violent and regrets his violence."

FIXING A HOLE

'Fixing A Hole' was another Sgt Pepper song assumed to refer to drugs. People assumed that Paul was talking about 'fixing' with heroin. But the song really was about renovating his life, allowing himself the freedom to close up the cracks and holes that allowed the enemies of his imagination to leak in. "It's the hole in your make up which lets the rain in and stops your mind from going where it will," as he put it.

Although it wasn't about DIY, Paul may have drawn the images from his Scottish hideaway, High Park, that he had bought in June 1966 on the advice of his accountants. The house, which had 400 acres of grazing land, hadn't been lived in for five years and was in poor condition from the regular battering of rain and sea winds. The brown walls were dark with damp, the only furniture consisted of potato boxes and there was no bath.

Paul decorated this property 'in a colourful way' as remembered by Alistair Taylor, Brian Epstein's assistant who accompanied Paul and Jane on their first visit to High Park. "The brown paint made the farmhouse look like the inside of an Aero bar," he wrote in his book *Yesterday: My Life With The Beatles*. "Paul decided he'd had enough of it so he went into Campbeltown and bought lots of packets of coloured pens. The three of us spent the next few hours just doodling in all these colours, spreading them all over the wall and trying to relieve the gloom."

In 1967, in an interview with artist Alan Aldridge, Paul was probed on the drug associations: "If you're a junky sitting in a room and fixing a hole then that's what it will mean to you, but when I wrote it I meant if there's a crack, or the room is uncolourful, then I'll paint it."

Paul is thought to have drawn the lyrical imagery of 'Fixing A Hole' from High Park, his Scottish bolthole.

FIXING A HOLE
Written: Lennon/McCartney
Length: 2' 36"
UK release: *Sgt Pepper's Lonely Hearts Club Band* album, June 1, 1967
US release: *Sgt Pepper's Lonely Hearts Club Band* album, June 2, 1967

SHE'S LEAVING HOME

In February 1967, Paul came across a newspaper article about a 17-year-old London schoolgirl studying for her A GCE level exams who'd been missing from home for over a week. Her distressed father was quoted as saying, "I cannot imagine why she should run away. She has everything here."

The subject of teenage runaways was topical in 1967. As part of the creation of an alternative society, counter-culture guru Timothy Leary had urged his followers to 'drop out', to abandon education and 'straight' employment. As a result, streams of young people headed for San Francisco, centre of Flower Power. The FBI announced 90,000 runaways that year – a record.

With only the newspaper story to go on, Paul created a moving song about a young girl sneaking away from her claustrophobically respectable home in search of fun and romance in the swinging Sixties. What he didn't know at the time was how accurate his speculation was. He also had no idea that he had met the girl in question just three years before.

The runaway in the story was Melanie Coe, the daughter of John and Elsie Coe, who lived in Stamford Hill, north London. The only differences between her story and the story told in the song are that she met a man from a gambling casino rather than from 'the motor trade', and that she walked out in the afternoon while her parents were at work, rather than in the morning while they were asleep. "The amazing thing about the song was how much it got right about my life," says Melanie. "It quoted the parents as saying 'we gave her everything money could buy,' which was true in my case. I had two diamond rings, a mink coat, hand-made clothes in silk and cashmere and even my own car.

SHE'S LEAVING HOME
Written: Lennon/McCartney
Length: 3' 35"
UK release: *Sgt Pepper's Lonely Hearts Club Band* album, June 1, 1967
US release: *Sgt Pepper's Lonely Hearts Club Band* album, June 2, 1967

Melanie Carr, seen above behind the Beatles at *Ready Steady Go!* in 1963, became the teenage runaway subject of 'She's Leaving Home'.

"Then there was the line 'after living alone for so many years', which really struck home to me because I was an only child and I always felt alone," Melanie continues. "I never communicated with either of my parents. It was a constant battle. I left because I couldn't face them any longer. I heard the song when it came out and thought it was about someone like me but never dreamed it was actually about me. I can remember thinking that I didn't run off with a man from the motor trade, so it couldn't have been me! I must have been in my twenties when my mother said she'd seen Paul on television and he'd said that the song was based on a story in a newspaper. That's when I started telling my friends it was about me."

Melanie's case was a textbook example of the generational friction of the late sixties. Melanie wanted a freedom she'd heard about but could not find at home. Her father was a successful executive and her mother a hairdresser, but their marriage was dry and brittle. They had no religion: to them the most important things in life were respectability, cleanliness and money. "My mother didn't like any of my friends," says Melanie. "I wasn't allowed to bring anyone home. She didn't like me going out. I wanted to act but she wouldn't let me go to drama school. She wanted me to become a dentist. She didn't like the way I dressed. She didn't want me to do anything that I wanted to do. My father was weak. He just went along with whatever my mother said, even when he disagreed with her."

It was through music that Melanie found consolation. At the age of 13, she began clubbing in the West End of London and, when the legendary live television show *Ready Steady Go!* started in late 1963, she became a regular dancer on the show. Her parents would often scour the clubs and drag her back home. If she came back late, she would be hit. "When I went out, I could be me," she said. "In fact, in the clubs I was encouraged to be myself and to have a good time. Dancing was my passion. I was crazy for the music of the time and couldn't wait until the next single came out. When the song says 'Something was denied', that something was me. I wasn't allowed to be *me*. I was looking for excitement and affection. My mother wasn't affectionate at all. She never kissed me."

On Friday October 4, 1963, Melanie won a *Ready Steady Go!* mime competition. By coincidence, it happened to be the first time the Beatles were on the show and she was presented with her award by Paul McCartney. Each of the Beatles then gave her a signed message. "I spent that day in the studios going through rehearsals," she says, "so I was around the Beatles most of that time. Paul wasn't particularly chatty and John seemed distant but I did spend time talking to George and Ringo."

Melanie's flight from home took her into the arms of David, a croupier she had met in a club. They rented a flat in Sussex Gardens near Paddington Station and, while out walking one afternoon, they saw her photo on the front page of an evening newspaper. "I immediately went back to the flat and put on dark glasses and a hat," she said. "From then on, I lived in terror that they'd find me. They did discover me after about ten days, because I think I'd let it slip where my boyfriend worked. They talked to his boss who persuaded me to call them up. When they eventually called to see me, they bundled me into the back of their car and drove me home."

To escape from her parents, Melanie married at 18. The marriage didn't last much more than a year and by the age of 21 she had moved to America to live in an ashram and tried to make it as an actress. Melanie now lives in Spain with two children and a partner, buying and selling Fifties Hollywood jewellery. "If I had my life to live over again, I wouldn't choose to do it the same way," Melanie remarks. "What I did was very dangerous but I was lucky. I suppose it is nice to be immortalised in a song but it would have been nicer if it had been for doing something other than running away from home."

BEING FOR THE BENEFIT OF MR KITE!

In January 1967, the Beatles went to Knole Park near Sevenoaks in Kent to make a promotional film for 'Strawberry Fields Forever'. "There was an antiques shop close to the hotel we were using," says former Apple employee Tony Bramwell. "John and I wandered in and John spotted this framed Victorian circus poster and bought it."

Printed in 1843, the poster proudly announced that Pablo Fanque's Circus Royal would be presenting the 'grandest night of the season' at Town Meadows, Rochdale, Lancashire. The production was to be 'for the benefit of Mr Kite' and would feature 'Mr J. Henderson the celebrated somerset (sic) thrower' who would 'introduce his extraordinary trampoline leaps and somersets over men and horses, through hoops, over garters and lastly through a hogshead of real fire. In this branch of the profession Mr H challenges the world'. Messrs Kite and Henderson were said to assure the public that 'this night's production will be one of the most splendid ever produced in this town, having been some days in preparation'.

John began to write a song using the poster's words. It now hung in his music room and Pete Shotton saw him squinting at the words while he picked out a tune on his piano. John changed a few facts to fit the song. On the poster, Mr Henderson offered to challenge the world, not Mr Kite: the Hendersons weren't 'late of Pablo Fanque's Fair', Kite was 'late of Wells's Circus'. In order to rhyme with 'don't be late', John moved events from Rochdale to Bishopsgate and to rhyme with 'will all be there' he changed the circus to a fair. The original horse was named Zanthus rather than Henry.

Pablo Fanque, Mr Kite and the Hendersons were never more than colourful names to John but records show that, 150 years ago,

BEING FOR THE BENEFIT OF MR KITE!
Written: Lennon/McCartney
Length: 2' 37"
UK release: *Sgt Pepper's Lonely Hearts Club Band* album, June 1, 1967
US release: *Sgt Pepper's Lonely Hearts Club Band* album, June 2, 1967

they were stars in the circus world. Mr Kite was William Kite, son of a circus proprietor, James Kite, and an all-round performer. In 1810 he formed Kite's Pavilion Circus and 30 years later he was with Wells's Circus. He is believed to have worked in Pablo Fanque's Circus from 1843 to 1845.

Pablo Fanque was a multi-talented performer, who became the first black circus proprietor in Britain. His real name was William Darby and he was born in Norwich in 1796 to John and Mary Darby. He started calling himself Pablo Fanque in the 1830s.

The Hendersons were John (wire-walker, equestrian, trampolinist and clown) and his wife Agnes, who was the daughter of circus owner Henry Hengler. The Hendersons travelled all over Europe and Russia during the 1840s and 1850s. The 'somersets' which Mr Henderson performed on 'solid ground' were somersaults, 'garters' were banners held between two people and a 'trampoline' in those days was a wooden springboard rather than stretched canvas.

At the time, John saw 'Being For The Benefit Of Mr Kite!' as a throwaway, telling Hunter Davies, "I was just going through the motions because we needed a new song for *Sgt Pepper* at that moment." By 1980, he had radically revised his opinion. He told *Playboy* interviewer David Sheff: "It's so cosmically beautiful... The song is pure, like a painting, a pure watercolour."

John standing beside the Victorian poster which provided almost all of the names and phrases that were used in 'Being For The Benefit of Mr Kite!'

WITHIN YOU WITHOUT YOU

George became interested in Eastern thought as a consequence of discovering the sitar in 1965 and, having studied the instrument under Ravi Shankar, made his first explicit statement of his new-found philosophy in 'Within You Without You'.

Written as a recollected conversation, the song put forward the view that Western individualism – the idea that we each have our own ego – is based on an illusion that encourages separation and division. In order for us to draw closer and get rid of the 'space between us all', we need to give up this illusion of ego and realize that we are essentially 'all one'. Although the view expressed in 'Within You Without You' was drawn from Hindu teaching, it touched a chord among those experimenting with acid at the time. Through a chemically-induced destruction of ego, acid trippers often felt as if they had been absorbed into a greater 'cosmic consciousness'. The line about gaining the world but losing your soul is taken from a warning given by Jesus and recorded in two of the gospels (Matthew 16, v 26, Mark 8, v 36).

George began to compose the song one night after a dinner party at the home of Klaus Voormann, a German artist and musician he had first met in Hamburg and who had designed the cover for *Revolver*. Voormann was now living in London, married to former *Coronation Street* actress Christine Hargreaves and playing bass for Manfred Mann. Also present at the party were Tony King and Pattie Harrison. King had known the Beatles since they first arrived in London in 1963 and he would later work for Apple in London. "Klaus had this pedal harmonium and George went into an adjoining room and started fiddling around on it," remembers King. "It made

WITHIN YOU WITHOUT YOU
Written: Harrison
Length: 5' 05"
UK release: *Sgt Pepper's Lonely Hearts Club Band* album, June 1, 1967
US release: *Sgt Pepper's Lonely Hearts Club Band* album, June 2, 1967

'Within You Without You' was the first time that George put into song the teachings of mentor Ravi Shankar.

these terrible groaning noises and, by the end of the evening, he'd worked something out and was starting to sing snatches of it to us. It's interesting that the eventual recording of 'Within You Without You' had the same sort of groaning sound that I'd heard on the harmonium because John once told me that the instrument you compose a song on determines the tone of a song. A number originally written on the piano sounds totally different to one worked out on a guitar."

King's recollection of the evening is of a typical hip Sixties affair with joints being smoked and lots of cosmic ideas floating around: "We were all on about the wall of illusion and the love that flowed between us but none of us knew what we were talking about. We all developed these groovy voices. It was a bit ridiculous really. It was as if we were sages all of a sudden. We all felt as if we had glimpsed the meaning of the universe.

"When I first met George in 1963, he was Mr Fun, Mr Stay Out All Night," King continues. "Then all of a sudden, he found LSD and Indian religion and he became very serious. Things went from rather jolly weekends, where we'd have steak and kidney pie and sit around giggling, to these rather serious weekends where everyone walked around blissed out and talked about the meaning of the universe. It was never really my cup of tea but we all got caught up in it because we were young, easily influenced, and around famous people. I

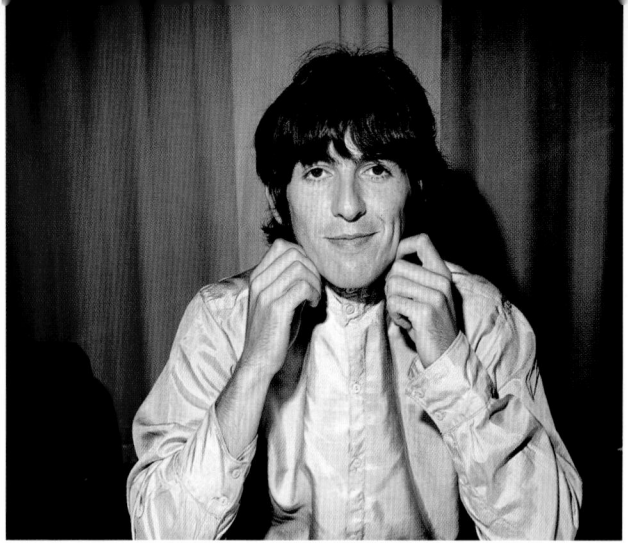

"These vibrations that you get through yoga, cosmic chants and things like that are such a buzz," said George, in typically karmic mode.

remember when the Dutch artists Simon and Marijke, who later painted the Apple shop front, were at George's, I got fed up with it all and went down the pub. Just as I was walking down George's drive, Simon and Marijke floated past in yards of chiffon and said in their groovy voices, 'Ooh. Where are you going, man?' I told them I was going for a Guinness. They said,. 'Oh. Say something beautiful for me, will you?'"

In an interview with *International Times* in 1967, George said: "We're all one. The realization of human love reciprocated is such a gas. It's a good vibration which makes you feel good. These vibrations that you get through yoga, cosmic chants and things like that, I mean it's such a buzz. It buzzes you out of everywhere. It's nothing to do with pills. It's just in your own head, the realization. It's such a buzz. It buzzes you right into the astral plane."

None of the other Beatles were present when 'Within You Without You' was recorded. George and Neil Aspinall played tambouras while session musicians played an assortment of instruments including dilruba, tabla, violin and cello. "The Indian musicians on the session weren't hard to organize," remembers George Martin. "What was difficult, though, was writing a score for the cellos and violins that the English players would be able to play like the Indians. The dilruba player, for example, was doing all kinds of swoops and so I actually had to score that for strings and instruct the players to follow.

"The laugh at the very end of the track was George Harrison. He just thought it would be a good idea to out on it," recalls Martin.

WHEN I'M SIXTY-FOUR

Paul has said that the melody to 'When I'm Sixty-Four' was composed on the piano at Forthlin Road, Liverpool, "when I was about 15". This places it in either 1957 or 1958, shortly after he joined John in the Quarry Men. By 1960, Paul was playing a version of it at gigs when the amplification broke down. At the time, he thought of it as "a cabaret tune", written out of respect for the music of the Twenties and Thirties, which his father had played as a young man.

In the midst of psychedelia, the fashions of Jim McCartney's younger days were being revived and it made sense for Paul to dust off his teenage song. Twenties pastiche 'Winchester Cathedral' had been a UK hit for The New Vaudeville Band in September 1966, and *Bonnie and Clyde*, the movie that started a craze for Thirties clothing, was released in 1967.

Although the song was written with his father in mind, it was coincidental that he was 64 when it was eventually released. "My dad

WHEN I'M SIXTY-FOUR

Written:	Lennon/McCartney
Length:	2' 37"
UK release:	*Sgt Pepper's Lonely Hearts Club Band* album, June 1, 1967
US release:	*Sgt Pepper's Lonely Hearts Club Band* album, June 2, 1967

was probably only 56 when I wrote it," Paul said, "Retirement age in Britain is 65, so maybe I thought 64 was a good prelude. But probably 64 just worked well as a number."

The song is written as a letter from a socially inept young man who seems to be trying to coax a female he hardly knows into promising him long-term devotion. The official tone of the letter ('drop me a line, stating point of view') paints a convincing picture of this formal young gent who wants to get it all in writing before he signs on the dotted line.

"It was a kind of pastiche," says George Martin. "It was a send-up of the old stuff. The words are slightly mocking. It was also something of his father's music coming out because his father had been a musician in the Twenties. Paul always had that sneaking respect for the old rooty-tooty music."

John claimed that he wouldn't have dreamt of writing anything like 'When I'm Sixty-Four'. "John sneered at a lot of things," says Martin. "But that was part of the collaborative style. They tended to be rivals. They were never Rodgers and Hart. They were more like Gilbert and Sullivan. One would do one thing and the other would say, yeah, I can do better than that and go and do better than that. At the same time, he was thinking – that was bloody good. I wish I could do it."

Paul originally wrote 'When I'm Sixty-Four' when he was 15 and made it an affectionate tribute to his father.

LOVELY RITA

An American friend was visiting Paul and, noticing a female traffic warden, a relatively new British phenomenon, commented: "I see you've got meter maids over here these days." Paul was taken with this alliterative term and began experimenting with it on the piano at his father's home. "I thought it was great," he said. "It got to be 'Rita meter maid' and then 'lovely Rita meter maid'. I was thinking it should be a hate song…but then I thought it would be better to love her." Out of this came the idea for a song about a shy office worker who, having been issued with a parking ticket, seduces the warden in an attempt to get let off the fine. "I was imagining the kind of person I would be to fall for a meter maid," Paul remarked.

Some years later, a traffic warden by the name of Meta Davies, who operated in the St John's Wood area of London, claimed she had inspired the song. Not that she had been seduced by a Beatle but, in 1967, she had booked a certain P McCartney who had, apparently, asked about her unusual name. "His car was parked on a meter where the time had expired," says Meta, "I had to make out a ticket which, at the time, carried a ten shilling fine. I'd just put it on the windscreen when Paul came along and took it off. He looked at it and read my signature that was in full, because there was another M Davies on the same unit. As he was walking away, he turned to me and said, 'Oh, is your name really Meta?' I told him that it was. We chatted for a few minutes and he said, 'That would be a good name for a song. Would you mind if I use it?' And that was that. Off he went."

It may be that Paul had already written 'Lovely Rita' and was flattering her a little, although Meta herself was 22 years his senior and the mother of a teenage daughter. "I was never a Beatles' fan," admits Meta. "But you couldn't help hearing their music. My own daughter used to wait outside the Abbey Road Studios to see them."

LOVELY RITA
Written: Lennon/McCartney
Length: 2' 42"
UK release: *Sgt Pepper's Lonely Hearts Club Band* album, June 1, 1967
US release: *Sgt Pepper's Lonely Hearts Club Band* album, June 2, 1967

GOOD MORNING GOOD MORNING

Paul dominated *Sgt Pepper* because John had become a lazy Beatle. He rarely ventured far from home, paid little attention to business and was drawing inspiration, not from contemporary art but from the stuff of domestic life – newspapers, school runs, daytime TV.

'Good Morning, Good Morning' was an accurate summary of his situation and an admission that he had run out of things to say. It was a song about his life of indolence – the result of too many drugs, a cold marriage and days measured out in meals, sleep and television programmes such as *Meet The Wife*. "When he was at home, he spent a lot of his time lying in bed with a notepad," remembers Cynthia of this period. "When he got up he'd sit at the piano or he'd go from one room to the other listening to music, gawping at television and reading newspapers. He was basically dropping out from everything that was happening. He was thinking about things. Everything he was involved in outside the home was pretty high-powered."

While sitting around in this state of mind, odd sounds and scraps of conversation would trigger ideas. It was a television commercial for Kellogg's Corn Flakes that gave John the title and chorus of 'Good Morning, Good Morning'. The black and white commercial featured nothing more than corn flakes being tipped into a bowl. The four-line jingle went: 'Good morning, good morning, The best to you each morning, Sunshine breakfast, Kellogg's Corn Flakes, Crisp and full of fun'.

The 'walk by the old school' was a reference to taking Julian to Heath House and it's likely that the person he hoped would 'turn up at a show' was Yoko Ono who he had met in November 1966. The 'show' would therefore have been an art show, not a theatre performance.

GOOD MORNING, GOOD MORNING
Written: Lennon/McCartney
Length: 2' 41"
UK release: *Sgt Pepper's Lonely Hearts Club Band* album, June 1, 1967
US release: *Sgt Pepper's Lonely Hearts Club Band* album, June 2, 1967

A DAY IN THE LIFE

For 'She Said She Said', John had combined two unfinished songs but here, for the first time, he put together an unfinished song of his own with one of Paul's to build the most ambitious track on the album.

John's songwas prompted by his interminable newspaper reading. The '4000 holes in Blackburn, Lancashire', was picked from the Far And Near column in the *Daily Mail* dated January 17, 1967, where it was reported that a Blackburn City Council survey of road holes showed that there was one twenty-sixth of a hole in the road for each resident of the city. When John was stuck for a rhyme for 'small' to finish off the line 'Now they know how many holes it takes to fill…' his old school friend Terry Doran suggested 'the Albert Hall'.

Paul dominated *Sgt Pepper's Lonely Hearts Club Band* as John had settled into a life of casual indolence.

The band pose with the *Sgt. Pepper* cover at their manager Brian Epstein's home in west London, May 22, 1967

The film about the English army winning the war was of course *How I Won The War*, that wouldn't be premiered until October 1967 but had been talked about a lot in the press.

The man who 'blew his mind out in a car' was Tara Browne, an Irish friend of the Beatles and a well-known socialite, who died in a car accident on December 18, 1966. The coroner's report was issued in January 1967. "I didn't copy the accident," John told Hunter Davies. "Tara didn't blow his mind out. But it was in my mind when I was writing that verse." The details of the accident in the song – not noticing traffic lights and a crowd forming at the scene – were made up. Paul, who contributed lines to this part of the song, didn't know at the time that John had Tara Browne in mind. He thought he was writing about 'a stoned politician'.

Browne was driving down Redcliffe Gardens in Earls Court after midnight, when a Volkswagen emerged from a side street into his path. He swerved and his Lotus Elan ploughed into a stationary van. He was pronounced dead on arrival at a local hospital. The autopsy revealed that his death was the result of "brain lacerations due to fractures of the skull". His passenger, model Suki Potier, escaped with bruises and shock.

Tara Browne, great grandson of the brewer Edward Cecil Guinness and son of Lord Oranmore and Browne, was part of a young aristocratic elite who loved to mingle with pop stars (but he wasn't a member of the House of Lords). Although only 21 at the time of his death, he would have inherited a £1,000,000 fortune at the age of 25 and was described on his death certificate as a man "of independent means" with a London home in Eaton Row, Belgravia. After schooling at Eton, Browne married at 18 and fathered two boys before separating from his wife and taking up with Suki Potier. He frequented London nightspots such as Sibylla's and the Bag O'Nails and had become particularly friendly with Paul and Mike McCartney and Rolling Stone Brian Jones. For his 21st birthday, he had the Lovin' Spoonful flown to his ancestral home in County Wicklow, Ireland. Mick Jagger, Mike McCartney, Brian Jones and John Paul Getty were amongst the guests. Paul was with Browne when he first took LSD in 1966.

Paul's unfinished song, a bright and breezy piece about getting out of bed and setting off for school, was spliced between the second and third verses of John's song. "It was another song altogether but it happened to fit," Paul said. "It was just me remembering what it was like to run up the road to catch a bus to school, having a smoke and going into class...It was a reflection of my schooldays. I would have a Woodbine (a cheap unfiltered British cigarette) and somebody would speak and I would go into a dream."

A DAY IN THE LIFE
Written: Lennon/McCartney
Length: 5' 33"
UK release: *Sgt Pepper's Lonely Hearts Club Band* album, June 1, 1967
US release: *Sgt Pepper's Lonely Hearts Club Band* album, June 2, 1967

The references to having a smoke, dreams and 'turn-ons' meant that the track was banned from the airwaves in many countries. There were even some who were convinced that the holes in Blackburn, like the holes Paul had been keen to fix, were those of a heroin user.

In 1968 Paul admitted that 'A Day In The Life' was what he called 'a turn-on song'. "This was the only one on the album written as a deliberate provocation," he said. "But what we want to do is to turn you on to the truth rather than on to pot." George Martin comments: "The 'woke up, got out of bed' bit was definitely a reference to marijuana but 'Fixing A Hole' wasn't about heroin and 'Lucy In The Sky With Diamonds' wasn't about LSD. At the time I had a strong suspicion that 'went upstairs and had a smoke' was a drug reference. They always used to disappear and have a little puff but they never did it in front of me. They always used to go down to the canteen and Mal Evans used to guard it."

MAGICAL MYSTERY TOUR

With *Sgt Pepper* behind them, the Beatles immediately plunged into recording soundtracks for two very different films – *Yellow Submarine* and *Magical Mystery Tour*.

Yellow Submarine, a feature-length animation project, wasn't initiated by the group but they took a keen interest in its development. The Beatles were happy to see themselves turned into cartoon characters and contributed storylines as well as four original songs. The script was by a team of screenwriters, one of whom was Erich Segal, author of the best-selling novel, *Love Story*. A psychedelic fantasy, *Yellow Submarine* concerns a happy kingdom called Pepperland, which is taken over by the villainous Blue Meanies. The fab four ride to the rescue in a yellow submarine from Liverpool, eventually conquering the Meanies through the combined power of Love and Music.

Magical Mystery Tour was an experimental 50-minute colour feature for television. It started off as Paul's project but the whole group was heavily involved in all aspects of production. They financed, directed, cast and scripted the film, as well as appearing in it themselves.

Along with the single 'All You Need Is Love'/'Baby You're A Rich Man', the songs from this period are the most psychedelic of the Beatles' career. *Magical Mystery Tour* was released in America as an album in November 1967 and in Britain as a double extended-play disc in December. The *Yellow Submarine* soundtrack, which included an orchestral side from George Martin, wasn't released until January 1968, shortly after *The Beatles*.

This eclectic bunch of songs would make a fitting farewell to 1967, the year of the Summer of Love, before the more sober reflections of

The *Magical Mystery Tour* double EP was the soundtrack to an experimental TV feature that critics failed to warm to.

1968. The new year marked a fresh period in the Beatles' songwriting, when cleaning up, straightening out and getting back to basics became the order of the day.

Magical Mystery Tour, which was first seen on British television on December 26, 1967, was a critical failure, which consequently received only limited exposure in America. The music was much more successful; the British double EP reached Number 2 in the singles charts and the American album went to Number 1.

The *Yellow Submarine* film was released in July 1968 and was a commercial success in America, although it was never put on full release in Britain. The album, which featured other artists as well as the Beatles, reached the Number 3 spot in Britain and Number 2 in America.

ALL YOU NEED IS LOVE

Early in 1967, the Beatles were approached by the BBC to take part in what would be the first-ever, live global television link: a 125-minute programme broadcast to 26 countries with contributions from national broadcasting networks in Europe, Scandinavia, North America, Central America, North Africa, Japan and Australia.

To mark the occasion, the Beatles were asked to write a simple song that would be understood by viewers of all nationalities. Writing began in late May, with Paul and John working on separate compositions, until John's 'All You Need Is Love' emerged as the obvious choice. The song was not only musically and lyrically uncomplicated but also it perfectly captured the aspirations of international youth in the summer of 1967. This was the time when the war in Vietnam was at its most intense and the 'love generation' showed its opposition by staging a number of peaceful protests. "It was an inspired song and they really wanted to give the world a

ALL YOU NEED IS LOVE

Written:	Lennon/McCartney
Length:	3' 48"
UK single release:	July 7, 1967
UK chart position:	1
US single release:	July 17, 1967
US chart position:	1

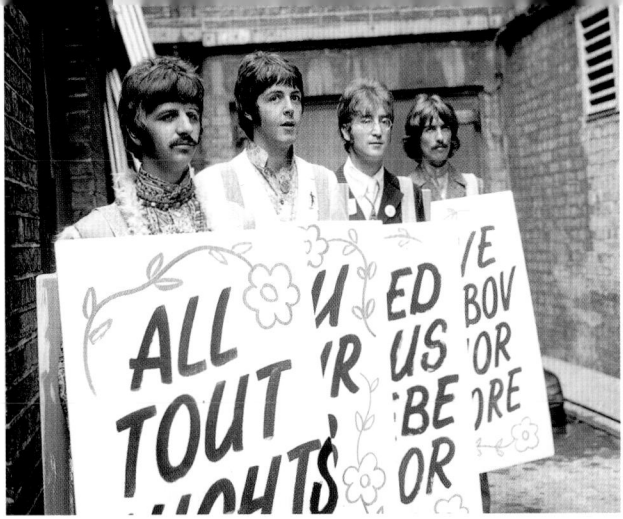

The Beatles' plea for universal love was debuted on a 1967 TV programme that was simultaneously shown in 26 countries.

message," said Brian Epstein. "The nice thing about it is that it cannot be misinterpreted. It is a clear message saying that love is everything."

In calling for universal love, 'All You Need Is Love' extended the message that John had first tried to put across in 'The Word' in 1965. He was fascinated by the power of slogans to unite people and was determined to create something with the timelessness of 'We Shall Overcome' (a labour union song popularized in the Sixties by folk singer Pete Seeger). When asked in 1971 whether songs like 'Give Peace A Chance' and 'Power To The People' were propaganda songs, he answered, "Sure. So was 'All You Need Is Love'.. I'm a revolutionary artist. My art is dedicated to change."

The viewers of *Our World* on June 25, 1967 saw a re-creation of a Beatles recording session: rhythm tracks had been laid down on June 14 and the live input was instantaneously added and mixed for transmission. A party atmosphere was created in Abbey Road's Studio One by inviting Mick Jagger, Marianne Faithfull, Eric Clapton and Keith Moon to hold balloons, wave placards and join in on the chorus. George Martin accentuated the message of international unity by opening the song with bars from La Marseillaise (France), and closing it with snatches from 'In The Mood' (America) the Brandenburg concerto (Germany) and 'Greensleeves' (England).

The single was released on July 7, and became the anthem of the Summer of Love, a paean to peace, love and understanding. "We had been told that we'd be seen recording it by the whole world at the same time," said Paul. "So we had one message for the world – love. We need more love in the world."

BABY YOU'RE A RICH MAN

As with 'A Day In The Life', two unfinished songs were sewn together to create 'Baby You're A Rich Man', which opens with John's section, originally titled 'One Of The Beautiful People', and then moves up a gear for Paul's 'rich man' chorus.

'The beautiful people' was a term applied to the hip in-crowd who, with their long hair, free love and dope, created an alternative to 'straight' society. They used the word 'beautiful' freely in their conversations to describe anything of which they approved. "At the back of my mind somewhere...there is something which tells me that everything is beautiful," said Paul in a stoned interview with *International Times* in January 1967. "Instead of opposing things like 'Oh, I don't like that television show' or 'No, I don't like the theatre' I know really that it's all great and that everything's great and there's no bad ever if I can think of it all as great."

In 1967, San Francisco was regarded as the city of the beautiful people because it was here that the hippy movement was first spotted by the media and where the first psychedelic 'happenings' and open-air 'tribal gatherings' had taken place. Although the Beatles played San Francisco in 1964, 1965 and 1966, they didn't really get to explore the city until 1967. Paul was the first to visit, on April 4, when he dropped in on a Jefferson Airplane rehearsal and jammed on guitar. George was next, on August 7, when he came to Haight Ashbury, the San Francisco district that had given birth to underground newspapers, psychedelic poster art, communes, crash pads, head shops, free clinics and legions of exotic street people. Pattie's sister Jenny was living in the area. "You are our leader, George," one hippy shouted as he set off walking from the corner

BABY, YOU'RE A RICH MAN
Written: Lennon/McCartney
Length: 3' 03"
UK single release: July 7, 1967 as B-side of 'All You Need Is Love'
US single release: July 17, 1967 as B-side of 'All You Need Is Love'

of Haight and Masonic with Pattie, Neil Aspinall and Derek Taylor beside him. "You know where it's at."

George was taken aback at the drug-glazed adoration of those who pushed flowers, poems, posters and drugs at him. "It's you who should be leading yourself," he told his would-be followers. "You don't want to be following leaders – me or anyone else." When he arrived at a park, George sat on the grass, listened to other people's songs and then started to sing 'Baby You're A Rich Man'.

The rich man in Paul's section is reputed to be manager Brian Epstein and in a demo version of the song, John maligns him by singing 'Baby, you're a rich fag Jew'. "The point was," said John, "stop moaning. You're a rich man and we're all rich men."

Paul may have used the Beatles' manager, Brian Epstein, as the 'rich man' of 'Baby You're A Rich Man'.

HELLO GOODBYE

Alistair Taylor, Brian Epstein's assistant, remembered once asking Paul how he wrote his songs, and Paul took him into his dining room to give a demonstration on a hand-carved harmonium. He told Taylor to shout out the opposite of whatever he sang as he struck the keys. And so it went – black and white, yes and no, stop and go, hello and goodbye. "I've no memory at all of the tune," Taylor later recounted. "You have to remember that melodies are as common around the Beatles as bugs in May. Some grow into bright butterflies and others shrivel and die. I wonder whether Paul really made up that song as he went along or whether it was running through his head already. Anyway, shortly afterwards, he arrived at the office with a demo tape of the latest single – 'Hello Goodbye.'"

The last part of the record, where the Beatles repeat the line 'Hela, hey, aloha' came about spontaneously in the studio. ('Aloha' is an affectionate form of Hawaiian greeting.)

If 'Hello Goodbye' was nothing more than a word game set to music, in the mystical climate of 1967, Paul was expected to offer a deeper interpretation. In an interview with *Disc*, he gallantly tried to produce an explanation: "the answer to everything is simple. It's a song about everything and nothing…to have white. That's the amazing thing about life."

'Hello Goodbye' was released as a single in November 1967 and topped the charts in both Britain and America. The final 'aloha' chorus was used in the *Magical Mystery Tour* film.

George expressed his resentment at the financial set-up of publishing company Northern Songs in 'Only A Northern Song' (right).

HELLO GOODBYE
Written: Lennon/McCartney
Length: 3' 31"
UK single release: November 24, 1967
UK chart position: 1
US single release: November 27, 1967
US chart position: 1

ONLY A NORTHERN SONG

Originally recorded in February 1967 as George's contribution to *Sgt Pepper's Lonely Hearts Club Band*, 'Only A Northern Song' first saw the light of day in *Yellow Submarine*. The song was a sly dig at the business arrangements of the Beatles. Their songs had always been published by Northern Songs Ltd, 30 per cent of whose shares belonged to John and Paul, with Ringo and George owning only 1.6 per cent each. This meant that John and Paul, in addition to being the group's main songwriters, were benefiting again as prime shareholders in the publishing company. As far as Northern Songs was concerned, George was a merely a contracted writer.

In 'Only A Northern Song', George complained that it didn't really matter what he wrote because the bulk of the money was going into other people's pockets. Underlying this was his feeling, only expressed publicly after the group had broken up, that his songs were being ignored and that he his contributions were used as mere tokens.

"At first it was just great (to get one song on each album), it was like, hey, I'm getting in on the act too!" George commented. "After a while I did (come to resent this), especially when I had good songs. Sometimes I had songs that were better than some of their songs and we'd have to record maybe eight of theirs before they'd *listen* to one of mine."

It's not surprising that George, who in 1964 claimed "security is the only thing I want. Money to do nothing with, money to have in case you want to do something", ultimately became the Beatle least keen to resurrect the Beatles.

ONLY A NORTHERN SONG
Written: Harrison
Length: 3' 27"
UK release: *Yellow Submarine* album, January 17, 1969
US release: *Yellow Submarine* album, January 13, 1969

ALL TOGETHER NOW

'All Together Now' was written in the studio in May 1967 with Paul as main contributor. It was intended as another 'Yellow Submarine' and John was delighted later when he heard that British soccer crowds were singing it.

One of the effects of psychedelia was a renewed interest in the innocence of childhood and nursery rhymes would begin to affect their post-Pepper work. Folklorist Iona Opie, editor of *The Oxford Dictionary of Nursery Rhymes*, believes that as the lines sound so familiar, it draws more on a shared memory: "I can't distinguish any particular influence on 'All Together Now'," she says. "So many ABC rhymes exist and there are counting rhymes like 'One, two, three, four, Mary at the cottage door...' which come pretty close. The song seems to come out of a universal subconscious."

Paul has confirmed that he saw it in the tradition of children's songs ("It's a *Play Away* command song") but that he was also playing with the dual meaning of 'all together now' which could be either a music-hall-style invitation to participate or a slogan for world unity. Paul Horn remembers the song being sung while they were in India but instead of singing 'H, I, J, I love you' they would sing 'H, I, Jai Guru Dev' in honour of Maharishi's spiritual master.

Paul, Ringo and George pose with a cardboard cut-out of John at the July 1968 press launch of their *Yellow Submarine* animated movie.

ALL TOGETHER NOW
Written: Lennon/McCartney
Length: 2' 13"
UK release: *Yellow Submarine* album, January 17, 1969
US release: *Yellow Submarine* album, January 13, 1969

HEY BULLDOG

'Hey Bulldog' was recorded on February 11, 1968, when the Beatles were at Abbey Road to make a promotional film for 'Lady Madonna'. Paul suggested that instead of wasting time pretending to record 'Lady Madonna', they should tape something new and so John produced some unfinished lyrics he'd written for *Yellow Submarine*. John explained to the others how he heard the song and they all threw in suggestions for the words. One line John had written – 'Some kind of solitude is measured out in news' – was misread and came out as 'Some kind of solitude is measured out in you'. They decided to keep it.

The bulldog of the title never existed before the recording. The original lyric mentioned a bullfrog but, to everyone's amusement, Paul started to bark at the end of the song. Because of this, they retitled it.

Erich Segal, the author of *Love Story*, was one of the screenwriters on *Yellow Submarine*. Years later, he claimed that 'Hey Bulldog' had been written for him because the bulldog was the mascot of Yale University where he was a lecturer in classics!

HEY BULLDOG

Written:	Lennon/McCartney
Length:	3' 14"
UK release:	*Yellow Submarine* album, January 17, 1969
US release:	*Yellow Submarine* album, January 13, 1969

IT'S ALL TOO MUCH

Paul stands by the bus that loomed large in the *Magical Mystery Tour* TV special.

George was the Beatle who most often spoke in spiritual terms about his experience of LSD. 'It's All Too Much', recorded in May 1967, was written, George said, "in a childlike manner from realizations that appeared during and after some LSD experiences and which were later confirmed in meditation".

Through images of silver suns and streaming time, the song attempted to articulate the feeling of personal identity being swallowed up by a benign force. Three months after this recording, George met the Maharishi Mahesh Yogi and began to view his LSD experience as a signpost rather than a destination. "LSD isn't a real answer," he said in September 1967. "It doesn't give you anything. It enables you to see a lot of possibilities that you may never have noticed before but it isn't the answer. It can help you go from A to B, but when you get to B you see C, and you see that to get really high, you have to do it straight. There are special ways of getting high without drugs – with yoga, meditation and all those things."

IT'S ALL TOO MUCH

Written:	Harrison
Length:	6' 28"
UK release:	*Yellow Submarine* album, January 17, 1969
US release:	*Yellow Submarine* album, January 13, 1969

MAGICAL MYSTERY TOUR

Flying home to London on April 11, 1967, after visiting Jane Asher in Denver for her 21st birthday party, Paul began to work on an idea for a Beatles television special. The group felt that they had outgrown the 'caper' format which had made them such a big hit in the cinema and now Paul was keen to make films himself, working with an 8mm camera and composing electronic soundtracks.

Encouraged by the experimental mood of the times, Paul envisaged making an unscripted film where characters and locations were chosen in advance , but the story was improvised on camera. His plan was to put the Beatles alongside an assorted collection of actors and colourful characters on a strange coach journey through the English countryside.

As Hunter Davies reported in the *Sunday Times* the day before *Magical Mystery Tour* was shown on British television: "(They had decided that the film) would be Magical, so that they could do any ideas which came to them, and Mysterious in that neither they nor the rest of the passengers would know what they were going to do

MAGICAL MYSTERY TOUR

Written:	Lennon/McCartney
Length:	2' 51"
UK release:	'Magical Mystery Tour' EP, December 8, 1967
US release:	*Magical Mystery Tour* album, November 27, 1967

next…'The whole thing will be a mystery to everyone,' Paul told the rest of the Beatles, 'including us.'"

There were two main inspirations behind *Magical Mystery Tour*. The first was the British working-class custom of the 'mystery tour', an organized day trip by coach, where only the driver knows the destination. The second was American novelist Ken Kesey's idea of driving through America on a psychedelically painted bus. The sign on the front of Kesey's bus read 'Furthur' (sic) and the one on the back – 'Caution. Weird load'. The bus was full of counter-culture 'freaks' who Kesey fed loud music and copious amounts of drugs just to see what would happen. His driver was Neal Cassady, the model for Dean Moriarty in Jack Kerouac's *On The Road*. The story of their adventures was eventually told in Tom Wolfe's book *The Electric Kool-Aid Acid Test*.

The Beatles were aware of Kesey's activities and later, when the Apple record label was founded, Kesey visited the office in Savile Row to record a spoken-word album.

On April 25, Paul arrived at Abbey Road studios with nothing more than the song title, the first line and a general idea for the tune. He said he wanted his new song to be like a commercial for the television programme, letting viewers know what was in store. Mal Evans was dispatched to find some real mystery tour posters from which they could lift phrases but, after visiting coach stations, returned empty-handed. When the backing track had been recorded, Paul asked everyone to shout out words connected with mystery tours which Mal wrote down. They came up with 'invitation', 'reservation', 'trip of a lifetime' and 'satisfaction guaranteed', but it wasn't enough and so the vocal track was filled with gobbledy-gook until Paul returned two days later with a completed lyric.

Paul's words were a mixture of traditional fairground barking and contemporary drug references. To the majority of the audience 'roll up, roll up' was the ringmasters invitation to the circus. To Paul it was also an invitation to roll up a joint. The Magical Mystery Tour was going to 'take you away', on a trip. Even the phrase 'dying to take you away' was a conscious reference to the *Tibetan Book Of The Dead*.

The track was used over an opening sequence made up of scenes from the film with an additional spoken section which declared: "When a man buys a ticket for a magical mystery tour, he knows what to expect. We guarantee him the trip of a lifetime, and that's just what he gets – the incredible Magical Mystery Tour."

"On yer 'ed!" George and Paul and take a break from filming on the set of *Magical Mystery Tour*.

FOOL ON THE HILL

Paul's encounter with a mysterious stranger on London's Primrose Hill was indirectly to lead to 'Fool On The Hill'.

Paul started work on 'Fool On The Hill' in March 1967 while he was writing 'With A Little Help From My Friends', although it wasn't recorded until September.

Hunter Davies observed Paul singing and playing "a very slow, beautiful song about a foolish man sitting on the hill", while John listened staring blankly out of the window at Cavendish Avenue. "Paul sang it many times, la la-ing words he hadn't thought of yet. When at last he finished, John said he'd better write the words down or he'd forget them. Paul said it was OK. He wouldn't forget them," comments Davies.

The song was about an idiot savant, a person everyone considers to be a fool but who is actually a misunderstood visionary. Paul was thinking of gurus like Maharishi Mahesh Yogi who were often derided and an Italian hermit he once read about who emerged from a cave in the late 1940s to discover that he'd missed the entire Second World War. An experience which is said to have contributed to Paul's image of the fool standing on the hill is recounted by Alistair Taylor in his book *Yesterday*.

Taylor recalls an early morning walk on Primrose Hill with Paul and his dog Martha, where they watched the sun rise before realizing that Martha had gone missing. "We turned round to go and suddenly there he was standing behind us," wrote Taylor. "He was a middle-aged man, very respectably dressed in a belted raincoat. Nothing in that, you may think, but he'd come up behind us over the bare top of the hill in total silence."

Both Paul and Taylor were sure that the man hadn't been there seconds earlier because they'd been searching the area for the dog.

FOOL ON THE HILL

Written:	Lennon/McCartney
Length:	3' 00"
UK release:	'Magical Mystery Tour' EP, December 8, 1967
US release:	*Magical Mystery Tour* album, November 27, 1967

He seemed to have appeared miraculously. The three men exchanged greetings, the man commented on the beautiful view and then walked way. When they looked around, he'd vanished. "There was no sign of the man," said Taylor. " He'd just disappeared from the top of the hill as if he'd been carried off into the air! No one could have run to the thin cover of the nearest trees in the time we had turned away from him, and no one could have run over the crest of the hill."

What added to the mystery was that immediately before the man's appearance Paul and Taylor had, provoked by the beautiful view over London and the rising of the sun, been mulling over the existence of God. "Paul and I both felt the same weird sensation that something special had happened. We sat down rather shakily on the seat and Paul said, 'What the hell do you make of that? That's weird. He was here, wasn't he? We did speak to him?'

"Back at Cavendish, we spent the rest of the morning talking about what we had seen and heard and felt," continues Taylor. "It sounds just like any acid tripper's fantasy to say they had a religious experience on Primrose Hill just before the morning rush hour, but neither of us had taken anything like that. Scotch and Coke was the only thing we'd touched all night. We both felt we'd been through some mystical religious experience, yet we didn't care to name even to each other what or who we'd seen on that hilltop for those few brief seconds."

In *Magical Mystery Tour*, the song was used over a sequence with Paul on a hilltop overlooking Nice.

FLYING

The Beatles had recorded two previous instrumentals – 'Cry For A Shadow' in Germany in 1961 (when backing Tony Sheridan as the Beat Brothers) and the unreleased '12-Bar Original' in 1965. 'Flying' was the only instrumental to be released on a Beatles' record.

Used as incidental music for *Magical Mystery Tour*, 'Flying' emerged out of a studio jam. Originally titled 'Aerial Tour Instrumental', it was registered as a group composition and featured a basic rhythm track with additional mellotron, backwards organ and vocal chanting. The cloud scenes over which 'Flying' was heard in the film, were originally shot by Stanley Kubrick for *2001 Space Odyssey* but never used.

FLYING
Written: Harrison/Lennon/McCartney
Length: 2' 16"
UK release: 'Magical Mystery Tour' EP, December 8, 1967
US release: *Magical Mystery Tour* album, November 27, 1967

George waiting to film the 'Blue Jay Way' sequence of *Magical Mystery Tour*.

BLUE JAY WAY

BLUE JAY WAY
Written: Harrison
Length: 3' 56"
UK release: 'Magical Mystery Tour' EP, December 8, 1967
US release: *Magical Mystery Tour* album, November 27, 1967

'Blue Jay Way' was written by George in August 1967 during his visit to California with Pattie, Neil Aspinall and Alex Mardas. On arrival in Los Angeles on August 1, they were driven to a small rented cottage with a pool on Blue Jay Way, a street high in the Hollywood Hills above Sunset Boulevard. It belonged to Robert Fitzpatrick, a music business lawyer who was on vacation in Hawaii.

Derek Taylor, formerly the Beatles' press officer and now a publicist working in Los Angeles, was due to visit them on their first night in town, but got lost in the narrow canyons on his way to the cottage, and was delayed. There was a small Hammond organ in the corner of the room and George whiled away the time by composing a song about being stuck in a house on Blue Jay Way while his friends were lost in the fog.

Blue Jay Way is a notoriously hard street to find – you can be geographically close and yet separated by a ravine. "By the time we got there the song was virtually intact," says Derek Taylor. "Of course, at the time I felt very bad. Here were these two wretchedly jet-lagged people and we were about two hours late. But here, indeed, was a song which turned up in *Magical Mystery Tour* (the film) through a prism with about eight images, with George in a red jacket sitting and playing piano on the floor."

Taylor was amused by what people made of the song. One critic thought the line in which George urged his guest not to 'be long' was advice to young people telling them not to 'belong' (to society, that is). Another acclaimed musicologist believed that, when George said that his friends had 'lost their way', he meant that a whole generation had lost direction. "It's just a simple little song," says Taylor.

YOUR MOTHER SHOULD KNOW

'Your Mother Should Know' by Paul could have been written as early as May 1967, when both John and Paul were working on songs for the *Our World* television special. Like 'When I'm 64', the song was a tribute to the music his father enjoyed singing when he was a young man in Jim Mac's Jazz Band. Jim McCartney formed his own ragtime band in 1919 and played dates around Liverpool, performing numbers like 'Birth Of The Blues' and 'Stairway To Paradise'. One day, Paul surprised his dad by recording one of his compositions under the title 'Walking In The Park With Eloise', under the alias of the Country Hams.

Paul wrote it at Cavendish Avenue and thinks it was affected by the fact that his Auntie Gin and Uncle Harry were staying with him at the time. It was the sort of song that they would have liked. Paul also had in mind the idea of 'mother knows best', a lament for those who were no longer close to their parents.

'Your Mother Should Know', however, found its way into the *Magical Mystery Tour* in a scene where the four Beatles, in white tail suits, descend a staircase and are joined by teams of formation dancers. Strictly speaking, any hit that Paul's mother would have known would have been a hit before she was born in 1909, in the days when hits were not determined by record sales but by sales of sheet music.

Paul and John may have written 'Your Mother Should Know' as early as May 1967.

YOUR MOTHER SHOULD KNOW
Written: Lennon/McCartney
Length: 2' 29"
UK release: 'Magical Mystery Tour' EP, December 8, 1967
US release: *Magical Mystery Tour* album, November 27, 1967

I AM THE WALRUS

The sprawling, disjointed nature of 'I Am The Walrus' owes much to the fact that it is an amalgamation of at least three song ideas that John was working on, none of which seemed quite enough in its own right. The first, inspired by hearing a distant police siren while at home in Weybridge, started with the words 'Mis-ter c-ity police-man' and fitted the rhythm of the siren. The second was a pastoral melody about his Weybridge garden. The third was a nonsense song about sitting on a corn flake.

John told Hunter Davies, who was still researching the Beatles' official biography at the time: "I don't know how it will all end up. Perhaps they'll turn out to be different parts of the same song." According to Pete Shotton, the final catalyst was a letter received from a pupil of Quarry Bank School, which mentioned that an English master was getting his class to analyze Beatles' songs. The letter from the Quarry Bank pupil was sent to John by Stephen Bayley who received an answer dated September 1, 1967 (which was sold at auction by Christie's of London in 1992). This amused John, who decided to confuse such people with a song full of the most perplexing and incoherent clues. He asked Shotton to remind him of a silly playground rhyme which English schoolchildren at the time delighted in. John wrote it down: 'Yellow matter custard, green slop pie, All mixed together with a dead dog's eye, Slap it on a butty, ten foot thick, Then wash it all down with a cup of cold sick'.

John proceeded to invent some ludicrous images ('semolina pilchards, elementary penguins') and nonsense words ('texpert, crabalocker'), before adding some opening lines he'd written down during an acid trip. He then strung these together with the three

Allen Ginsberg was mocked by John as an 'elementary penguin' in the typically acerbic 'I Am The Walrus'.

unfinished songs he'd already shown Hunter Davies. "Let the fuckers work that one out", he apparently said to Shotton when he'd finished. Asked by *Playboy* to explain 'Walrus' some 13 years later, he remarked that he thought Dylan got away with murder at times and that he'd decided "I can write this crap too."

The only serious part of the lyric, apparently, was the opening line with its vision of the unity behind all things.

The 'elementary penguin' which chanted 'Hare Krishna' was John having a dig at Allen Ginsberg who, at the time, was chanting the Hare Krishna mantra at public events. The walrus itself came from Lewis Carroll's poem 'The Walrus and the Carpenter'.

The 'eggman' was supposedly a reference to Animals' vocalist Eric Burdon who had an unusual practice of breaking eggs over his female conquests while making love and became known among his musical colleagues as the 'egg man'. Marianne Faithfull believes that 'semolina pilchard' was a reference to Det. Sgt. Norman Pilcher, the Metropolitan police officer who made a name for himself by targeting pop stars for drug possession.

The recording of 'I Am The Walrus' began on September 5. It lasted on and off throughout the month because George Martin was trying to find an equivalent to the flow of images and word play in the lyrics by using violins, cellos, horns, clarinet and a 16-voice choir, in addition to the Beatles themselves. On September 29, some lines from Shakespeare (*King Lear* Act IV Scene VI) were fed into the song from a BBC broadcast.

I AM THE WALRUS
Written: Lennon/McCartney
Length: 4' 37"
UK single release: November 24, 1967 as B-side to 'Hello Goodbye'
US single release: November 27, 1967 as B-side to 'Hello Goodbye'

LADY MADONNA

'Lady Madonna' was the first single to show that the way forward for the Beatles now lay in returning to the basic rock'n'roll of their early days. After *Sgt Pepper's Lonely Hearts Club Band* and *Magical Mystery Tour*, it was assumed that musical progression would mean more complexity, but the Beatles again defied expectations.

The main riff was taken from Johnny Parker's piano playing on the instrumental 'Bad Penny Blues', a 1956 hit in Britain for jazz trumpeter Humphrey Lyttelton and his band, that had been produced by George Martin. "We asked George how they got the sound on 'Bad Penny Blues'," said Ringo. "George told us that they used brushes. So I used brushes and we did a track with just brushes and piano and then we decided we needed an off-beat, so we put an off-beat in." Lyttelton didn't mind at all, as Parker had taken the riff from Dan Burley anyway. "You can't copyright a rhythm and rhythm was all that they had borrowed," he said. "I was very complimented. Although none of the

LADY MADONNA

Written: Lennon/McCartney
Length: 2' 18"
UK single release: March 15, 1968
UK chart position: 1
US single release: March 18, 1968
US chart position: 4

After the psychedelic stylings of *Magical Mystery Tour*, the Beatles returned to the basic rock 'n' roll of their early tours with 'Lady Madonna'.

Beatles cared for traditional jazz, they all knew and liked 'Bad Penny Blues' because it was a bluesy, skiffley thing rather than a trad exercise." (Dan Burley and His Skiffle Boys, formed in 1946, was the source of the description 'skiffle music' first applied to the folk-blues-country style of Lonnie Donegan in Britain during the early 1950s.)

The song was intended by Paul to be a celebration of motherhood which started with an image of the Virgin Mary but then moved on to consider all mothers. "How do they do it?", he asked when interviewed by *Musician* in 1986. "Baby at your breast – how do they get the time to feed them? Where do they get the money? How do you do this thing that women do?"

The singer Richie Havens remembered being with Paul in a Greenwich Village club when a girl came up to him and asked whether 'Lady Madonna' had been written about America. "No," said Paul. "I was looking through this African magazine and I saw this African lady with a baby. And underneath the picture it said 'Mountain Madonna'. But I said, oh no – Lady Madonna – and I wrote the song."

Released as a single in March 1968, 'Lady Madonna' went to Number 1 in Britain but stalled at Number 4 in America.

THE INNER LIGHT

On September 29, 1967, John and George were guests of David Frost on the live late-night television show *The Frost Report*. The subject of this edition was Transcendental Meditation and it included an interview with the Maharishi Mahesh Yogi, filmed earlier the same day at London Airport.

In the invited audience at the studio in Wembley, north London was Sanskrit scholar Juan Mascaró, a Cambridge professor. The following month, Mascaró wrote to George enclosing a copy of *Lamps Of Fire*, a collection of spiritual wisdom from various traditions that he had edited. He suggested that George might consider putting verses from the Tao Te Ching to music, in particular a poem titled 'The Inner Light'.

In his preface to *Lamps Of Fire*, first published in 1958, Mascaró wrote: "The passages of this book are lamps of fire. Some shine more and some shine less, but they all merge into that vast lamp called by St John of the Cross 'the lamp of the being of God'."

'The Inner Light' was the first song of George's to appear on a single when it became the B side of 'Lady Madonna'.

THE INNER LIGHT
Written: Harrison
Length: 2' 36"
UK single release: March 15, 1968 as B-side to 'Lady Madonna'
US single release: March 18, 1968 as B-side to 'Lady Madonna'

Costumes aplenty at the 1967 launch of *Magical Mystery Tour.*

HEY JUDE

As John and Yoko started living together, not surprisingly, divorce proceedings began between John and Cynthia. An interim agreement was reached whereby Cynthia and Julian were allowed to stay at Kenwood while the two respondents took up residence in a Montagu Square flat in central London.

Paul had always enjoyed a close relationship with John's son Julian, then five years old and, to show support for mother and child during the break-up, he drove down to Weybridge from his home in St John's Wood bearing a single red rose. Paul often used driving time to work out new songs and, on this day, with Julian's uncertain future on his mind, he started singing 'Hey Julian' and improvising lyrics on the theme of comfort and reassurance. At some point during the hour-long journey, 'Hey Julian' became 'Hey Jules' and Paul developed the lines 'Hey Jules, don't make it bad, Take a sad song and make it better'. It was only later, when he came to flesh out the lyric, that he changed Jules to Jude, feeling that Jude was a name that sounded stronger. He had liked the name Jud when he'd seen the musical *Oklahoma*.

The song then became less specific. John believed it was addressed to him, encouraging him to make the break from the Beatles and build a new future with Yoko ('You were made to go out and get her…'). Paul felt that, if it was addressed to anyone, it was to himself, dealing with the adjustments he knew that he was going to have to make as old bonds were broken within the Beatles.

The music drove the lyric, with sound taking precedence over sense. One line in particular – 'the movement you need is on your shoulder' – was intended as a temporary filler. When Paul played the song to John, he pointed out that this line needed replacing, saying it sounded as if he was singing about his parrot. "It's probably the best line in the song," said John. "Leave it in. I know what it means."

Julian Lennon grew up knowing the story behind 'Hey Jude' but it wasn't until 1987 that he heard the facts first-hand from Paul, whom he bumped into in New York. "It was the first time in years that we'd sat down and talked to each other," says Julian. "He told me that he'd been thinking about my circumstances all those years ago, about what I was going through and what I would have to go through in the future. Paul and I used to hang out quite a bit – more than dad and I did. Maybe Paul was into kids a bit more at the time. We had a great friendship going and there seem to be far more pictures of me and Paul playing together at that age than pictures of me and dad."

"I've never really wanted to know the truth about how dad was and how he was with me," Julian admits. "I kept my mouth shut. There was some very negative stuff talked about me – like when he said that I'd come out of a whisky bottle on a Saturday night. Stuff like that. That's tough to deal with. You think, where's the love in that? It was very psychologically damaging and for years that affected me. I used to think, how could he say that about his own bloody son!"

Julian hasn't studied the words of 'Hey Jude' for some time but finds it hard to get away from the song. He'll be in a restaurant when he'll hear it played, or it'll come on the car radio when he's driving. "It surprises me whenever I hear it," he says. "It's very strange to think that someone has written a song about you. It still touches me."

'Hey Jude' was the most successful Beatles' single ever. It topped the charts around the world and, before the end of 1967, over five million copies had been sold.

HEY JUDE

Written:	Lennon/McCartney
Length:	7' 08"
UK single release:	August 30, 1968
UK chart position:	1
US single release:	August 26, 1968
US chart position:	1

THE BEATLES

The Beatles, or *The White Album* as it is commonly referred to,, confounded expectations because of its simplicity. It was as if the group had decided to produce the exact opposite of *Sgt Pepper*. Long album title? Let's just call it *The Beatles*. Multi-coloured cover? Let's go white. Clever overdubs and mixes? Let's use acoustic guitars on a lot of the tracks. Other-worldly subject matter? Let's sing about cowboys, pigs, chocolates and doing it in the road.

The change was in part due to the Beatles' interest in the teachings of Indian guru, Maharishi Mahesh Yogi. Pattie Harrison had attended a lecture given by him in February 1967 and six months later she encouraged George and the rest of the Beatles to hear him speak at the Hilton Hotel in Park Lane, London. As a result of this meeting, they all embarked on a ten-day course on Transcendental Meditation, at University College, Bangor, in North Wales.

While in Bangor, on Sunday, August 27, 1967, they learned that Brian Epstein had been found dead at his Belgravia flat. The loss of Epstein, who had managed their career since early 1962 and had become something of a father figure, may well have made the Beatles even more open to the guidance of the Maharishi, whom they visited in India in February 1968.

The trip to India not only brought calm and self-reflection to their fraught lives but also rekindled their musical friendships. Paul Horn, an American flautist who was there at the same time, believes that meditation was a great stimulus for them. "You find out more about yourself on deeper levels when you're meditating," he said. "Look how prolific they were in such a relatively short time. They were in the Himalayas away from the pressures and away from the

The time spent in India under the guidance of Maharishi Mahesh Yogi gave the Beatles the breathing space to write the follow-up to *Sgt Pepper*.

telephone. When you get too involved with life, it suppresses your creativity. When you're able to be quiet, it starts coming up."

On their return from India, the Beatles claimed that they had brought back 30 songs which they would be using on their next album. There were indeed 30 new songs on *The Beatles* but not all of them were written in India, and some of the Indian songs (like George's 'Sour Milk Sea' and 'Circles') were never recorded by the Beatles. It's probably fairer to say that about half of the album was written or at least started while they were away. Because they had no access to electric guitars or keyboards, many of these songs were acoustic.

John would later refer to *The Beatles* as being the first unself-conscious album after the Beatles' great period of self-consciousness beginning with *Rubber Soul* and ending with *Magical Mystery Tour* and *Yellow Submarine*. *The Beatles* was released as a double album in November 1968 and rose to the Number 1 spot on both sides of the Atlantic.

BACK IN THE USSR

Friendly rivalry existed between the Beatles and the Beach Boys, and between 1965 and 1968 each new effort by either band spurred the other on to greater heights. When Brian Wilson heard *Rubber Soul*, he reported that it blew his mind to hear an album of such variety and consistency. "It flipped me out so much," he said, "that I determined to try the same thing – to make an entire album that was a gas." His reply was *Pet Sounds*, the Beach Boys' crowning achievement, which contained 'Sloop John B', 'Caroline No', 'Wouldn't It Be Nice' and 'God Only Knows'. When Paul heard *Pet Sounds*, he was equally impressed and the influence could be heard on *Revolver* and *Sgt Pepper*.

Although they admired each other, the two groups had little social contact. Carl Wilson and Mike Love had seen the Beatles play in Portland, Oregon, on August 22, 1965, and called by the dressing room after the show. Brian Johnson had been present at the Waldorf Hotel in London when John and Paul were played a pressing of *Pet Sounds* in April 1966 and in April 1967, Paul dropped by the studios in LA where Brian Wilson was working on the Beach Boys track 'Vegetables'.

The most prolonged contact came in February 1968, when all four Beatles and their partners travelled to Rishikesh, India, to study Transcendental Meditation under the Maharishi Mahesh Yogi. On the course were three other professional musicians – Scottish singer Donovan, American flautist Paul Horn and Beach Boy Mike Love. The musicians spent a great deal of time together talking, jamming and songwriting.

One of the songs that came out of this encounter was 'Back In The USSR', written by Paul as a pastiche of the Beach Boys and

The Beach Boys and the Beatles constantly strove to outperform each other.

Chuck Berry. The genesis of the song was a comment made by Love to Paul one morning over breakfast. "Wouldn't it be fun to do a Soviet version of 'Back In The USA'," Love suggested, referring to Berry's jingoistic 1959 single in which the singer expressed how mighty glad he was to be back home in civilized America with its cafes, drive-ins, skyscrapers, hamburgers and juke boxes. The Beach Boys had earlier drawn on this song and Berry's 'Sweet Sixteen' for their tracks 'California Girls' and 'Surfin' USA', in which they extolled the virtues of local ladies and surf beaches.

Paul acted on Love's suggestion and came up with a parody that did for the USSR what Berry had done for the USA and for Soviet women what the Beach Boys had done for the girls of California. After a decade of songs which had made poetry out of the names of places such as Memphis, Chicago and New Orleans, it was striking to hear Moscow mentioned in rock'n'roll. "I just liked the idea of Georgia girls and talking about places like the Ukraine as if it was California," said Paul. As a tribute to Love, the Beatles' eventual recording imitated the vocal harmonies of the Beach Boys.

In a radio interview given in November 1968 Paul said, "In my mind it's just about a (Russian) spy who's been in America for a long time and he's become very American but when he gets back to the USSR he's saying 'Leave it 'til tomorrow to unpack my case, Honey, disconnect the phone.' and all that, but to Russian women."

'Back In The USSR' disturbed conservative Americans, because at a time of Cold War and conflict in Vietnam it appeared to be

'Back In The USSR' led some right-wing US commentators to condemn the band as communist subversives

celebrating the enemy. Having admitted to drug-taking, were these long-haired boys now embracing communism? American anti-rock campaigner David A Noebel, author of *Communism, Hypnotism and the Beatles*, while unable to produce their party membership cards, was sure that they were furthering the cause of revolutionary socialism. "John Lennon and the Beatles were an integral part of the revolutionary milieu and received high marks from the Communist press," he wrote, "especially for the *White Album* which contained 'Back In The USSR' and 'Piggies'. One line from 'Back In The USSR' left the anti-Communists speechless: 'You don't know how lucky you are boy/Back in the USSR.'"

Through more diligent research, Noebel would have discovered that the official Soviet line was that the Beatles were evidence of capitalism's decadence. Just as the Nazis declared jazz music and abstract painting 'degenerate' so the Communists railed against the evil of rock'n'roll and promoted folk music that extolled the virtues of the State. Young people in the Soviet Union were just as excited by the Beatles' music as their Western counterparts but had to rely on bootleg recordings, smuggled imports and radio broadcasts from America and Britain. In 1988, with the Cold War about to be consigned to history, Paul paid tribute to his Soviet fans by recording an album of rock'n'roll standards on the official government recording label, Melodia. In May 2003 he played a concert in Red Square and had a private meeting at the Kremlin with Vladimir Putin who told him that he had listened to Beatles music as a teenager. "It was very popular," he told Paul. "More than popular. It was a breath of fresh air, a window onto the outside world."

"'Back In The USSR' is a hands-across-the-water song," said Paul in 1968. "They like us out there. Even though the bosses in the Kremlin may not, the kids do."

BACK IN THE USSR
Written: Lennon/McCartney
Length: 2' 43"
UK release: *The Beatles* album, November 22, 1968
US release: *The Beatles* album, November 25, 1968

DEAR PRUDENCE

Prudence was Prudence Farrow (younger sister of the American actress Mia Farrow) who attended the same course with the Beatles in India. The song was a plea to her to come out from her excessively long periods of meditation and relax with the rest of the group.

At the end of the demo version of 'Dear Prudence', John continues playing guitar and says: "No one was to know that sooner or later she was to go completely berserk, under the care of Maharishi Mahesh Yogi. All the people around were very worried about the girl because she was going insane. So, we sang to her." Later, John was to explain that Prudence had gone slightly 'barmy', locked in her room meditating for three weeks, "trying to reach God quicker than anyone else".

DEAR PRUDENCE
Written: Lennon/McCartney
Length: 3' 56"
UK release: *The Beatles* album, November 22, 1968
US release: *The Beatles* album, November 25, 1968

Paul Horn, the American flautist, says that Prudence was a highly sensitive person and that, by jumping straight into deep meditation, against the Maharishi's advice, she had allowed herself to fall into a catatonic state. "She was ashen-white and didn't recognize anybody," he says. "She didn't even recognize her own brother, who was on the course with her. The only person she showed any slight recognition towards was Maharishi. We were all very concerned about her and Maharishi assigned her a full-time nurse."

Prudence, whose living quarters were in the same building as the four Beatles and their partners, denies that she went mad but agrees that she was more fanatical about meditating than the Beatles were. "I'd been meditating since 1966 and had tried to get on the course in 1967, so it was like a dream come true for me," she explains. "Being on that course was more important to me than anything in the world. I was very focused on getting in as much meditation as possible, so that I could gain enough experience to teach it myself. I knew that I must have stuck out because I would always rush straight back to my room

Maharishi Mahesh Yogi was concerned about over-sensitive student Prudence Farrow.

after lectures and meals so that I could meditate. It was all so fascinating to me. John, George and Paul would all want to sit around jamming and having a good time and I'd be flying into my room. They were all serious about what they were doing but they just weren't as fanatical as me. The song that John wrote was just saying, 'Come out and play with us. Come out and have fun.'"

This she eventually did and got to know the Beatles well. The Maharishi put her in an after-lecture discussion group with John and George – who he thought would be good for her. "We talked about the things we were all going through," she says. "We were questioning reality, asking questions about who we were and what was going on. I liked them and I think they liked me."

Although the song was written in India and Prudence overheard various jam sessions between the Beatles, Mike Love and Donovan, John never played the song to her. "George was the one who told me about it," she recalls. "At the end of the course, just as they were leaving, he mentioned that they had written a song about me but I didn't hear it until it came out on the album. I was flattered. It was a beautiful thing to have done."

Prudence is now married and lives in Florida where she teaches meditation. In October 1983, Siouxie and the Banshees had a British Top 10 hit with their version of 'Dear Prudence'.

GLASS ONION

In an age of rapid social change, the Beatles were often regarded as prophets and every song was scrutinized for symbols and allusions. Who was the egg man in 'I Am The Walrus'? Was the tea that was mentioned in 'Lovely Rita' really marijuana? Was 'Henry The Horse' street slang for heroin?

The Beatles had perhaps laid themselves open to this by mixing poetry with nonsense. John, in particular, had enjoyed obfuscating his point of view, perhaps because of his insecurity. However, by 1968, he was trying to write more directly and most of the work he brought back from India was less complicated. When a pupil from his old school wrote and asked him to explain the motives behind his songwriting, John replied that the work was done for fun and laughs. "I do it for me first," he said. "Whatever people make of it afterwards is valid, but it doesn't necessarily have to correspond to my thoughts about it, OK? This goes for anyone's 'creations', art, poetry, song etc. The mystery and shit that is built around all forms of art needs smashing anyway."

GLASS ONION
Written: Lennon/McCartney
Length: 2' 17"
UK release: *The Beatles* album, November 22, 1968
US release: *The Beatles* album, November 25, 1968

'Glass Onion' was a playful response by John to those who pored over his work looking for hidden meanings. He started to piece together the song using odd lines and images from some of the most enigmatic Beatles' songs – 'Strawberry Fields Forever', 'There's A Place', 'Within You Without You', 'I Am The Walrus', 'Lady Madonna', 'The Fool On The Hill' and 'Fixing A Hole'. In 'Glass Onion', he jokingly claimed that the walrus, from 'I Am The Walrus', was really Paul. (In some primitive cultures the walrus is a symbol of death and this was taken as confirmation by those who believed that Paul had been killed in a road accident in 1966, to be replaced by a double.) Finally, he came up with four new tantalizing images for his 'literary' fans to pore over – bent-

Apple press officer Derek Taylor saw odd flower arrangements in a London restaurant.

back tulips, a glass onion, the Cast-Iron Shore and a dovetail joint. The bent-back tulips, explains former Apple press officer Derek Taylor, was a reference to a particular flower arrangement in Parkes, a fashionable London restaurant in the Sixties.

"You'd be in Parkes sitting around your table and you'd realize that the flowers were actually tulips with their petals bent all the way back, so that you could see the obverse side of the petals and also the stamen. This is what John meant about 'seeing how the other half lives'. He meant seeing how the other half of the flower lives but also, because it was an expensive restaurant, how the other half of society lived."

There were simple explanations for the other perplexing references: the Cast-Iron Shore was Liverpool's own beach (also known as the Cassie); a dovetail joint referred to a wood joint using wedge-shaped tenons and Glass Onion was the name John wanted to use for The Iveys, the band that signed with Apple in July 1968.

The Iveys didn't like the name Glass Onion and, instead, called themselves Badfinger after 'Badfinger Boogie', the original title of 'With A Little Help From My Friends'.

OB-LA-DI OB-LA-DA

Paul first heard the words 'Ob-la-di Ob-la-da' uttered by Nigerian conga player Jimmy Scott, whom he met at the Bag o' Nails club in Soho, London. A flamboyant and unforgettable character in dark glasses and African clothing, Scott was renowned for his catch phrases. His wife Lucrezia says that 'ob la di, ob la da' is a phonetic translation of something that his father would say to him in the Urhobo language used by the Warri people in the mid-West region of Nigeria. "It had a special meaning which he never told anyone," she says. "Even the Beatles didn't know what it meant. When I once asked Paul what it meant he said he thought it meant 'Comme ci, comme ça' but that isn't right. To Jimmy, it was like a philosophy that he took with him through life."

Jimmy Anonmuogharan Scott Emuakpor was born in Sapele, Nigeria, and came to England in the Fifties, where he found work in the jazz clubs of Soho. He played with Georgie Fame and the Blue Flames in the Sixties, backed Stevie Wonder on his 1965 tour of Britain and later formed his own Ob-la-di Ob-la-da Band. He provided music for some of the dance scenes in the Hammer film *She* (1965) that starred Ursula Andress, Peter Cushing and Christopher Lee. Lucrezia says that the phrase was quite well known because in concert he would call out 'Ob la di' and the audience would shout back 'Ob la da' and then Scott would reply 'Life goes on'. The fact that Paul used his catch phrase as the basis of a song ignited controversy. "He got annoyed when I did a song of it because he wanted a cut," Paul told *Playboy* in 1984. "I said 'Come on, Jimmy. It's just an expression. If you'd written the song, you could have had the cut.'"

'Ob-la-di Ob-la-da' has been cited as the first example of white ska; although the phrase was Urhobo, the song Paul created around it and the characters he invented were from Jamaica. When recording the vocals, Paul made a mistake in singing that Desmond, rather than Molly, 'stayed at home and did his pretty face'. The other Beatles liked the slip and so it was kept. Paul loved the song and wanted it to be a single. John always hated it.

Jimmy Scott played congas on the session (July 5, 1968) – the only time he worked with the Beatles. Lucrezia remembers being called in to hear a playback and taking in a headed letter made for the Ob-la-di Ob-la-da Band to show Paul how the phrase was spelt. Later that year, he appeared on the Rolling Stones' *Beggars Banquet* album and in 1969 at the Stones' free concert in Hyde Park. Around this time he was arrested and taken to Brixton prison to await trial on a charge of failing to pay maintenance to his ex-wife. He asked the police to contact the Beatles' office to see if Paul would foot his huge outstanding legal bill. This Paul did, on condition that Scott dropped his case against him over the song.

Scott left England in 1969 and didn't return until 1973 when he immersed himself in the Pyramid Arts project in east London, giving workshops on African music and drumming. In 1983, he joined Bad Manners and was still with them when he died in 1986. "We'd just done this tour of America and he caught pneumonia," remembers Bad Manners' front man Doug Trendle, aka Buster Bloodvessel. "When he got back to Britain he was strip-searched at the airport because he was Nigerian. They left him naked for two hours. The next day he was taken into hospital and he died. Nobody is too sure how old he was because he lied about his age when he got his first British passport. He was supposed to be around 64."

OB-LA-DI OB-LA-DA

Written:	Lennon/McCartney
Length:	3' 08"
UK release:	*The Beatles* album, November 22, 1968
US release:	*The Beatles* album, November 25, 1968

Marmalade saw their version of 'Ob-la-di Ob-la-da' top the UK chart in late 1968.

In July 1986, a concert featuring Bad Manners, Hi Life International, the Panic Brothers, and Lee Perry and the Upsetters was mounted at the Town and Country Club, London, to raise money for the Jimmy Scott Benevolent Fund. He left at least 12 children from two marriages. "Jimmy was essentially a rhythmic, charming, irresistible man with the gift of the gab," Lucrezia wrote in the benefit's programme. "If life was sometimes dull, it shouldn't have been, for his stories of people, of places, of incidents, were an endless stream bubbling with fun."

Paul, who kept in contact with Jimmy, also contributed a quote. "He was a great friend of mine," he wrote. "In the Sixties we used to meet in a lot of clubs and spent many a happy hour chatting until closing time. He had a great positive attitude to life and was a pleasure to work with."

Two British cover versions of 'Ob-la-di Ob-la-da' were recorded and the one by Scottish group Marmalade went to Number 1. The Beatles' version was only released in America, but not until 1976.

WILD HONEY PIE

The shortest and most repetitive of any Beatles' lyric, 'Wild Honey Pie' emerged from a spontaneous singalong in Rishikesh.

"It was just a fragment of an instrumental which we were not sure about," said Paul. "But Pattie Harrison liked it very much, so we decided to leave it on the album."

Coincidentally, Mike Love had recently co-written a Beach Boys' track entitled 'Wild Honey'.

WILD HONEY PIE
Written: Lennon/McCartney
Length: 0' 52"
UK release: *The Beatles* album, November 22, 1968
US release: *The Beatles* album, November 25, 1968

The Beatles hanging out in Hyde Park in London in 1967. The identity of the city gent remains unknown.

THE CONTINUING STORY OF BUNGALOW BILL

Bungalow Bill, the song says, 'Went out tiger hunting with his elephant and gun. In case of accidents he always took his mum.' Written by John while in India, it recounts the true story of Richard Cooke III, a young American college graduate, who visited his mother Nancy while she was on the course in Rishikesh.

John described Bungalow Bill as "the all-American bullet-headed Saxon mother's son" and Cooke agrees that it was an accurate description of him when he first met the Beatles. Cooke was over 6ft tall, dressed in white and sporting a crew cut. "The other Beatles were always real nice to me but John was always aloof," he says. "They epitomized the counter culture and I was the classic good American boy and college athlete. There wasn't a whole bunch that we got to connect on."

The tiger-hunt the song refers to took place three hours from Rishikesh. Cooke and his mother travelled by elephant and then hid in a tree on a wooden platform known as a marchand to await the arrival of a tiger.

"Rik sat down and I stood behind him," remembers Nancy. "It wasn't long before I saw this flash of yellow and black. I let out a yell and Rik twirled and shot the tiger right through the ear."

"I was pretty excited that I had shot a tiger," remembers Cooke. "But the Texan who organized the shoot came over to me and said, 'You shot it, but don't say a word. As far as the world is concerned you didn't shoot this tiger.' He wanted to be the one who went back home with the skin and the claws as his trophy."

It was when they arrived at the ashram that Cooke began to feel some remorse, wondering whether the killing of the animal would bring him 'bad karma'. He and his mother had a meeting with Maharishi that was also attended by John and Paul.

"It was a fluke that they happened to be sitting there when I had this conversation with Maharishi," says Cooke. "My mother is a very vocal person and she was talking excitedly about killing the tiger and Maharishi looked pretty aghast that his followers could actually go out and do something like this. It was the only time I ever saw him almost angry."

"Rik told him that he felt bad about it and said that he didn't think he'd ever kill an animal again," recalls Nancy. "Maharishi said – 'You had the desire, Rik, and now you no longer have the desire?' Then John asked, 'Don't you call that slightly life-destructive?' I said, 'It was either the tiger or us. The tiger was jumping right where we were'. That came up in the lyric as 'If looks could kill it would have been us instead of him.'"

Bungalow Bill was an allusion to Buffalo Bill, the performing name of American cowboy showman William Frederick Cody (1846–1917) who was a hero in post-war schoolboy comics. It became 'Bungalow' because all the accommodation in Rishikesh was in bungalows. Ian MacDonald points out in *Revolution In The Head* that the tune appears to be based on 'Stay As Sweet As You Are' which was written by Mack Gordon and Henry Revel and was used in the 1934 film *College Rhythm*.

Cooke knew nothing of 'Bungalow Bill' until he started getting postcards saying 'Hey Bungalow Bill. What did you kill?' from friends who had recognized him in the song. He now divides his time between Hawaii and Oregon and works as a photographer for *National Geographic* magazine. His mother Nancy lives in Beverly Hills, California.

THE CONTINUING STORY OF BUNGALOW BILL

Written:	Lennon/McCartney
Length:	3' 14"
UK release:	*The Beatles* album, November 22, 1968
US release:	*The Beatles* album, November 25, 1968

WHILE MY GUITAR GENTLY WEEPS

WHILE MY GUITAR GENTLY WEEPS
Written: Harrison
Length: 4' 45"
UK release: *The Beatles* album, November 22, 1968
US release: *The Beatles* album, November 25, 1968

George was reading the I Ching, the Chinese book of changes, and decided to apply its principles of chance to his songwriting. At his parents' Lancashire home, he picked a novel off the shelf with the intention of writing a song based on the first words that he came across. The words were 'gently weeps' and so George began to write.

He started recording in July 1968 but felt that the other Beatles weren't showing sufficient interest in the song. In September, he brought in his friend Eric Clapton to play lead guitar while he played rhythm.

Firmly in his mystical period, George used the I Ching Chinese principle of chance as he wrote 'While My Guitar Gently Weeps'.

John often called Yoko 'Mother'; in 'Happiness Is A Warm Gun' she was 'Mother Superior'.

HAPPINESS IS A WARM GUN

For this song, John stitched together three songs that he had started but which didn't seem to be going anywhere. The first was a series of random images picked up from a night of acid tripping with Derek Taylor, Neil Aspinall and Pete Shotton at a house Taylor was renting near Dorking in Surrey. "John said he had written half a song and wanted us to toss out phrases while Neil wrote them down," says Taylor. "First of all, he wanted to know how to describe a girl who was really smart and I remembered a phrase of my father's which was: 'She's not a girl who misses much'. It sounds like faint praise but on Merseyside, in those days, it was actually the best you could get.

"Then I told a story about a chap my wife Joan and I met in the Carrick Bay Hotel on the Isle of Man. It was late one night drinking in the bar and this local fellow who liked meeting holidaymakers and rapping to them suddenly said to us, 'I like wearing moleskin gloves you know. It gives me a little bit of an unusual sensation when I'm out with my girlfriend.' He then said, 'I don't want to go into details.' So we didn't. But that provided the line, 'She's well acquainted with the touch of the velvet hand'. Then there was 'like a lizard on a window pane'. That, to me, was a symbol of very quick movement. Often, when we were living in LA, you'd look up and see tiny little lizards nipping up the window," continues Taylor.

"'The man in the crowd with multi-coloured mirrors on his hobnail boots', was from something I'd seen in a newspaper about a Manchester City soccer fan who had been arrested by the police for having mirrors on the toe caps of his shoes so that he could look up girls' skirts. We thought this was an incredibly complicated and tortuous way of getting a cheap thrill and so that became 'multi-coloured mirrors' and 'hobnail boots' to fit the rhythm. A bit of poetic licence," adds Taylor. "The bit about 'lying with his eyes while his hands were working overtime' came from another thing I'd read where a man wearing a cloak had fake plastic hands, which he would rest on the counter of a shop while underneath the cloak he was busy lifting things and stuffing them in a bag around his waist.

"I don't know where the 'soap impression of his wife' came from but the eating of something and then donating it 'to the National Trust' came from a conversation we'd had about the horrors of walking in public spaces on Merseyside, where you were always coming across the evidence of people having crapped behind bushes and in old air-raid shelters. So to donate what you've eaten to the National Trust (a British organization with responsibilities for upkeeping countryside of great beauty) was what would now be known as 'defecation on common land owned by the National Trust.' When John put it all together, it created a series of layers of images. It was like a whole mess of colour," Taylor concludes.

The second section begins 'I need a fix' and came out of his relationship with Yoko who played a motherly, and some might say superior, role in his life. For most of their relationship he would refer to her as 'Mother'. This was also a time when he was dabbling in heroin, a drug that was later to get a grip on him.

HAPPINESS IS A WARM GUN
Written: Lennon/McCartney
Length: 2' 43"
UK release: *The Beatles* album, November 22, 1968
US release: *The Beatles* album, November 25, 1968

The final section was inspired by something in an American gun magazine that George Martin had pointed out to him. There was a line on the cover reading 'Happiness is a warm gun in your hand…', an obvious play on Peanuts cartoonist Charles Schulz's 1962 book *Happiness is a Warm Puppy*. The apparently bizarre juxtaposition of killing and pleasure stimulated John's imagination at a time. "I thought, what a fantastic thing to say," said John. "A warm gun means that you've just shot something."

The music and vocal delivery of this section emulated 'Angel Baby' by Rosie and the Originals (1960) a track that John loved. *Rolling Stone* writer Jonathan Cott interviewed John on September 18, 1968 and noted that, "John played Rosie and the Originals' version of 'Give Me Love'." This was the B side of 'Angel Baby'. Five days later, John began recording 'Happiness is a Warm Gun'.

On his copy of the lyric sheet John wrote 'dirty old man' by the first section, 'the junkie' by the second and 'the gunman (satire of 50's R + R)' by the third. Sex, drugs and rock 'n' roll!.

MARTHA MY DEAR

The name Martha came from Paul's two-year-old Old English Sheepdog, but this song is a plea to a girl who has always been the singer's muse: he asks her to remember him because he still believes that they were meant for each other. In January 1968, Paul and Jane Asher had announced that they were going to get married during the year but Paul began dating other girls while Jane was away acting and in July she called off the engagement.

"We still see each other and love each other, but it hasn't worked out," Jane said. "Perhaps we'll be childhood sweethearts and meet again and get married when we're about 70."

The song began as a two-handed piano excercise, something designed to stretch him musically. Explaining the genesis of the song in 1968 he said; "Mainly I come up with a tune and some words come into my head. In this case these happened to be 'Martha my dear'. They don't mean anything. I don't ever try to make serious social comment. You can read anything you like into it but really it's just a song. It's me singing to my dog!"

'Martha My Dear' was recorded in October 1968 – by which time Linda Eastman had become Paul's girl-friend. Jane began a relationship with cartoonist Gerald Scarfe in the early Seventies and they married in 1981.

Paul and Jane Asher went separate ways in 1968 but remained in touch as close friends.

MARTHA MY DEAR
Written: Lennon/McCartney
Length: 2' 28"
UK release: *The Beatles* album, November 22, 1968
US release: *The Beatles* album, November 25, 1968

I'M SO TIRED

During the Beatles' stay in Rishikesh, there were two 90-minute lectures each day and much of the rest of the time was taken up with meditating. Students were expected to build up their periods of meditation slowly as their technique improved. One person on the course reportedly claimed to have clocked up a 42-hour session. John found that this life of stillness and inner absorption meant that he couldn't sleep at night and consequently he began feeling tired during the day.

'I'm So Tired', written after three weeks in India, was also about the things he was beginning to miss. The Academy of Meditation was alcohol- and drug- free and John's mind was turning to his beloved cigarettes and the possibility of a drink. Sometimes a friend of his would smuggle some wine in.

Most of all he was missing Yoko Ono. The couple had not yet begun an actual affair because John wasn't sure how to end his marriage. He had briefly entertained the idea of inviting her to India but realized that the complications of having Cynthia and Yoko under the same roof would be too great.

I'M SO TIRED
Written: Lennon/McCartney
Length: 2' 03"
UK release: *The Beatles* album, November 22, 1968
US release: *The Beatles* album, November 25, 1968

BLACKBIRD

There are a number of stories surrounding the creation of 'Blackbird'. One has it that Paul woke early one morning in Rishikesh to hear a blackbird singing, picked up his guitar to transcribe the bird song and came up with the music. Another suggests that he was inspired by news reports of race riots in America and translated the plight of oppressed racial minorities beginning to flex their muscles into the image of a bird with broken wings struggling to fly.

Paul's step-mother, Angie McCartney, says that it was written for her mother, Edie Stopforth, and that she has a copy of a studio take where Paul says, "This one's for Edie" before recording it. "My mother was staying with Jim and I after a long illness," she says. "During that time Paul visited us and spent some time sitting on mum's bed. She told him that she would often listen to a bird singing at night. Paul eventually took a little tape recorder up to her room and recorded the sound of this bird."

Paul has said that the tune was inspired, not by a blackbird's singing, but by his memory of Bach's Bourrée in E minor (from the lute suite BWV 996) that he had learned as a teenager from a guitar manual. He was partly thinking of the racial situation in America and wrote it as if offering encouragement to the typical black woman facing oppression.

Although written in 1968 it's difficult to pinpoint the exact month since Paul has said that he wrote it not in India but on his Scottish farm. It's likely that he started the music in India, influenced by Donovan, and completed it between his return on March 26 and the demo recordings at George's house late in May. This makes it more likely that the lyric was written in the aftermath of Martin

BLACKBIRD
Written: Lennon/McCartney
Length: 2' 18"
UK release: *The Beatles* album, November 22, 1968
US release: *The Beatles* album, November 25, 1968

Luther King's death on April 4. On June 11 he performed it for an Apple promotional film that was being directed by Tony Bramwell.

The use of the term 'blackbird' to refer to people of African origin dates back to the slave trade and was always used pejoratively. In the sixties it was appropriated by the civil rights campaigners and given a positive spin. A civil rights musical, *Fly Blackbird*, with songs by C. Bernard Jackson and James Hatch, opened off-Broadway in 1962 and went on to win an Obie for Best Musical.

In the summer of 1968, Paul serenaded the fans gathered outside his home with an acoustic version of 'Blackbird'. Margo Bird, a former Apple Scruff (the term for the group of fans who used to congregate outside the Apple offices in Savile Row) remembers: "I think he had a young lady round, Francie Schwartz. We'd been hanging around outside and it was obvious she wasn't going to be leaving. He had a music room right at the top of the house and he opened the sash window, sat on the edge and played it to us. It was the early hours of the morning."

Paul often cites 'Blackbird' as evidence that the best of his songs come spontaneously, when words and music tumble out as if they had come into being without conscious effort on his behalf.

The lyric of 'Blackbird' was partly a reflection on the murder of US civil rights activist Martin Luther King.

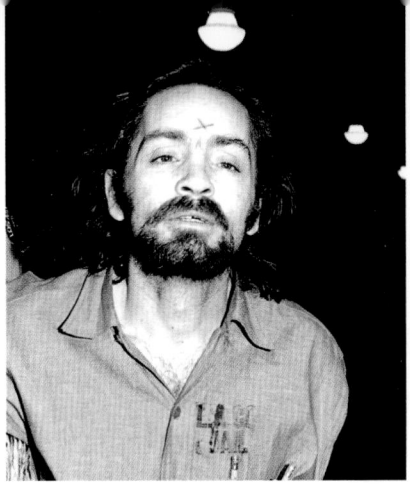

PIGGIES

George referred to 'Piggies' as "a social comment" although the song did little more than mock the middle-classes by calling them pigs, a Sixties term of derision usually reserved for the police. Pigs were also the animal chosen by George Orwell in *Animal Farm* to represent tyrannical leaders.

The song became notorious in 1971 when it was revealed that Charles Manson, the self-appointed leader of the infamous Manson 'family', had interpreted the words as a warning to the white establishment that they were to get ready for an uprising.

Particularly significant, in Manson's disturbed mind, was the suggestion that the piggies were in need of 'a damn good whacking'. According to witnesses, this was one of Manson's favourite lines, and one that he quoted frequently before his imprisonment for involvement in the murders which many saw as the final dark chapter in the hippie era.

The clue that eventually linked the eight murders – five at the residence of film star Sharon Tate, two at Leno LaBianca's and one at Gary Hinman's – was the painting of the word 'pig', 'pigs' or 'piggy' in the victims' blood. The LaBiancas were even stabbed with knives and forks, apparently because these utensils are mentioned in the last verse.

George was horrified at Manson's misguided interpretation of what he felt was a rather tame song, pointing out that the 'damn good whacking' line had been suggested by his mother when he was looking for something to rhyme with 'backing' and 'lacking'. "It was nothing to do with American policemen or Californian shagnasties," he said.

After murdering eight people in 1971, the Beatles-fixated Charles Manson wrote the word 'Pig' on the walls in their blood.

PIGGIES
Written: Harrison
Length: 2' 04"
UK release: *The Beatles* album, November 22, 1968
US release: *The Beatles* album, November 25, 1968

ROCKY RACCOON

'Rocky Raccoon' was a musical Western, written by Paul while in India. Set in the mountains of Dakota (probably because of the Doris Day song 'Black Hills Of Dakota' from the movie *Calamity Jane*), it tells the tale of young Rocky whose girl, Nancy Magill, runs off with Dan. Rocky pursues Dan and attempts to shoot him down but is beaten to the draw. Afterwards, Rocky is treated in his hotel room by a doctor stinking of gin. "We were sitting on the roof at Maharishi's just enjoying ourselves when I wrote this one," said Paul. "I started laying the chords and originally the title was 'Rocky Sassoon'. Then me, John and Donovan started making up the words, they came very quickly and eventually it became 'Rocky Raccoon' because it sounded more cowboyish."

The lyric bears more that a passing resemblance to Robert Service's 'The Shooting of Dan McGrew' (1907), a poem that also tells a story of love and revenge with similar-sounding characters. In both works a shooting takes place in a saloon. The femme fatale in Rocky's case is described in the line 'she called herself Lil…but everyone knew her as Nancy'. In Dan McGrew's case the lady is 'known as Lou'.

Apple Scruff Margo Bird heard that the character of the doctor was drawn from real life. "Paul had a quad bike which he came off one day towards the end of 1966. He was a bit stoned at the time and cut his mouth and chipped his tooth," she says. "The doctor who came to treat him was stinking of gin and because he was a bit worse for wear he didn't make a very good job of the stitching. That is why Paul had a nasty lump on his lip for a while and he grew a moustache to cover it."

ROCKY RACCOON
Written: Lennon/McCartney
Length: 3' 32"
UK release: *The Beatles* album, November 22, 1968
US release: *The Beatles* album, November 25, 1968

DON'T PASS ME BY

'Don't Pass Me By' was Ringo's first complete Beatles' song. Until then, his only contribution to the Beatles' songwriting had been the titles for 'A Hard Day's Night' and 'Tomorrow Never Knows', plus whatever musical contributions he made to 'Flying' and 'What Goes On'.

Asked in December 1967 whether he had aspirations as a songwriter, Ringo replied: "I try. I have a guitar and a piano and play a few chords, but they're all just chinga-lingas. No great tune comes out as far as I'm concerned."

The truth is he'd been trying to get the Beatles to record 'Don't Pass Me By' for years. During an interview for radio in New Zealand on their June 1964 tour of Australasia, Ringo could be heard urging the others to "sing the song I've written, just for a plug". Paul responded by saying: "Ringo has written a song called 'Don't Pass Me By'. A beautiful melody. This is Ringo's first venture into songwriting."

After Paul and John had sung a verse, Ringo was asked more about it: "It was written as a country and western but Paul and John singing it with that blues feeling has knocked me out. Are the Beatles going to record it? I don't know. I don't think so, actually. I keep trying to push it on them every time we make a record."

It was to remain unrecorded for another five years. "Unfortunately, there's never enough time to fit Ringo's song on an album," Paul explained in 1964. "He never finished it."

Ringo spent four years trying to persuade his bandmates to include 'Don't Pass Me By' on a Beatles album.

DON'T PASS ME BY
Written: Starr
Length: 3' 50"
UK release: *The Beatles* album, November 22, 1968
US release: *The Beatles* album, November 25, 1968

WHY DON'T WE DO IT IN THE ROAD?

One of the great strengths of the Lennon and McCartney team was that, although they now rarely sat down and created a song from scratch together, they did urge each other on to greater heights in what was increasingly to become solo work.

Sometimes they would try to outdo each other by composing in a style more often associated with the other. *The White Album* contained the sensitive 'Julia' and sentimental 'Goodnight' by John in Paul's style, as well as gritty Lennon-like rock'n'roll numbers like 'Helter Skelter' and 'Why Don't We Do It In The Road?' from Paul. 'Why Don't We Do It In The Road?' upset John because Paul recorded it with Ringo in a separate studio at Abbey Road and Paul's chosen style – a risqué lyric and sparse arrangements – was close to the style he had become associated with.

Paul had the idea for the song while in India when he saw two monkeys copulating in the open. He was struck by the apparently uncomplicated way in which animals mate compared with the rules, rituals and routines of human sex.

"The Beatles have always been a rock group," Paul explained in November 1968. "It's just that we're not completely rock'n'roll. That's why we do 'Ob-La-Di Ob-La-Da' one minute, and this the next. When we played in Hamburg we didn't just play rock'n'roll all evening because we had these fat old businessmen coming in – and thin old businessmen as well – and they would ask us to play a mambo or a samba. I never usually write a song and think: 'Right, now this is going to be about something specific.' It's just that the words happen. I never try to make any serious social point. Just words to go with the music. And you can read anything you like into it."

WHY DON'T WE DO IT IN THE ROAD?
Written: Lennon/McCartney
Length: 1'41"
UK release: *The Beatles* album, November 22, 1968
US release: *The Beatles* album, November 25, 1968

I WILL

Paul spent 67 takes getting 'I Will' right on September 16, 1968, with Ringo playing on cymbal and maracas and John tapping the rhythm with a piece of wood. It was the first of Paul's songs to be written about Linda and he was still adding and changing lines as it was being recorded.

Unsurprisingly, there's a sense of anticipation in the lyric, provoked no doubt by the knowledge that Linda and her daughter were arriving in London the very next week. Paul had previously only met Linda in London during the *Sgt Pepper* period and on two subsequent visits to America, but he obviously felt he knew enough about her to be confident in offering her his love 'forever and forever'.

He had started the song in India but being unhappy with the original lyric he stripped it off and started again.

I WILL
Written: Lennon/McCartney
Length: 1' 46"
UK release: *The Beatles* album, November 22, 1968
US release: *The Beatles* album, November 25, 1968

'I Will', Paul''s first song about wife-to-be Linda, was written just before she moved to London to live with him.

JULIA

JULIA
Written:
Lennon/
McCartney
Length: 2' 54"
UK release:
The Beatles album,
November 22,
1968
US release:
The Beatles album,
November 25,
1968

Although many of John's songs were shaped by the trauma of losing his mother as a teenager, 'Julia' was the first time he directly introduced his mother into a Beatles' song.

Julia Stanley was born in Liverpool in 1914 and married Frederick Lennon in 1938. John was the only child they had together. By the time John was five, Julia gave birth to another man's child and John was taken into the care of Julia's sister Mimi. His mother was attractive and unconventional. She taught John to play banjo and it was through her that John heard his first Elvis Presley records.

Julia's sudden death in a road accident in 1958 came just when John was becoming close to her again. He'd started using her home in Blomfield Road for band practices with the Quarry Men because Aunt Mimi didn't like loud music in her house.

Although 'Julia' was addressed to his mother, it was also a coded message to his new love, Yoko Ono. The 'ocean child', who John says is calling him, is clearly a reference to Yoko whose name in Japanese means 'child of the ocean'. "It was in India that she began writing to me," John said. "She would write things like 'I am a cloud. Watch for me in the sky.' I would get so excited about her letters."

The first two lines of the song are taken from *Sand And Foam,* a collection of proverbs by the Lebanese mystic, Kahlil Gibran, first published in 1927. Gibran wrote: "Half of what I say is meaningless; but I say it so the other half may reach you." The rest of the song, John said, was finished with help from Yoko herself when they met up back in England because, besides being an artist and film maker, she was a poet who wrote in a minimalist style.

BIRTHDAY

Paul wrote 'Birthday' in 1968 to celebrate Linda's 26th birthday.

The songs on The Beatles composed in India were guitar-orientated because guitars were the only instruments available at the ashram.

However, 'Birthday' was written in Abbey Road Studios, on September 18, 1968, with Paul thumping out the basic tune on a piano. According to John, Paul had been thinking of 'Happy, Happy Birthday', a 1957 hit in America for the Tuneweavers, but wanted to produce something which sounded contemporary and rock'n'roll. It was also Linda Eastman's 26th birthday in six days' time and Paul knew that she was arriving in London the following week, just in time to celebrate.

Paul went in the studio late in the afternoon and worked out the basic keyboard riff, the start of which was based on the introduction of Rosco Gordon's 'Just A Little Bit' (1960). Later, George, John and Ringo came in and added a backing track. During the evening, the four of them took a break and went round to Paul's house to watch the British television premiere of *The Girl Can't Help It* (1956), which starred Jayne Mansfield and featured music by Fats Domino, Gene Vincent, the Treniers, the Platters, Little Richard and Eddie Cochran.

Perhaps inspired by this dose of early rock'n'roll, the Beatles returned to the studio around 11pm and completed the vocals. Each of the Beatles threw in lines and Yoko Ono and Pattie Harrison helped with the backing. "We just made up the words in the studio," said Paul. "It's one of my favourite tracks on the album because it was instantaneous. It's a good one to dance to."

John's opinion, volunteered 12 years later, was par for the course: "It's a piece of garbage."

BIRTHDAY
Written: Lennon/McCartney
Length: 2' 42"
UK release: *The Beatles* album, November 22, 1968
US release: *The Beatles* album, November 25, 1968

YER BLUES

'Yer Blues' was the most despairing song John had written to date, representing an anguished cry to Yoko for help. John felt he was at a crossroads in his life: his career as a performing Beatle was nearly over, his manager was dead and now he was contemplating bringing an end to his marriage.

He felt loyalty to Cynthia and yet he knew that in Yoko he'd met his artistic and intellectual match. She was, he later said, the girl he had always dreamed of meeting; the girl he had imagined when he wrote 'Girl'.

During the stay in Rishikesh, John and Cynthia were often separated because of their different meditation routines and it wasn't until the flight back to London from Delhi that John mentioned to Cynthia his indiscretions during their six-year marriage. She was shocked: "I never dreamt that he had been unfaithful to me during our married life. He hadn't revealed anything to me. I knew of course that touring abroad and being surrounded by all the temptations any man could possibly want would have been impossible to resist. But even so my mind just couldn't and wouldn't accept the inevitable. I had never had anything concrete to go on, nothing tell-tale."

John later said that this dilemma had made him feel suicidal. In this song, he jokingly compares himself to 'Mr Jones', the witless central character in Dylan's 'Ballad Of A Thin Man'. Musically, 'Yer Blues' was indicative of the direction he would eventually take with his post-Beatles career.

YER BLUES
Written: Lennon/McCartney
Length: 4' 01"
UK release: *The Beatles* album, November 22, 1968
US release: *The Beatles* album, November 25, 1968

MOTHER NATURE'S SON

Both John and Paul wrote songs after hearing a lecture by the Maharishi about the unity of man and nature, but it was to be Paul's 'Mother Nature's Son' that made the album's final selection.

John's song, 'A Child Of Nature', made similar observations about the sun, sky, wind and mountains but, whereas Paul fictionalized his response by writing in the character of a 'poor young country boy', John wrote about himself 'on the road to Rishikesh'.

A demo of 'A Child Of Nature' was made by John in May 1968, but the Beatles didn't record it. Three years later and with a new set of lyrics it became 'Jealous Guy'.

Paul had always been a lover of the countryside and when he wrote 'Mother Nature's Son' he had in mind a song he had heard when he was younger called 'Nature Boy' (1947) , made popular by Nat 'King' Cole. Although the song was started in India it was completed at his father's house.

Nat 'King' Cole's 1947 hit 'Nature Boy' was in Paul's mind when he composed 'Mother Nature's Son'.

MOTHER NATURE'S SON

Written:	Lennon/McCartney
Length:	2' 48"
UK release:	*The Beatles* album, November 22, 1968
US release:	*The Beatles* album, November 25, 1968

EVERYBODY'S GOT SOMETHING TO HIDE EXCEPT ME AND MY MONKEY

Initially known as 'Come On, Come On', the song was built up from its title. John said it was a clear reference to his relationship with Yoko. "That was just a nice line which I made into a song," he said. "Everybody seemed to be paranoid except for us two, who were in the glow of love...everybody was sort of tense around us."

It wasn't until his return from India that the friendship turned into an affair and Cynthia knew what was happening. Yoko started to attend recording sessions for the new album, much to the annoyance of the other Beatles. The British press also found it difficult to accept Yoko and this irked John and was to play a part in his eventual move to America. "In England, they think I'm someone who has won the pools and gone off with a Japanese Princess," he once said. "In America, they treat her with respect. They treat her as the serious artist she is."

The rapid 'Come on, come on, come on....' chorus sounds similar to what became known as the 'gobble chorus' section of the Fugs' track 'Virgin Forest' that appeared on *The Fugs' Second Album* (1966). Barry Miles, then running the Indica Bookshop, supplied the Beatles with the latest underground releases from America, including work by The Fugs.

EVERYBODY'S GOT SOMETHING TO HIDE EXCEPT ME AND MY MONKEY
Written: Lennon/McCartney
Length: 2' 24"
UK release: *The Beatles* album, November 22, 1968
US release: *The Beatles* album, November 25, 1968

SEXY SADIE

'Sexy Sadie' appears to be a song about a girl who leads men on, only to make fools of them, but was written about the Maharishi Mahesh Yogi, after John had become disillusioned with him. Knowing that he could never record a potentially libellous song called Maharishi, he titled it 'Sexy Sadie', but on the demo recording of the track he let rip with a string of obscenities directed towards his real quarry.

There were two reasons why the Beatles decided to leave Rishikesh. They had been told that the Maharishi was only after their money and a rumour suggested he had made a sexual advance to a women on the course. It unnerved them and the three Beatles told the guru they were leaving. Pressed to explain their decision, John reportedly said, "Well, if you're so cosmic, you'll know why."

Paul Horn, who remembers them leaving, believes the fall-out was inevitable: "These courses were designed for people who had a solid background in meditation. The Beatles didn't have the experience and I think they were expecting miracles. George was really interested but Ringo wasn't into Eastern philosophy at all. John was and always sceptical about anything until it had been proven to him. Paul was easy-going and could have gone either way.

"The big fuss came because there were some people there who were more interested in the Beatles than learning to meditate and they became hangers-on. One woman was really into the Beatles and started all this crap about the Maharishi making passes at her. There were a lot of rumours, jealousies and triangles going on and she got back at the Beatles through saying this about the Maharishi. The bottom line, though, is that it was time for them to go home. This was just the catalyst."

The band's relationship with the Maharishi did not end well, and John poured his bitterness into 'Sexy Sadie'.

SEXY SADIE
Written: Lennon/McCartney
Length: 3' 15"
UK release: *The Beatles* album, November 22, 1968
US release: *The Beatles* album, November 25, 1968

HELTER SKELTER

The concept for 'Helter Skelter' came from a music paper's rave review of a new single by the Who. Paul didn't think the single matched the hyperbole and set himself the challenge of writing something that could legitimately be described in that language.

The single, 'I Can See For Miles', was released in October 1967 and reviewed by Chris Welch in *Melody Maker*. "Forget Happy Jack sitting in sand on the Isle of Man," wrote Welch. "This marathon epic of swearing cymbals and cursing guitars marks the return of the Who as a major freak-out force. Recorded in America, it's a Pete Townshend composition filled with Townshend mystery and menace."

It's impossible to be certain that this was the review, because Paul's description has changed over the years. In 1968, he said the review had said "The group really goes wild with echo and screaming and everything," but 20 years later he claimed it described the Who single as, "the loudest, most raucous rock'n'roll, the dirtiest thing they'd ever done." However, Paul's account of the effect that the review had on him had't changed: "I thought 'That's a pity. I would

HELTER SKELTER

Written:	Lennon/McCartney
Length:	4' 29"
UK release:	*The Beatles* album, November 22, 1968
US release:	*The Beatles* album, November 25, 1968

Crazed killer Charles Manson felt 'Helter Skelter' was warning America of imminent racial conflict.

like to do something like that.' Then I heard it and it was nothing like it. It was straight and sophisticated. So we did this. I like noise."

Despite being described as having 'swearing cymbals' and 'cursing guitars', 'I Can See For Miles' had a discernible melody throughout and could not properly be described as raucous. Paul wanted to write something that really did 'freak people out' and, when the Beatles first recorded 'Helter Skelter' in July 1968, they did it in one take which was almost half an hour long. They returned to it in September 'out of their heads', and produced a shorter version. At the end of it, Ringo can be heard shrieking, "I've got blisters on my fingers."

Most British listeners were aware that a helter skelter was a spiral fairground slide but Charles Manson, who heard the *White Album* in December 1968 thought that the Beatles were warning America of a racial conflict that was 'coming down fast'. In the scenario that Manson had developed, the Beatles were the four angels mentioned in the New Testament book of Revelation who, through their songs, were telling him and his followers to prepare for the coming holocaust by escaping to the desert.

Manson referred to this future uprising as 'Helter Skelter' and it was the daubing of these words in blood at the scene of one of the murders that became another vital clue in the subsequent police investigation. It was because of the song's significance that Vincent Bugliosi, the LA District Attorney who prosecuted at Manson's trial, named his best-selling account of the murders *Helter Skelter*.

LONG LONG LONG

More than any other Beatle, George was inspired to write by hearing other songs. The chords of 'Long Long Long' were suggested to him by Bob Dylan's haunting track 'Sad Eyed Lady Of The Lowlands'. George was fascinated with the movement from D to E minor to A and back to D and wanted to write something which sounded similar. He scribbled the lyric out in the pages of an empty 'week at a glance' diary for 1968 and called it 'It's Been A Long Long Long Time' which then became the working title.

'Long Long Long' sounds like a straightforward love song but, according to George, the 'you' in question here is God. He was the first Beatle to show an interest in Eastern religion and the only one to carry on with it after the others became disenchanted with the Maharishi following their visit to India. George did, however, alter his allegiances, distancing himself from Maharishi and Transcendental Meditation and becoming publicly identified with the International Society for Krishna Consciousness, later producing their Hare Krishna mantra as a hit single.

LONG LONG LONG

Written:	Harrison
Length:	3' 04"
UK release:	*The Beatles* album, November 22, 1968
US release:	*The Beatles* album, November 25, 1968

REVOLUTION

John's refusal to concur with revolutionary politics saw militants condemn his 'betrayal'.

The Summer of Love was followed by the Spring of Revolution. In March 1968, thousands marched on the American Embassy in London's Grosvenor Square to protest against the war in Vietnam. In May, students rioted in Paris. Unlike Mick Jagger, who made an appearance at Grosvenor Square, John surveyed these events from home, keeping in touch through the news media and the underground press. He began work on 'Revolution' while in India and completed it at home when Cynthia was away in Greece. He took it to Paul as a potential single but Paul said the song wasn't commercial enough.

This wasn't the song of a revolutionary but rather the song of someone under pressure from revolutionaries to declare his allegiance. Easily the most politically conscious of the Beatles and unapologetically left-wing in outlook, John had become a target for various Leninist, Trotskyist and Maoist groups, who felt he should lend both moral and financial support to their causes.

'Revolution' was John's reply to these factions, informing them that, while he shared their desire for social change, he believed that the only worthwhile revolution would come about through inner change rather than revolutionary violence. However, he was never absolutely sure of his position, hedging his bets on the slow version of the song released on the album. After admitting that destruction can come with revolution, he sang 'you can count me out/in' obviously unsure of which side of the debate to come down on. On the fast version, recorded six weeks later and released as the B side of 'Hey Jude', he omitted the word 'in'.

The omission provoked much hand-wringing in the underground press. The American magazine *Ramparts* called it a 'betrayal' and the

New Left Review: "a lamentable petty bourgeois cry of fear". *Time* magazine, on the other hand, devoted a whole article to the song which it said, "criticized radical activists the world over".

The nature of John's dilemma was revealed in an exchange of letters published in a Keele University magazine. In an open letter, student John Hoyland said of 'Revolution', "That record was no more revolutionary than *Mrs Dale's Diary* (a BBC radio soap). In order to change the world, we've got to understand what's wrong with the world. And then – destroy it. Ruthlessly. This is not cruelty or madness. It is one of the most passionate forms of love. Because what we're fighting is suffering, oppression, humiliation – the immense toll of unhappiness caused by capitalism. And any 'love' which does not pit itself against these things is sloppy and irrelevant. There is no such thing as a polite revolution."

In his reply, John wrote: "I don't remember saying that 'Revolution' was revolutionary. Fuck Mrs Dale. Listen to all three versions of 'Revolution' – 1, 2 and 9 and then try again, dear John (Hoyland). You say 'in order to change the world, we've got to understand what's wrong with the world and then destroy it. Ruthlessly'. You're obviously on a destruction kick. I'll tell you what's wrong with it – people. So, do you want to destroy them? Ruthlessly? Until you/we change your/our heads – there's no chance. Tell me one successful revolution. Who fucked up communism, Christianity, capitalism, Buddhism etc? Sick heads, and nothing else. Do you think all the enemy wear capitalist badges so that you can shoot them? It's a bit naive, John. You seem to think it's just a class war."

Interviewed later by journalists from the magazine, John (Lennon) said: "All I'm saying is I think you should do it by changing people's heads, and they're saying we should smash the system. Now the system-smashing scene has been going on forever. What's it done? The Irish did it, the Russians did it and the French did it and where has it got them? It's got them nowhere. It's the same old game. Who's going to run this smashing up? Who's going to take over? It'll be the biggest smashers. They'll be the ones to get in first and, like in Russia, they'll be the ones to take over. I don't know what the answer is but I think it's down to people."

It was a position John was to hold to. In 1980, he said that 'Revolution' still stood as an expression of his politics. "Count me out if it's for violence. Don't expect me on the barricades unless it's with flowers."

REVOLUTION
Written: Lennon/McCartney
Length: 4' 15"
UK single release: August 30, 1968 as B-side to 'Hey Jude'
US single release: August 26, 1968 as B-side to 'Hey Jude'

HONEY PIE

'Honey Pie' was a tribute to Jim McCartney from his son. "My dad's always played fruity old songs like this, and I like them," Paul said. "I would have liked to have been a writer in the Twenties because I like the top hat and tails thing."

Just as he believed 'Helter Skelter' was written for him personally, Charles Manson found further instructions in 'Honey Pie'. After all, it was addressed to people in the USA, inviting them to display the magic of their 'Hollywood song'? Manson lived near Los Angeles. What could be clearer?

HONEY PIE
Written: Lennon/McCartney
Length: 2' 41"
UK release: *The Beatles* album, November 22, 1968
US release: *The Beatles* album, November 25, 1968

SAVOY TRUFFLE

George had been friendly with Eric Clapton since meeting him in April 1966 and 'Savoy Truffle' was a playful song about Clapton's love of chocolate. This habit contributed to Clapton's tooth decay and George was warning him that one more soft-centred chocolate and he'd have to have his teeth pulled out.

The song's lyric is made up of the exotic names then given to individual chocolates in Mackintosh's Good News assortment such as Creme Tangerine, Montelimar, Ginger Sling and Coffee Dessert. Savoy Truffle was another authentic name, whereas Cherry Cream and Coconut Fudge were invented to fit the song.

Derek Taylor helped with the middle eight by suggesting the title of a film he'd just seen called *You Are What You Eat* which was made by two American friends, Alan Pariser and Barry Feinstein. It didn't scan properly so George changed it to 'you know that what you eat you are'.

SAVOY TRUFFLE
Written: Harrison
Length: 2' 54"
UK release: *The Beatles* album, November 22, 1968
US release: *The Beatles* album, November 25, 1968

CRY BABY CRY

CRY BABY CRY
Written:
Lennon/
McCartney
Length: 3' 01"
UK release:
The Beatles album,
November 22,
1968
US release:
The Beatles album,
November 25,
1968

In 1968, as Hunter Davies was finishing his band biography, John told him: "I've got another (song) here, a few words, I think I got them from an advert: 'Cry baby cry, Make your mother buy'. I've been playing it over on the piano. I've let it go now. It'll come back if I really want it." The lines came back to him while he was in India where Donovan remembers him working on it. "I think the eventual imagery was suggested by my own songs of fairy tales. We had become very close in exchanging musical vibes."

Partly based on the nursery rhyme 'Sing A Song Of Sixpence' and, via the advert, partly on the playground taunt 'Cry, baby, cry,/ Stick a finger in your eye/ And tell your mother it wasn't I', the song includes John's own creations the Duchess of Kirkaldy and the King of Marigold. Kirkaldy is in Fife, Scotland, and was where John used to stop off on his way to Durness for family holidays as a boy.

John's keen embrace of psychedelia extended to his Rolls-Royce.

REVOLUTION 9

'Revolution 9' was neither a Lennon and McCartney song nor a Beatles' recording but an eight minute, 15 second-long amalgamation of taped sounds which John and Yoko mixed together.

The album track of 'Revolution' originally clocked in at over 10 minutes; more than half of it consisting of John and Yoko screaming and moaning over a range of discordant sounds, created to simulate the rumblings of a revolution. Subsequently, they decided to clip the chaotic section and use it as the basis of another track, which turned into 'Revolution 9'.

At this point, home-made tapes of crowd disturbances were brought in and other sound effects were found in EMI's library. Due to the lack of sophisticated multi-track recording, all three Abbey Road studios had to be commandeered, with machines being specially linked together and tape loops held in place with pencils. John operated the faders to create a live mix.

With so many overlapping sounds, it is almost impossible to identify all the individual noises and spoken comments. Mark

REVOLUTION 9

Written:	Lennon/McCartney
Length:	8' 22"
UK release:	*The Beatles* album, November 22, 1968
US release:	*The Beatles* album, November 25, 1968

The sonic collage of 'Revolution 9' included a recording of John and Yoko screaming the word 'right'.

Lewisohn, who studied the original four-track recording, divided these into: a choir; backwards violins; a backwards symphony; an orchestral overdub from 'A Day In The Life'; banging glasses; applause; opera; backwards mellotron; humming; spoken phrases by John and George and a cassette tape of Yoko and John screaming the word 'right' from 'Revolution'.

The most memorable tape, (which supplied part of the title), was the sonorous voice intoning 'Number Nine, Number Nine'. This was apparently discovered on a library tape, which may have formed part of a taped examination question for students of the Royal Academy of Music.

Once again, Charles Manson thought that John was speaking personally to him through the hubbub, taking the number 9 as a reference to Revelation chapter 9 with its vision of the coming apocalypse. Manson thought John was shouting 'rise', rather than 'right', and interpreted it as an incitement to the black community to rise against the white middle class. 'Rise' became one of Manson's key phrases and was found painted in blood at one of the murder scenes.

Paul was in America when 'Revolution 9' was put together and was disappointed at its inclusion on *The Beatles*, particularly as he had been making sound collages at home since 1966 and realized that John would now be seen as the innovator.

GOOD NIGHT

'Good Night' is certainly the most schmaltzy song ever written by John. If it had been one of Paul's songs, John would probably have dismissed it as "garbage" but his final comment was only that it was possibly "over-lush".

John wrote it, he said, for Julian as a bedtime song just as, 12 years later, he would write 'Beautiful Boy' for his second son, Sean. The melody appears to have been 'inspired' by Cole Porter's 'True Love' (1956) song from the musical *High Society* that became a hit for Bing Crosby and Grace Kelly.

Julian wasn't aware that John had written the song for him until he was interviewed for this book. This was probably due to the fact that his parents split up within a few weeks of its composition.

GOOD NIGHT

Written:	Lennon/McCartney
Length:	3' 11"
UK release:	*The Beatles* album, November 22, 1968
US release:	*The Beatles* album, November 25, 1968

DON'T LET ME DOWN

DON'T LET ME DOWN
UK single release:
April 11, 1969, as B-side of 'Get Back'
US single release:
May 5, 1969, as B-side of 'Get Back'

John had always expressed fears of being let down by those he had put his trust in. 'If I Fell' was the template for a number of songs in which he confessed his need for love and his anxiety over being rejected.

Written about Yoko and released as the B side of 'Get Back' in April 1969, this same old worry was expressed as an agonizing cry having found someone who loved him more than anyone had ever done before. Influenced by Yoko's minimalist approach to art, he has cut out all embellishments, reducing his perennial plea to the form of an urgent telegram.

John and Yoko in 1968 leaving Marylebone Court, where he had admitted possession of cannabis resin.

LET IT BE

Committed to completing a final movie for United Artists, but with no inclination of emulating *Help* or *A Hard Day's Write*, the Beatles fulfilled their contract with *Let It Be*, an 80-minute colour documentary of the group rehearsing at Twickenham Film Studios, recording at Apple Studios and playing live on the roof of the Apple office in London. These three strands were filmed in January 1969 but the film wasn't premiered until May 1970, when a boxed album and book set was prepared for the release. The album wasn't available separately until November 1970.

The plan had been to make an album called *Get Back* and to film the recording process for a television documentary. There was a possibility of including a live show and a number of venues were considered – the Roundhouse in London, Liverpool Cathedral, the QE2, Tripoli, Tahiti and a Roman amphitheatre in Tunisia.

The film and album that evolved involved compromises. Instead of being a document of musical creativity, *Let It Be* became a record of musical disintegration. To get the album finished, Paul assumed control, pushing and prodding where necessary, while John and George sulked, openly displaying their resentment.

Rows over the album contributed to the group's final break-up. The American Allen Klein, now acting as their manager, wasn't happy with the quality of the tapes which engineer Glyn Johns had edited down, and so he brought in a fellow American, the producer Phil Spector, to beef up the production. When Paul heard what Spector had done to 'The Long And Winding Road', he requested that it be restored to its original form. After this request was ignored, Paul announced his departure from the Beatles.

The Beatles pictured with Yoko listening to *Let It Be*. At one time they all stood together. Now they sat apart, barely able to conceal their differences.

The album was scrappy. Because it was the last album released, it's often assumed it was the last album recorded. But, after the squabbling that characterized *Let It Be*, the Beatles went on to record *Abbey Road*, an album which George Martin still ranks as his favourite.

By the time *Let It Be* was released the Beatles had disbanded. Paul had already released his first solo album, although it wasn't until December 1970 that their union was officially dissolved following Paul's lawsuit. *Let It Be* reached the top of the British and American album charts after its release in May 1970. The advance orders of almost four million in the US were the largest for any album ever. In 2003 the album was re-released with Spector's contributions wiped off and titled *Let It Be… Naked*. The running order was re-shuffled, 'I've Got A Feeling' (originally the B side to 'Get Back') was added and 'Dig It' and 'Maggie Mae' were left off. The plan was to restore the album to what the four Beatles had originally intended.

TWO OF US

Performed in the documentary by John and Paul on acoustic guitars, 'Two Of Us' sounds like a song about their Liverpool teenage years together – burning matches, lifting latches and going home to play more music together. But the 'two of us' were not Paul and John but Paul and Linda. One of the most attractive things to Paul about his new girlfriend was her unpretentious 'hang-loose' approach to everything. In a life restricted by schedules and contractual obligations, he relished being with someone who seemed consistently laid-back, someone with whom he could forget he was a Beatle.

Soon after they met in London during the autumn of 1968, Linda taught Paul the joys of getting completely lost. She would drive him out of the city with no destination in mind and with the sole intention of ending up miles from anywhere. To a Beatle, who was constantly told where and when he was needed this was an exhilarating return to freedom. "As a kid I loved getting lost," explains Linda. "I would say to my father – let's get lost. But you could never seem to be able to get really lost. All signs would eventually lead back to New York or wherever we were staying! Then, when I moved to England to be with Paul, we would put Martha in the back of the car and drive out of London. As soon as we were on the open road I'd say 'Let's get lost' and we'd keep driving without looking at any signs. Hence the line in the song 'two of us going nowhere'.

"Paul wrote 'Two Of Us' on one of those days out," Linda explains. "It's about us. We just pulled off in a wood somewhere and parked the car. I went off walking while Paul sat in the car and started writing. He also mentions the postcards because we used to send a lot of postcards to each other."

Loving Linda's laid-back nature, Paul wrote 'Two Of Us' about their relationship.

TWO OF US
Written:
Lennon/McCartney
Length:
3' 36"
UK release:
Let It Be album, May 8, 1970
US release:
Let It Be album, May 18, 1970

DIG A PONY

'Dig A Pony' was largely composed in the studio and the words make very little sense. At one point it was called 'Con A Lowry' (possibly a reference to a make of organ used in the studio) but John changed it to 'Dig A Pony', "because 'I con a Lowry' didn't sing well… It's got to be d's and p's, you know."

Similarly, the line 'I do a road hog' started as 'I dig a skylight' and then became 'I did a groundhog'. "It had to be rougher," John argued. "I don't care if skylight was prettier." The chorus was taken from a separate song of John's written about Yoko called 'All I Want Is You'. The original song listing for the album used this title rather than 'Dig A Pony'.

In January 1969 when the song was recorded, John explained the secret of its composition, "I just make it up as I go along". In September 1980, he laconically concluded, "(just) another piece of garbage".

DIG A PONY

Written:	Lennon/McCartney
Length:	3' 54"
UK release:	*Let It Be* album, May 8, 1970
US release:	*Let It Be* album, May 18, 1970

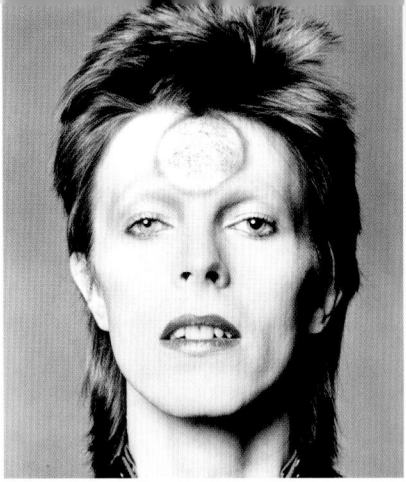

ACROSS THE UNIVERSE

The oldest song on the *Let It Be* album, 'Across The Universe' was recorded in February 1968 and first featured on a charity album for the World Wildlife Fund in December 1969.

A song about writing songs, or at least about the mysteries of the creative process, John was often to refer to it as one of his favourite Beatles' songs because of the purity of the lyric. The words had come to him while in bed at Kenwood. He had been arguing with Cynthia and, as he lay there trying to sleep, the phrase 'pools of sorrow, waves of joy' came to him and wouldn't leave until he got up and started writing the words down. "It drove me out of bed," John said. "I didn't want to write it. I was just slightly irritable and I couldn't go to sleep."

Written after having met the Maharishi Mahesh Yogi in England but before studying with him in India the chorus mentions Guru Dev, who was Maharishi's guru. John wanted this to be the single that the Beatles put out while they were away in India but it lost out to 'Lady Madonna'. David Bowie later recorded a cover version for his *Young Americans* album (1975) on which John played guitar.

David Bowie recorded a cover of 'Across The Universe' for his *Young Americans* album. John helped out on guitar.

ACROSS THE UNIVERSE

Written:	Lennon/McCartney
Length:	3' 48"
UK release:	*Let It Be* album, May 8, 1970
US release:	*Let It Be* album, May 18, 1970

I ME MINE

As George became more deeply involved in Eastern thought, he tried to reconcile his position as a rock star with the religious demands of relinquishing his ego in order to attain enlightenment.

It was his belief that it is our preoccupation with our individual egos – what 'I' want, what belongs to 'me', what's 'mine' – that prevents us from being absorbed into the universal consciousness, where there is no duality and no ego. "There is nothing that isn't part of the complete whole," George said. "When the little 'i' merges into the big 'I', then you are really smiling!"

The waltz tune of 'I Me Mine' was inspired by Johann Strauss II's 'Kaiserwalzer', a 60-second extract of which had been used as background music on a BBC2 TV documentary *Europa: The Titled and the Unentitled* the evening before. The version was by the Vienna Philarmonic Orchestra conducted by Willi Boskovsky. George had seen the programme and developed a tune from what he remembered.

I ME MINE

Written:	Harrison
Length:	2' 25"
UK release:	*Let It Be* album, May 8, 1970
US release:	*Let It Be* album, May 18, 1970

DIG IT

Credited to all four Beatles, 'Dig It' started as a fledgling song by John called 'Can You Dig It' which consisted of variations of the title being sung over a riff.

The version released on *Let It Be* was an excerpt from a much longer jam in which all the Beatles made up lines on the spot, hence the shared composer credit.

There was a lot of time spent hanging around reading newspapers when they recorded which might account for the references to the FBI and CIA. Transcripts of studio conversations reveal George talking about blues guitarist B B King and distinguishing him from fellow blues man Freddie King. Matt Busby was the heroic manager of Manchester United, one of England's most popular and successful football teams. Busby would have been in the news because twelve days before this recording he had announced his retirement after 24 years with the club.

DIG IT
Written: Harrison/Lennon/McCartney/Starr
Length: 0' 50"
UK release: *Let It Be* album, May 8, 1970
US release: *Let It Be* album, May 18, 1970

George was keen to tell his blues men apart during the recording session for 'Dig It'.

LET IT BE

LET IT BE
Written: Lennon/McCartney
Length: 4' 03"
UK single release: March 6, 1970
UK chart position: 2
US single release: March 11, 1970
US chart position: 1

Released as a single in March 1970, 'Let It Be' sounded as if it had been recorded as the Beatles' swansong yet it dated from January 1969. No one had any idea that it was going to be the last single.

Paul had written 'Let It Be' out of his general feelings of despair, as the Beatles began to fall apart at the seams. The documentary had started out as a record of a rehearsal followed by a live performance, but it was to become a record of the group's death throes.

By now, John preferred to spend his time with Yoko whose presence around the studio was not welcomed by everyone. George had already quit the group once and was discouraged at the way his songs were being instantly rejected. Even Ringo had taken off for a short holiday during the recording of *The White Album* when the atmosphere got really bad.

Paul was clearly trying to take over the role of leader because he felt that without organization and discipline nothing would be achieved. "I think we've been very negative since Mr Epstein passed away," Paul can be heard saying in the film. "We haven't been positive. That's why all of us in turn have been sick of the group. There's nothing positive in it. It's a bit of a drag. The only way for it not to be a bit of a drag is for the four of us to think – should we make it positive or should we forget it?"

Although Paul's role may have been necessary, it didn't make him popular. The others began to resent his role as organiser. 'Let It Be' was written by Paul as a response to all this pressure: "I wrote it when all those business problems started to get me down," he said. "I really was passing through my 'hour of darkness' and writing the song was my way of exorcizing the ghosts."

I'VE GOT A FEELING

'I've Got A Feeling' was again two unfinished songs strung together, this time Paul's 'I've Got A Feeling' and John's 'Everybody's Had A Hard Year'. Paul's song, optimistic as ever, was presumably written for Linda just to tell her that she was the girl he'd always been looking for. John's song was a litany where every line began with the word 'everybody'.

John had indeed been through a hard year. His marriage to Cynthia had ended, he was separated from his son Julian, Yoko had suffered a miscarriage, he had been arrested on a charge of drug possession and he reckoned his personal fortune had dwindled to about £50,000.

During the filming of *Let It Be*, John ran through 'Everybody Had A Hard Year' and said, somewhat tongue in cheek, that it was something he had started writing the night before. If this were true, it would date the song's origin to January 1969, but there is BBC film of him shot in December 1968, where he is singing the song with an acoustic guitar in the garden of his Ascot home.

I'VE GOT A FEELING

Written:	Lennon/McCartney
Length:	3' 37"
UK release:	*Let It Be* album, May 8, 1970
US release:	*Let It Be* album, May 18, 1970

THE LONG AND WINDING ROAD

THE LONG AND WINDING ROAD
Written: Lennon/McCartney
Length: 3' 37"
UK release: *Let It Be* album, May 8, 1970
US release: *Let It Be* album, May 18, 1970

Like 'Yesterday', 'The Long And Winding Road' evokes loss without describing any specific situation. The images of wind and rain suggest feelings of being abandoned in the wilderness, while the long and winding road leading to 'her door' is the sign of hope.

The imagery actually comes from Paul's experience of staying at High Park, his farm in Scotland, which is exposed to high winds and frequently lashed with rain. The long and winding road itself is the B842, over twenty five miles of twists and turns which runs down the east coast of Kintyre into Campbeltown, the nearest town to the farm.

Paul has said that he had the voice of Ray Charles in mind when he wrote it and that this influenced the use of jazzy chords. The road he envisaged as an endless road because the song is about what is eventually unattainable.

It was released as a single in America in May 1970 and reached the Number 1 spot.

Paul was thinking of Ray Charles when he wrote 'The Long And Winding Road'.

ONE AFTER 909

'One After 909' could well be the oldest Lennon and McCartney song ever to be recorded by the Beatles. It was one of 'over a hundred songs' which they often talked about having written before recording 'Love Me Do' and goes back to that time together at Forthlin Road.

The Beatles first recorded 'One After 909' in March 1963 during the same session which produced 'From Me To You' but George Martin was so unimpressed with it that it had never been released. It was an attempt by John, in 1957, to write an American railroad song, after skiffle hits such as 'Last Train To San Fernando' by Johnny Duncan, 'Cumberland Gap' and 'Rock Island Line' by Lonnie Donegan and 'Freight Train' by the Chas McDevitt Skiffle Group.

"We used to sag (play truant) off school, go back to my house and the two of us would write," Paul recalled. "There are a lot of songs from back then that we've never reckoned on because they're all very unsophisticated songs...We hated the words to 'One After 909'."

When they came to play around with it during the sessions there was chat between John and Paul where they mentioned how they had originally dropped it because they'd always considered the lyric illogical and unfinished.

ONE AFTER 909
Written: Lennon/McCartney
Length: 2' 55"
UK release: *Let It Be* album, May 8, 1970
US release: *Let It Be* album, May 18, 1970

FOR YOU BLUE

FOR YOU BLUE
Written:
Harrison
Length: 2' 32"
UK release:
Let It Be album,
May 8, 1970
US release:
Let It Be album,
May 18, 1970

Completed in six takes, 'For You Blue' was known as 'George's Blues' and on George's original lyric sheet as 'For You Blues' but became 'For You Blue' on the album.

George was always the Beatle most keen to develop his musical skills and it was through this that he developed close friendships with musicians as diverse as Ravi Shankar and Eric Clapton. It also led him to constantly experiment with different tunings, instruments and styles of playing.

Written for Pattie, 'For You Blue' was an exercise in writing a traditional blues song. George's only comment on it was to say: "It's a simple 12-bar song following all the normal 12-bar principles except that it's happy-go-lucky!"

George wrote his trad blues song 'For You Blue' for Pattie Boyd.

GET BACK

Paul said that he'd originally written 'Get Back' "as a political song" and surviving demos show that he was planning a satire on the attitudes of those who felt that immigrants to Britain should be repatriated. It was to be sung from the point of view of someone who didn't 'dig no Pakistanis taking all the people's jobs' and so was urging them to 'get back' to where they came from, its satirical intentions could easily have been misconstrued.

Years later, Paul was still having to field questions from journalists who'd heard bootleg editions of this version and who wondered if he'd gone through a racist period. "(The verses) were not racist at all," he said. "If there was any group that was not racist, it was the Beatles. All our favourite people were always black."

By the time it was recorded, 'Get Back' had been transformed into a song about Jojo from Tucson, Arizona, (Linda Eastman lived for a while in Tucson) and Loretta Martin who 'thought she was a woman, But she was another man'. No story was developed and the original 'Get back' chorus was retained. Because it was a rock'n'roll song, 'Get Back' was taken to refer to a return to musical roots and Apple's newspaper advert which bore the slogan 'The Beatles as nature intended' appeared to confirm this notion. "'Get Back' is the Beatles' new single," ran the copy. "It's the first Beatles' record which is as live as can be, in this electronic age. There's no electronic watchamacallit. 'Get Back' is a pure spring-time rock number."

It went on to quote Paul saying, "We were sitting in the studio and we made it up out of thin air…we started to write words there and then…when we finished it, we recorded it at Apple Studios and made it into a song to rollercoast by."

Paul originally penned 'Get Back' as a satire aimed at racists.

GET BACK
Written: Lennon/McCartney
Length: 3' 07"
UK single release: April 11, 1969
UK chart position: 1
US single release: May 5, 1969
US chart position: 1

THE BALLAD OF JOHN AND YOKO

'The Ballad Of John And Yoko' – in which John related the details of his marriage to Yoko in Gibraltar and their subsequent 'honeymoon' – was recorded in mid-April and released before the end of May. Paul helped with the final verse. The song portrayed the couple as victims about to be 'crucified': the two are turned back at Southampton docks, can't get a wedding licence in France, then they're misunderstood as they lie in bed 'for peace' and laughed at when they sit in a bag.

Something John failed to mention was the fact that they were turned back at Southampton dock not because of his notoriety but because they were trying to travel to France without passports. The plane they 'finally made' into Paris was not a scheduled airliner but an executive jet which John impatiently asked for when he realized that it was impossible to get married on a cross-Channel ferry.

THE BALLAD OF JOHN AND YOKO
Written: Lennon/McCartney
Length: 2' 55"
UK single release: May 30, 1969
UK chart position: 1
US single release: June 4, 1969
US chart position: 8

John's decision to get married appeared to have been made suddenly on March 14, 1969, when he and Yoko were being driven down to Poole in Dorset to visit his Aunt Mimi. This was two days after Paul's registry office wedding to Linda. John asked his chauffeur Les Anthony to go on into Southampton and enquire about the possibility of their being married at sea. When this was found to be impossible, John decided to go to Paris and instructed his office to come up with a way of arranging a quiet wedding there. Peter Brown discovered that this couldn't be organized at short notice but that they could marry in Gibraltar because it was a British protectorate and John was a British citizen.

In the end, the couple flew by private plane to Gibraltar on March 20, and went straight to the British Consulate where the registrar, Cecil

Wheeler, conducted a ten-minute marriage ceremony. They were on the ground for less than an hour before taking off for Amsterdam where they had booked the Presidential Suite at the Hilton. Their stay in Amsterdam was to be an extraordinary 'honeymoon'. Instead of requiring the usual privacy, they invited the world's press to invade their bedroom daily between 10:00 am and 10:00 pm during which time, they said, they would be staying in bed for peace.

Not unnaturally, the world's press hoped that John and Yoko might be intending to consummate their marriage in public. After all, they'd exposed their naked bodies on the cover of their album *Two Virgins* and had recorded the heartbeat of the child that Yoko later miscarried. There seemed to be no area of their lives that they weren't willing to turn into performance art.

To the journalists' frustration, the sight that greeted them in suite 902 was of John and Yoko in neatly pressed pyjamas sitting bolt upright in bed doing nothing more than talking about 'peace'. It was the perfect deal. The media had an insatiable appetite for articles about the Beatles and John would do almost anything to put over his message about peace. The Amsterdam 'Bed In' meant that all parties went away satisfied.

For seven days, they lay there holding court while a stream of media people sat and asked serious questions. The coverage was incredible. They did live interviews with American radio stations, made a sixty-minute documentary for themselves and saw their faces appear on the front pages of newspapers world-wide. "Yoko and I are quite willing to be the world's clowns, if by doing it we do some good," said John. "For reasons known only to themselves people do print what I say. And I'm saying peace. We're not pointing a finger at anybody. There are no good guys and bad guys. The struggle is in the mind. We must bury our own monsters and stop condemning people. We are all Christ and all Hitler. We want Christ to win. We're trying to make Christ's message contemporary. What would he have done if he had advertisements, records, films, TV and newspapers? Christ made miracles to tell his message. Well, the miracle today is communications, so let's use it."

From Amsterdam, they went to Vienna where they stopped overnight at the Hotel Sacher and ate some of its famous Sacher Torte (a rich chocolate cake) before watching the television premiere of their film *Rape*.

On April 1, they arrived back in London and gave a press conference at the airport. John expected a hostile reception because Yoko (a foreign divorcée, no less) was not considered the ideal partner for a British Beatle. To his surprise, the welcome was warm.

'The Ballad Of John And Yoko' was recorded by Paul and John with Paul playing bass, piano, maracas and drums, while John played lead and acoustic guitars and sang the vocals.

John and Yoko's famous 'Bed In' for peace saw them conduct a week's worth of interviews between the sheets.

OLD BROWN SHOE

'Old Brown Shoe' was one of three songs which George made a demo of at Abbey Road on February 25, 1969. The other two were 'Something', a future Beatles' single, and 'All Things Must Pass', the title track of his first solo album in 1970.

The lyric had its origins in George's religious view that we must free ourselves from the reality of the material world as it is illusory. Once absorbed into the divine consciousness, there would be no right versus wrong, body versus soul, spirit versus matter. Rather like Paul had done with 'Hello Goodbye', George's words were a game based on opposites. It wasn't a song which told much of a story and the intriguing title was pinched from a line about stepping out of 'this old brown shoe'. (George always had a problem coming up with titles.)

The main inspiration was musical. George had been messing around on a piano one day and hit on a chord sequence he liked. Words were added later.

Recorded two months after being demoed, 'Old Brown Shoe' became the B side of 'The Ballad Of John And Yoko'. Much later it was used as a track on the compilation albums *Hey Jude* and *The Beatles 1967–1970*.

George poured his cosmic worldview into 'Old Brown Shoe'.

OLD BROWN SHOE
Written: Harrison
Length: 3' 16"
UK single release: May 30, 1969 as B-side of 'The Ballad of John and Yoko'
US single release: June 4, 1969 as B-side of 'The Ballad of John and Yoko'

YOU KNOW MY NAME

Released as the B side of 'Let It Be', 'You Know My Name' was the strangest single ever released by the Beatles and remains one of their least-known songs.

It had first been recorded shortly after the completion of *Sgt Pepper*, after John arrived at Abbey Road wanting to record a song called 'You Know My Name, Look Up The Number'. When Paul asked to see the lyric, John told him that was the lyric. He wanted it repeated in the style of the Four Tops' 'Reach Out, I'll Be There' until it sounded like a mantra. The line was a variation on a slogan John had noticed on the front cover of the Post Office's London telephone directory for 1967 which read; 'You have their NAME? Look up their NUMBER.'

For three days in May and June 1967, the Beatles worked on the song but then abandoned it until April 1969 when the track was taken out for reworking. Although John's original idea of repeating the title phrase was adhered to, the song was transformed from a mantra into what sounded like a karaoke night in Hell, organized by the Goons or the Bonzo Dog Doo Dah Band.

The only departure from the scripted words came when John twice asked for a big hand for 'Denis O'Bell', a reference to the Irish-born film producer Denis O'Dell who had been Associate Producer on *A Hard Day's Night* and who had become director of Apple Films and Apple Publicity.

None of the Beatles told O'Dell that they had referred to him in the song and so it came as a shock to him when he started receiving anonymous telephone calls at his home in St George's Square, Pimlico.

YOU KNOW MY NAME
Written: Lennon/McCartney
Length: 4' 19"
UK single release: March 6, 1970, as B-side of 'Let It Be'
US single release: March 11, 1970, as B-side of 'Let It Be'

ABBEY ROAD

Seven years on from their first recordings at the Abbey Road Studios, the Beatles returned for what proved to be their final sessions. Back in June 1962, they were wide-eyed provincial lads keen to make their mark on the music business. By July 1969, they had become world-weary sophisticates, their lives blighted by struggles over power and money.

The songs on *Abbey Road* reflected their frustrations. They're about legal negotiations, unpaid debts, being ripped off, bad karma and generally bearing the weight of the world on your shoulders. There was even a mock-jolly song about a silver hammer (namely Maxwell's) that is waiting to come down hard on you just when things are starting to get better.

Despite this mood – or perhaps because of it – *Abbey Road* was an outstandingly inventive farewell offering. It features two of George's best songs, 'Here Comes The Sun' and 'Something'; a stand-out track by John, 'Come Together', and a fascinating medley of half-finished songs skilfully woven together by Paul.

George Martin remembered that after *Let It Be*, Paul came to him and asked him to produce a Beatles' album with the kind of feeling they used to generate together. Martin agreed to help out if the Beatles were prepared to give him their co-operation. "That's how we made *Abbey Road*. It wasn't quite like the old days because they were still working on their old songs and they would bring in the other people to work as kind of musicians for them rather than being a team."

In Britain, *Abbey Road* was released in September 1969 and stayed at Number 1 for 18 weeks. In America, it was released in October and was at Number 1 for 11 weeks.

COME TOGETHER

'Come Together' started life as a campaign song for Timothy Leary , when he decided in 1969 that he was going to run as governor of California against America's future president Ronald Reagan.

Leary and his wife Rosemary were invited up to Montreal, where John and Yoko were between the sheets for another major 'bed in' on the 19th floor of the Queen Elizabeth Hotel. They arrived on June 1, 1969, and were promptly roped into singing on the chorus of 'Give Peace A Chance', which was recorded in the hotel bedroom. Leary and his wife were rewarded for their participation by having their names included in the lyric.

Abbey Road saw the band vent feelings of frustration and ennui but was still a hugely inventive album.

The next day, John asked Leary if there was anything that he could do to help him in his campaign and was asked if he could write a song to be used in commercials and performed at rallies. Leary's slogan was 'come together, join the party' – the 'come together' part coming from the *I Ching*, the Chinese book of changes. "There was obviously a double meaning there," said Leary. "It was come together and join the party – not a political party but a celebration of life."

John immediately picked up his guitar and began building on the phrase: 'Come together right now, Don't come tomorrow, Don't come alone, Come together right now over me, All that I can tell you, Is you gotta be free.' After coming up with a few more versions along the same lines, he made a demo tape and handed it to Leary.

Leary had the song played on alternative radio stations throughout California and began to think of it as his own. However, unknown to him, John had returned to England and within seven weeks had recorded a version with the Beatles. In October, it was released on the flip side of 'Something', the first single to be taken from Abbey Road.

Leary's campaign to become governor of California came to an abrupt halt in December 1969, when he was charged with possessing marijuana and eventually imprisoned. It was while in prison that Leary first heard *Abbey Road* on a local rock station and 'Come Together' came as a complete surprise. "Although the new version was certainly a musical and lyrical improvement on my campaign song, I was a bit miffed that Lennon had passed me over this way... When I sent a mild protest to John, he replied with typical Lennon charm and wit that he was a tailor and I was a customer who had ordered a suit and never returned. So he sold it to someone else."

The recorded version was largely made up in the studio, the swampy New Orleans bass having been added by Paul. Two of the song lines referring to 'old flat top' were lifted from Chuck Berry's 'You Can't Catch Me' and John was later sued for plagiarism. It was hard to deny where the words had come from, although, in this new context, they were nothing more than an affectionate nod towards the music of his youth. John strenuously denied any musical theft.

The conflict was resolved when John promised to record three songs belonging to the publisher of 'You Can't Catch Me'. He fulfilled this promise when he recorded Berry's 'Sweet Little Sixteen' and 'You Can't Catch Me' for his *Rock'n'Roll* album and Lee Dorsey's 'Ya Ya' on *Walls and Bridges*.

COME TOGETHER
Written: Lennon/McCartney
Length: 4' 20"
UK release: *Abbey Road* album, September 26, 1969
US release: *Abbey Road* album, October 1, 1969

SOMETHING

'Something' was the first Beatles' A side to be written by George. Its sources of inspiration were Ray Charles, who he imagined singing it, and a 1968 album track by James Taylor titled 'Something In The Way She Moves', and his wife Pattie.

James Taylor, an American, was signed to the Apple label and his eponymous first album was produced by Peter Asher between July and October 1968. Paul played bass on one track. 'Something In The Way She Moves' was the last track on the first side of the album and the opening lines were: 'There's something in the way she moves, Or looks my way or calls my name, That seems to leave this troubled world behind.'

The White Album was being recorded at Abbey Road at exactly the same time as Taylor was recording at Trident Studios in London's

'Come Together' began life as a campaign song for LSD guru Timothy Leary when he ran for governor of California against Ronald Reagan.

Soho. Indeed, on October 3, George was at Trident recording 'Savoy Truffle' with Paul and Ringo and probably heard the track then.

"I've always assumed George must have heard it but I never actually spoke to him about it," says Taylor. "I'd written 'Something In The Way She Moves' about two years before I recorded it and, strangely enough I'd wanted to call it 'I Feel Fine', but of course that was a Beatles' track.

"I often notice traces of other people's work in my own songs," Taylor continues. "If George either consciously or unconsciously took a line from one of my songs then I find it very flattering. It's certainly not an unusual thing to happen. I'd made a tape of 'Something In The Way She Moves' and about seven other songs about a couple of months before I met Peter Asher. I know Paul listened to it at Apple but I'm not sure who else listened to it."

The basic writing of 'Something' must have taken place in October because George has said that he worked it out on piano in Studio 1, while Paul was overdubbing in Studio 2. The only reason it wasn't included on the White Album was because the track selection had already been completed.

George first offered 'Something' to Joe Cocker and Jackie Lomax but then, in May 1969, decided to record it with the Beatles for *Abbey Road*. 'Something' was an enormously successful song for George, becoming the second most covered Beatles' song after 'Yesterday' (Ray Charles and Smokey Robinson both did versions) and giving him his first American Top 10 hit.

It had always been assumed that he wrote the song about Pattie but in a 1996 interview he said, "I didn't. I just wrote it and then somebody put together a video that used some footage of me and Pattie, Paul and Linda, Ringo and Maureen and John and Yoko... actually, when I wrote it I was thinking of Ray Charles." However, Pattie still believes that he had her in mind. "He always told me that it was about me," she says.

SOMETHING

Written:	Harrison
Length:	3' 03"
UK release:	*Abbey Road* album, September 26, 1969
US release:	*Abbey Road* album, October 1, 1969

MAXWELL'S SILVER HAMMER

MAXWELL'S SILVER HAMMER
Written: Lennon/McCartney
Length: 3' 27"
UK release: *Abbey Road* album, September 26, 1969
US RELEASE: *Abbey Road* album, October 1, 1969

A song, driven by strong rhymes, in which medical student Maxwell Edison uses his silver hammer to kill first his girlfriend, then a lecturer and finally a judge. Delivered in a jaunty, vaudevillian style, the only indication of Paul's recent avant-garde leanings was the mention of 'pataphysics', a word invented by Alfred Jarry, the French pioneer of absurd theatre, to describe a branch of metaphysics.

"John told me that 'Maxwell's Silver Hammer' was about the law of karma," says former Apple employee Tony King. "We were talking one day about 'Instant Karma' (John's 1970 single with Yoko Ono and the Plastic Ono Band) because something had happened where he'd been clobbered and he'd said that this was an example of instant karma. I asked him whether he believed that theory. He said that he did and that 'Maxwell's Silver Hammer' was the first song that they'd made about that. He said that the idea behind the song was that the minute you do something that's not right, Maxwell's silver hammer will come down on your head."

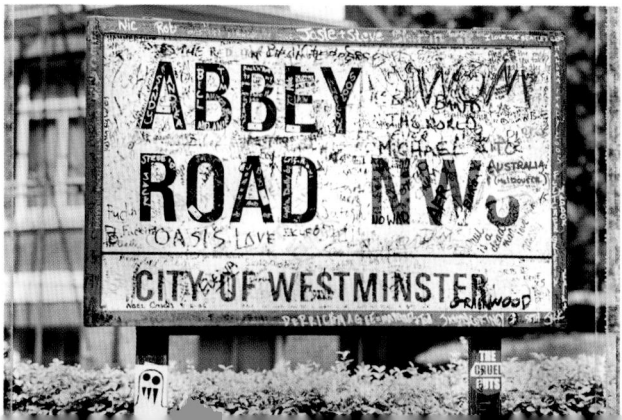

Beatles fans have for years covered the Abbey Road street sign in graffiti.

OH! DARLING

Paul wanted his voice to sound raw on 'Oh! Darling', so he sang it through again and again each day for a week before finally recording it. "I wanted it to sound as though I'd been performing it on stage all week," he said.

Inspired by the rock'n'roll ballads of the late Fifties, Jackie Wilson's in particular, it was a simple song pleading for a loved one to stay in exchange for lifelong devotion.

John never rated Paul's job on vocals and reckoned he could have done better. "It was more my style than his," he said.

OH! DARLING
Written: Lennon/McCartney
Length: 3' 26"
UK release: *Abbey Road* album, September 26, 1969
US release: *Abbey Road* album, October 1, 1969

OCTOPUS'S GARDEN

Ringo's second (and last) Beatles' song was inspired by a family holiday in Sardinia which he took in 1968 on board Peter Sellers' yacht. After Ringo had turned down the offer of an octopus lunch, the vessel's captain started to tell him all he knew about the life of octopuses.

"He told me how they go around the sea bed picking up stones and shiny objects to build gardens with," said Ringo. "I thought this was fabulous because at the time I just wanted to be under the sea too. I wanted to get out of it for a while."

To most listeners, it was a children's seaside song in the vein of 'Yellow Submarine' but, in 1969, George revealed that there were hidden dimensions. Even though Ringo only knew three chords on the piano, George said, the drummer was writing "cosmic songs without really noticing it."

OCTOPUS'S GARDEN
Written: Starr
Length: 2' 51"
UK release: *Abbey Road* album, September 26, 1969
US release: *Abbey Road* album, October 1, 1969

I WANT YOU

I WANT YOU
Written: Lennon/McCartney
Length: 7' 47"
UK release: *Abbey Road* album, September 26, 1969
US release: *Abbey Road* album, October 1, 1969

Consisting only of the repeated title line and the information that the desire is driving John mad, the lyric of 'I Want You' was once read out on BBC TV's current affairs programme *24 Hours* as an example of the banalities of pop music.

This incensed John, who was convinced that its simplicity made it superior to 'Eleanor Rigby' and 'I Am The Walrus'. To him, this was not a reversion to mindless monosyllabic pop but simply economy of language.

'I Want You' was written as a love song to Yoko. John admitted the influence she had on his new style of writing, saying that eventually he wanted to compose a perfect song using only one word. A 1964 poem of Yoko's consisted of the single word 'Water'.

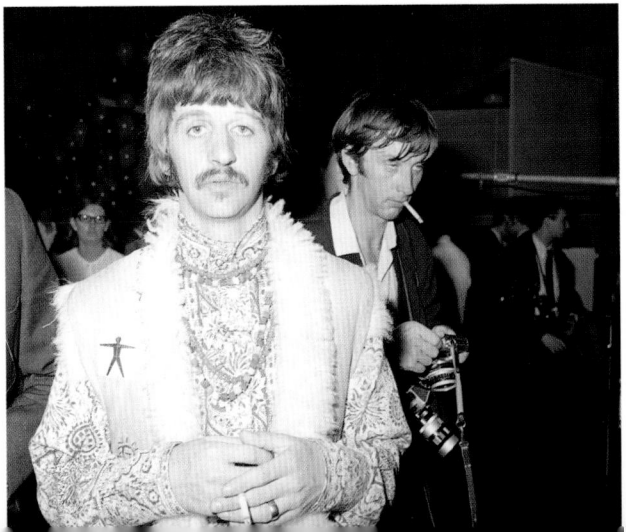

Ringo wrote 'Octopus's Garden' (left) after an informative encounter with the captain of Peter Seller's yacht.

HERE COMES THE SUN

Written by George, 'Here Comes The Sun' was an expression of delight at being able to slip away from the interminable business meetings which were now taking up so much of the Beatles' time.

In January 1969, John and Yoko met with music business manager Allen Klein and shortly afterwards declared that he would be looking after their business affairs, despite the fact that the New York lawyer John Eastman, brother of Linda, had recently been brought in to represent the Beatles collectively. This was the beginning of a bitter drawn-out conflict over who should manage the Beatles and what should be done about the chaotic state of their finances. Despite the tremendous sales of Beatles' music over the past six years, John claimed, "all of us could be broke in six months".

Klein offered to restructure Apple, organize a takeover bid for the shares the Beatles didn't own in Northern Songs and renegotiate a better royalty deal with EMI. He was able to persuade John, George and Ringo of his ability to do these things but Paul remained loyal to Eastman. As a result the Beatles' existence was now under threat and the frequent meetings at Apple were fraught with tension. One morning in the early spring, George decided it was all getting a bit too much like school, and so he took a day off from the round table routine and went to see his friend Eric Clapton at his country home in Ewhurst, Surrey.

Borrowing one of Eric's acoustic guitars, George took a walk around the gardens and, basking in the first real sunshine of the year, he felt a sudden flush of optimism and started to write 'Here Comes The Sun'. "It was such a great release for me simply being out in the sun," said George at the time. "The song just came to me."

The arrival of Allan Klein in the Beatles' world led to a period of damaging in-fighting.

HERE COMES THE SUN
Written: Harrison
Length: 3' 05"
UK release: *Abbey Road* album, September 26, 1969
US release: *Abbey Road* album, October 1, 1969

BECAUSE

John was relaxing on a sofa at home, while Yoko played the first movement of Beethoven's Piano Sonata No 14 in C Sharp Minor ('Moonlight Sonata') on the grand piano. John has said that he asked her if she could play the same chords in reverse order. This she did, and it proved to be the inspiration for 'Because'.

The similarity between the opening of the 'Moonlight Sonata' and 'Because' is striking, although close scrutiny reveals it to be a straightforward lift rather than the reversal of notes John suggested. Musicologist Wilfrid Mellers, author of *Twilight Of The Gods: The Music of the Beatles* puts it this way, "The affinity between the enveloping, arpeggiated C sharp minor triads, with the sudden shift to the flat supertonic, is, in the Lennon and Beethoven examples, unmistakable."

There was a touch of irony in the idea of a Beatle borrowing from Beethoven because there was a common perception at the time that rock'n'roll was antithetical to classical music and that no one could genuinely appreciate both. It also probably didn't help that the Beatles had recorded Chuck Berry's 'Roll Over Beethoven', an irreverent piece of advice to classical composers asking them to make way for rock'n'roll.

One of the first questions the Beatles were always asked in America was, 'What do you think of Beethoven?' It was Ringo who answered. "I love him," he said. "Especially his poems." But it was John, in particular, who came to regard Beethoven as the supreme composer, and one with whom he felt kinship. By 1969, he was no longer trying to be the artistic equal of Elvis or the Rolling Stones, but of Picasso, Van Gogh, Dylan Thomas and Beethoven.

BECAUSE
Written: Lennon/McCartney
Length: 2' 45"
UK release: *Abbey Road* album, September 26, 1969
US release: *Abbey Road* album, October 1, 1969

YOU NEVER GIVE ME YOUR MONEY

'You Never Give Me Your Money' announced the medley of half-finished songs which dominate the second side of *Abbey Road*. Paul collected the songs and carefully worked out a way of linking them together. 'You Never Give Me Your Money' itself is made up of three distinct fragments. The first, which develops the line in the title, was an allusion to the Beatles' financial problems saying that instead of money all they ever seemed to get was 'funny paper'.

"That's what we get," said George. "We get bits of paper saying how much is earned and what this and that is but we never actually get it in pounds, shillings and pence. We've all got a big house and a car and an office but to actually get the money we've earned seems impossible."

The next fragment, which mentions being penniless after leaving college, may have referred to the same problems but was written in the jolly, nostalgic style of Paul's 'woke up/ got out of bed' section of 'A Day In The Life'. The final piece was about the freedom of Paul's new life with Linda, where he could just pack the car and drive out of town leaving his worries behind.

YOU NEVER GIVE ME YOUR MONEY

Written:	Lennon/McCartney
Length:	4' 02"
UK release:	*Abbey Road* album, September 26, 1969
US release:	*Abbey Road* album, October 1, 1969

SUN KING

Fleetwood Mac's hit 'Albatross' exerted a major sonic influence over 'Sun King'.

As with 'Being For The Benefit Of Mr Kite!', John's opinions on 'Sun King' came to alter over the years but this time, changing from good to bad. In 1971, he referred to it as something that had come to him in a dream, implying that it was an inspired piece of work. By 1980, it had been revalued as just another piece of 'garbage'.

Historically, the Sun King was Louis XIV of France and it could have been he who John dreamt about, a dream wherein the King entered his palace to find all his guests were laughing and happy. Nancy Mitford had recently published a biography of Louis which was titled *The Sun King* and John may have read it or at least seen it. It may also have been a jokey reference to George's song 'Here Comes The Sun'.

The closing lines of the song are composed of those Italian, Spanish and Portuguese words which tourists pick up, strung together in no particular order – 'paparazzi', 'obrigado', 'parasol', 'mi amore'. The original title of the song was 'Los Paranoias'.

According to George, the point of musical departure was Fleetwood Mac's 'Albatross', a dreamy instrumental which had been a British Top 10 hit in the early part of 1969.

SUN KING
Written: Lennon/McCartney
Length: 2' 26"
UK release: *Abbey Road* album, September 26, 1969
US release: *Abbey Road* album, October 1, 1969

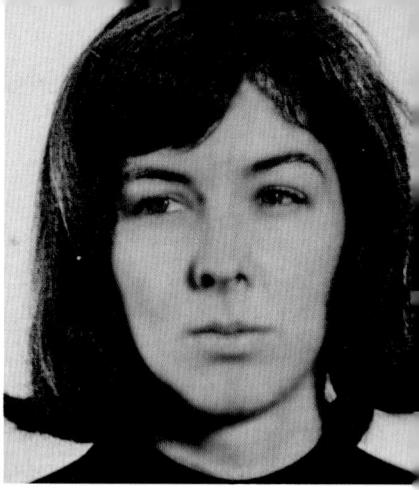

MEAN MR MUSTARD

John said that 'Mean Mr Mustard' was inspired by a newspaper story about a miser who concealed his cash wherever he could in order to prevent people forcing him to spend it. The line about stuffing a 'ten bob note' (a British ten shilling note) up his nose John admitted was his own invention, claiming that it had absolutely nothing to do with snorting cocaine.

Tony Bramwell believes another colourful London character also provided John with inspiration for this song. "There was an old 'bag lady' who used to hang around the Knightsbridge end of Hyde Park, close to the army barracks," he remembers. "She had all her possessions in plastic bags and slept in the park. I'm sure that she had something to do with the song."

The reference to a 'dirty old man' in the last line may have been to the character of Albert Steptoe in the BBC TV situation comedy *Steptoe & Son* (1962–1974) who was always referred to by his son Harold as a 'You dirty old man'. It became a catch phrase in Britain around the same time that the actor who played Steptoe, Wilfrid Brambell, took on the part of Paul's grandfather in *A Hard Day's Night*. (This explains the many references in the movie to Paul's granddad being 'very clean'.)

Written in India, 'Mean Mr Mustard' was recorded with 'Sun King' in one continuous piece. In the original version, Mr Mustard had a sister called Shirley but John changed it to Pam when he realized that it could more easily segue into 'Polythene Pam'.

Royston Ellis's lover, Stephanie, was one of two major inspirations behind John's song 'Polythene Pam' (right).

MEAN MR MUSTARD
Written: Lennon/McCartney
Length: 1' 06"
UK release: *Abbey Road* album, September 26, 1969
US release: *Abbey Road* album, October 1, 1969

POLYTHENE PAM

Although John initially insisted that 'Polythene Pam' was about "a mythical Liverpool scrubber (promiscuous girl or groupie) dressed up in her jackboots and kilt", the song was actually based on two people who he had known. The name came from Pat Dawson (then Pat Hodgett), a Beatles' fan from the Cavern Club days who, because of her habit of eating polythene, was known to the group as Polythene Pat. "I started going to see the Beatles in 1961 when I was 14 and I got quite friendly with them," she remembers. "If they were playing out of town they'd give me a lift back home in their van. It was about the same time that I started getting called Polythene Pat. It's embarrassing really. I just used to eat polythene all the time. I'd tie it in knots and then eat it. Sometimes I even used to burn it and then eat it when it got cold. Then I had a friend who got a job in a polythene bag factory, which was wonderful because it meant I had a constant supply."

But Polythene Pat never dressed up in polythene bags as the song says. That little quirk was taken from an incident involving a girl called Stephanie, who John met in the Channel Islands while on tour in August 1963.

Although John wouldn't elaborate when he spoke to *Playboy* in 1980, he did supply a few clues. "(Polythene Pam) was me remembering a little event with a woman in Jersey, and a man who was England's answer to Allen Ginsberg, who gave us our first exposure..."

England's answer to American beat poet Ginsberg turned out to be Royston Ellis, a young writer who first met the Beatles in May or June of 1960 when invited to read poetry at Liverpool University. What John went on reluctantly to tell *Playboy* was that Ellis was the first person to introduce the Beatles to drugs when he showed them how to get high from the strips inside a Benzedrine inhaler.

The "little event with a woman", as John described it, actually took place on the Channel island of Guernsey, not Jersey, when John met up with Ellis who had a summer job there as a ferry boat engineer. After the Beatles' concerts at the Auditorium in Guernsey on August 8, Ellis and his girlfriend Stephanie took John back to the attic flat Ellis was renting and this is where the polythene came into the story. "(Ellis) said Miss X (a girl he wanted me to meet) dressed up in polythene," John later remembered. "She did. She didn't wear jackboots and kilts. I just sort of elaborated. Perverted sex in a polythene bag. I was just looking for something to write about."

Ellis, who now lives in Sri Lanka and writes travel books, can't recall any 'perverted sex' but he can recall the night spent in a bed with Stephanie and John. "We'd read all these things about leather and we didn't have any leather but I had my oilskins and we had some polythene bags from somewhere," he says. "We all dressed up in them and wore them in bed. John stayed the night with us in the same bed. I don't think anything very exciting happened and we all wondered what the fun was in being 'kinky'. It was probably more my idea than John's. It could have all happened because in a poetry booklet of mine which I had dedicated to the Beatles there was a poem with the lines: 'I long to have sex between black leather sheets, And ride shivering motorcycles between your thighs.'

"At the time, it meant nothing to me. It was just one event during a very eventful time of my life," Ellis adds. Besides being a poet, Ellis was a pundit on teenage life and a chronicler of emergent British rock'n'roll. When they met, he had just completed *The Big Beat Scene*, an excellent survey of late Fifties British beat music.

POLYTHENE PAM

Written:	Lennon/McCartney
Length:	1' 12"
UK release:	*Abbey Road* album, September 26, 1969
US release:	*Abbey Road* album, October 1, 1969

John was fascinated by Ellis because he stood at the converging point of rock'n'roll and literature. Ellis arranged for the Beatles to back him early on at a beat music and poetry event at the Jacaranda Club. In July 1960, *Record Mirror* reported that 'the bearded sage' was thinking of bringing a Liverpool group called the 'Beetles' to London to play behind him as he performed his poetry. "I was quite a star for them at that time because I had come up from London and that was a world they didn't really know about," says Ellis. "I stayed with them for about a week in their flat at Gambier Terrace. John was fascinated by the fact that I was a poet and that led to deep conversations."

Shortly after introducing John to the delights of polythene, Ellis left England and has spent much of the time since travelling. So far removed has he been from the British pop scene, that he had never even heard 'Polythene Pam' until contacted for this book. He does recall with some pride, though, that in 1973 John wrote to the alternative newspaper *International Times* to correct them about the circumstances of the Beatles' first drug experiences: "The first dope, from a Benzedrine inhaler, was given the Beatles (John, George, Paul and Stuart) by an English cover version of Allen Ginsberg – one Royston Ellis, known as 'beat poet'... So, give the saint his due."

Stephanie reads while 'beat poet' Royston Ellis takes a nap in the Channel Islands in 1963, the year Ellis met up again with John.

SHE CAME IN THROUGH THE BATHROOM WINDOW

This song was inspired by the activities of an Apple Scruff who climbed into Paul's house in St John's Wood when he was away for the day. "We were bored, he was out and so we decided to pay him a visit," remembers Diane Ashley. "We found a ladder in his garden and stuck it up at the bathroom window which he'd left slightly open. I was the one who climbed up and got in."

Once she was inside the house, she opened the front door and let the rest of the girls in. Fellow Apple Scruff Margo Bird remembers: "They rummaged around and took some clothes. People didn't usually take anything of real value but I think this time a lot of photographs and negatives were taken. There were really two groups of Apple Scruffs – those who would break in and those who would just wait outside with cameras and autograph books. I used to take Paul's dog for a walk and got to know him quite well. I was eventually offered a job at Apple. I started by making the tea and ended up in the promotions department working with Tony King."

Paul asked Margo if she could retrieve any of his belongings. "I knew who had done it and I discovered that a lot of the stuff had already gone to America," she said. "But I knew that there was one picture he particularly wanted back – a colour-tinted picture of him in a Thirties frame. I knew who had taken this and got it back for him."

Paul completed 'She Came In Through The Bathroom Window' in June 1968 during a trip to America to do business with Capitol Records. It was here that he resumed his relationship with Linda Eastman, whom he'd been introduced to the previous summer in London and had since met in New York.

SHE CAME IN THROUGH THE BATHROOM WINDOW
Written: Lennon/McCartney
Length: 1' 57"
UK release: *Abbey Road* album, September 26, 1969
US release: *Abbey Road* album, October 1, 1969

Paul wrote 'She Came In Through The Bathroom Window' about some of the band's obsessive fans.

"Paul and Heather and I were in New York going to the airport to come back to England," remembers Linda."The name of the taxi driver talking to us was Eugene Quits, so then Paul wrote the line 'So I quite the police department.'"

According to Carol Bedford, an Apple Scruff who wrote the book *Waiting For The Beatles*, Paul later said to her: "I've written a song about the girls who broke in. It's called 'She Came In Through The Bathroom Window'." Diane was surprised to have become the subject of a Beatles' song. "I didn't believe it at first because he'd hated it so much when we broke in," she says. "But then I suppose anything can inspire a song, can't it? I know that all his neighbours rang him when they saw we'd got in and I'm sure that gave rise to the lines,'Sunday's on the 'phone to Monday/Tuesday's on the 'phone to me'."

Now married with four teenage children, Diane keeps a framed photo of herself with Paul on her kitchen shelf and looks back on her days as an Apple Scruff with affection. "I don't regret any of it. I had a great time, a really great time."

GOLDEN SLUMBERS

Paul was at his father's house in Cheshire tinkering around on the piano. Flicking through a songbook belonging to his step-sister Ruth (James McCartney had since remarried), he came across the traditional lullaby 'Golden Slumbers'. Unable to read the music, he went ahead and made up his own melody, adding new words as he went along.

'Golden Slumbers' was written by the English writer and dramatist Thomas Dekker, who was a contemporary of Shakespeare. The song was first published in *The Pleasant Comedy of Old Fortunatus* (1600).

A Londoner born around 1570, Dekker was the author of *The Shoemaker's Holiday* (1600), *The Honest Whore* (1604), *The Gull's Hornbook* (1609), *The Roaring Girl* (1611) and the posthumously published *The Syn's Darling* (1656).

For 'Golden Slumbers' Paul wrote a new melody for an old British lullaby.

GOLDEN SLUMBERS

Written:	Lennon/McCartney
Length:	1'31"
UK release:	*Abbey Road* album, September 26, 1969
US release:	*Abbey Road* album, October 1, 1969

HER MAJESTY

Written by Paul in Scotland, 'Her Majesty' was originally part of the medley, coming between 'Mean Mr Mustard' and 'Polythene Pam' but, on hearing a playback, Paul didn't like it and asked for it to be edited out.

The engineer who cut it out then recycled it to the end of the tape so that it wouldn't be destroyed. Paul must have heard another playback with 'Her Majesty' now tacked on as an apparent afterthought. He liked it enough to keep it there. Because the edit was only meant to be rough, the last chord of 'Mean Mr Mustard' was pressed into service to start 'Her Majesty', which ends abruptly because its own final note was left behind at the beginning of 'Polythene Pam'.

The Beatles met Queen Elizabeth to receive their MBEs on October 26, 1965. Afterwards, asked what they thought of her, Paul answered: "She's lovely. She was very friendly. She was just like a mum to us." Years later, Paul confessed to having had a crush on the young Elizabeth when he was a boy.

'Her Majesty' has the dubious distinction of being the final track on the last album the Fab Four were ever to record together.

HER MAJESTY

Written:	Lennon/McCartney
Length:	0' 23"
UK release:	*Abbey Road* album, September 26, 1969
US release:	*Abbey Road* album, October 1, 1969

CARRY THAT WEIGHT

Although 'Carry That Weight' appears to be just another song in the medley and is credited as such on the album, it was in fact recorded with 'Golden Slumbers' as a single. It's a nice touch because it brings the sequence back to where it started with the subject of money, business and the burdens of being a superstar.

The lyric expressed Paul's fears about the Beatles in their twilight days. He later said that the arguments over finance and management plunged him into the "darkest hours" of his life so far. The atmosphere around the Beatles had changed from light to heavy. "At certain times things get to me so much that I can't be upbeat any more and that was one of the times," he told his biographer Barry Miles.

CARRY THAT WEIGHT
Written: Lennon/McCartney
Length: 1' 36"
UK release: *Abbey Road* album, September 26, 1969
US release: *Abbey Road* album, October 1, 1969

In the later years, the Beatles' intra-band tensions affected even Paul's famously upbeat demanour, as related in 'Carry That Weight'.

THE END

As the final proper track on the last album recorded by the Beatles, 'The End' was to become the song which signed off their studio career. Philosophical to the last, Paul says that ultimately the love you 'take' is equal to the love you 'make'. He may have been saying no more that 'you take out what you put in', but John was sufficiently impressed to declare it a "very cosmic line" proving that "if Paul wants to, he can think."

Paul saw the couplet as a musical equivalent of the rhyming couplets with which Shakespeare ended some of his plays, a summary and also a signal that the events of the drama were now ended.

It certainly provided a neat symmetry to their recording career – which started with the gawky pleadings of lovesick teenagers in 'Love Me Do', and matured to reveal enigmatic words of wisdom from the group who transformed popular music.

THE END

Written:	Lennon/McCartney
Length:	2' 19"
UK release:	*Abbey Road* album, September 26, 1969
US release:	*Abbey Road* album, October 1, 1969

LIVE AT THE BBC

In 1982 Kevin Howlett looked through the BBC's archives of radio sessions with the Beatles and produced a programme called *Beatles At The Beeb.* Shortly afterwards, discussions began between EMI and the BBC to get the material released. However, it wasn't until 1994 that the right climate prevailed between the Beatles, Apple and EMI which enabled the project to be actualised.

Howlett took the BBC tapes to George Martin at Abbey Road where Martin digitally remastered the 58 tracks which survived from the 88 songs which the Beatles had played live on BBC radio. In fact, only 57 of the tracks had survived in the BBC archives. The 58th was secured from a fan who had contacted Howlett in 1988, during the transmission of another Beatles series.

These robust live performances didn't have the benefit of multitrack recording facilities, overdubs or remixes and so provide an undoctored example of what the Beatles sounded like during the peak of their performing career. John and Paul learned to write songs by emulating the great singles of their youth. Trying these cover versions out on audiences taught them what worked and helped them to understand why. Bit by bit they began to drop the cover versions for songs of their own which created the same mood.

Live At The BBC illustrates this growth. Of the songs they cover, 76% were from between 1954 and 1959, when they were serving their apprenticeship in Liverpool. Almost half the cover songs were written by a handful of writers they revered – Chuck Berry, Little Richard, Carl Perkins, Goffin and King and Leiber and Stoller.

The double album *Live At The BBC* was released in November 1994 and went on to sell over 8 million copies.

I'LL BE ON MY WAY

A very early Beatles song, 'I'll Be On My Way' was composed in youthful emulation of Buddy Holly.

'I'll Be On My Way' was the only unreleased Lennon-McCartney song to be included on Live At The BBC and, as such, the first Lennon-McCartney song played by the Beatles to be released since May 1970.

Written by Paul in 1961 in emulation of Buddy Holly it was included in the group's repertoire over the next two years but wasn't played at the Decca audition, an indication that it had already fallen out of favour. It was given to their stable mate Billy J. Kramer who used it as the flip side of 'Do You Want To Know A Secret?' in April 1963.

The lyric serves as a reminder that the Beatles didn't start out as artistic visionaries but simply rearranged existing clichés. Here 'June light' turns to 'moon light' (naturally) and the lovelorn narrator is forced into exile where 'golden rivers flow' and 'the winds don't blow'. It sounds like the rim of an active volcano, but maybe Paul had something else in mind.

John, typically, poured scorn on the song when asked about it in 1980: it was precisely the sort of pop that had always made him uncomfortable because it stifled the individual point of view with a raft of stock phrases. Paul wasn't quite so harsh when he looked back. It was "a bit too June-moon" he conceded, but it had "worked out quite well" for the group in their early shows.

I'LL BE ON MY WAY
Written: Lennon/McCartney
Length: 1' 57"
UK release: *Live at the BBC album*, November 30, 1994
US release: *Live at the BBC album*, November 30, 1994

ANTHOLOGY 1-3

The three double albums that comprise the *Anthology* set owe their genesis to an exercise in 1984 when engineer John Barrett was given the task of collating all the Beatles material in EMI's archives. Out of hundreds of hours of recordings he identified three unreleased tracks. EMI made test pressings and approached the remaining Beatles with the suggestion of an album. At the time, no agreement on a release could be reached.

Five years later, in an unrelated move, Apple's long-time manager Neil Aspinall revived a documentary idea he'd abandoned in 1969. He wanted to collect together all the best film footage of the Beatles for a television series that would tell their story in their words. He wanted the remaining Beatles to come together and record some new incidental music. The project would be called *The Long And Winding Road.*

The album of unreleased songs and the documentary series eventually coalesced into *Anthology*. The planned incidental music was dropped in favour of recording two new Beatles tracks. "As the thought of the three of us sitting down in a studio got nearer, I got cold feet about it," said Paul. "I thought, Does the world need a three-quarter Beatle record? But what if John was on, the three of us and John, like a real new record? If only we could pull off the impossible, that would be more fun, a bigger challenge."

The apparently impossible was pulled off when Yoko agreed to let them use two demo cassettes of unfinished songs by John as the basis for new Beatles tracks. These eventually became singles which helped to promote not only the six-hour documentary series but the *Anthology* albums.

Ringo, Paul, George and producer George Martin reconvene in 1994 for *Anthology*.

Anthology was not a soundtrack to the documentary series but an aural counterpart made up of alternative takes, unreleased tracks, live performances, early demos and brief snatches of interview. Out of the 139 songs on the collection, 28 were cover versions.

The greatest interest was naturally in the 21 new Beatles compositions, some of which had only previously been heard performed by other artists or on rare bootlegs. These ranged from poor-quality home recordings that were purely of historical value to completed studio tracks that had been ousted from albums only for reasons of space.

The general critical response to these rarities was that the Beatles original judgment to drop them or give them away had been sound. They could probably have had a hit with 'Come And Get It' and it's hard to see why 'Not Guilty' didn't find a place on *The White Album* but otherwise none of these 'new' songs enhanced their reputation. They merely confirmed what we had assumed, which was that the Beatles had already given us their best.

FREE AS A BIRD

'Free As A Bird' was essentially a novelty single designed to attract attention to the *Anthology* project. The novelty was that it would be the first new Beatles single in 25 years and would, in sound at least, reunite the most popular pop group the world has known.

There was feverish media excitement surrounding the release of the record, which was encouraged by EMI's publicity department. An early press release read, "The single, copies of which are currently under armed guard outside the UK, will be released worldwide on MONDAY DECEMBER 4 [1995]."

Nothing could hope to live up to these expectations but, in the event, 'Free As A Bird' was plausibly Beatles-sounding (circa 1969) although obviously hampered by the restraints of having been built around a discarded fragment of a John Lennon song that had been recorded on a cassette machine.

The events that led to the recording began on January 1, 1994 when Paul called Yoko to wish her a Happy New Year. This act of reconciliation led to further conversations and then a meeting when Paul attended John's induction into the Rock'n'Roll Hall Of Fame. During this time together they discussed the possibility of the remaining Beatles working on John's home demos. Yoko offered three tracks for consideration – 'Real Love', 'Grow Old With Me' and 'Free As A Bird'.

"I liked 'Free As A Bird' immediately," Paul said. "I liked the melody. It had strong chords and it really appealed to me... The great thing was that John hadn't finished it. On the middle eight he was just blocking out lyrics that he didn't have yet. That meant that we had to come up with something, and that now I was actually working 'with John'."

'Free As A Bird' was an expression of John's love of his happy home life with Yoko and Sean.

John probably first worked on the song at home in New York during the latter part of 1977. On October 4th of that year he and Yoko held a press conference in Japan to announce that they were both putting their careers on hold to concentrate on raising their son Sean.

Several of the songs he began during this period dealt with his new life as a house husband. In 'I'm Stepping Out', 'Watching The Wheels', 'Beautiful Boy' and 'Cleanup Time' he wrote of the strange sense of freedom he felt in abandoning the life of a celebrity for domestic duties.

Like many people psychologically wounded in early life, John craved attention and then spurned it when it came. Interviewed by *Rolling Stone* in 1970 his first comment was, "If I had the capabilities of being something other than I am, I would. It's no fun being an artist." His final comment, after being asked how he saw himself at 64, was in a similar vein. "I hope we're a nice old couple living off the coast of Ireland or something like that – looking at our scrapbook of madness."

For John, a stable family home had been the one thing that had always eluded him. With Sean and Yoko, he was determined to hang on to what he had got. 'Free As A Bird' was written to express his delight at being set free from the demands of celebrity and from the artistic pressure of having to compete with his earlier selves. He was, as he sings, 'home and dry'.

For the middle section of the song John had only the couplet 'Whatever happened to/The life that we once knew?', lines reminiscent of the belief he had expressed in 'Help!', 'Strawberry

The surviving Beatles pretended that John was still alive as they recorded *Anthology*.

Fields Forever' and 'In My Life' that his childhood was the most idyllic time of his life. Paul's additional lines subvert this train of thought, turning it into a longing for healed relationships – presumably his own with John.

Recording took place in February and March of 1994 at Paul's studio in Sussex with production credits being shared between the Beatles and former Electric Light Orchestra vocalist/guitarist Jeff Lynne. John's original cassette was transferred to tape and the sound digitally remastered. "We then took the liberty of beefing the song up with different chord changes and different arrangements," said George Harrison.

The project was approached as if John was still alive and that he and Paul were still working on each other's unfinished songs. "We came up with this holiday scenario," said Paul. "I rang up Ringo and said let's pretend that John's gone on holiday and he's sent us a cassette and said, 'Finish it up for me'."

George Martin, who had produced every other Beatles single, gave it a cautious blessing but felt that it lacked dynamics because they hadn't been able to successfully separate the piano and vocals on the original cassette and had put it in a rigid time beat to make overdubbing easier.

"They stretched it and compressed it and put it around until it got to a regular waltz control click and then they were done," he said. "The result was that, in order to conceal the bad bits, they had to plaster it fairly heavily so that what you ended up with was quite a thick homogeneous sound that hardly stops."

'Free As A Bird' reached number two in the British charts and number six in America.

FREE AS A BIRD
Written: Lennon
Length: 4' 24"
UK single release: December 4, 1995
UK chart position: 2
US single release: December 4, 1995
US chart position: 6

REAL LOVE

'Real Love' was a song John had worked on for at least two years and, although many people weren't aware of it, a version was used in the 1988 soundtrack to Andrew Solt's documentary *Imagine*.

It began as a song called 'Real Life', the verses of which later became 'I'm Stepping Out', posthumously released on *Milk And Honey*. The remaining chorus – 'It's real life/Yes, it's real life' – he obviously thought too good to throw away. The theme of the tune – I'm back to what really counts in life – was the essential theme of all his post-Beatle work. He was still stripping away myths, dispensing with the unnecessary and in this case, getting down to the reality of kitchens, cigarettes, babies, newspapers and early morning blues.

The revamped song was coming closer to the version that the Beatles would work on. The references to 'little girls and boys' and 'little plans and schemes' were now there.

When he finally changed the chorus from 'real life' to 'real love' the theme became the transforming love of Yoko Ono. He said many times in interview that he felt that she was the woman that all his longings for love and acceptance had been directed towards even before he met her. She was the 'girl with kaleidoscope eyes'. She was, as he wrote in his essay *The Ballad Of John And Yoko*, "Someone who I had already known, but somehow had lost."

In February 1995, Jeff Lynne deleted extraneous noises on John's cassette copy of 'Real Love' and transferred the mono recording to two 24-track analogue tapes at Paul's Sussex studio. Paul, George and Ringo added guitars, drums, bass, percussion and backing vocals. At one point Paul even used his upright bass which once belonged to Bill Black and was used on Elvis Presley's 'Heartbreak Hotel'.

REAL LOVE
Written: Lennon
Length: 3' 54"
UK single release: March 4, 1996
UK chart position: 4
US single release: March 4, 1996
US chart position: 11

CHRISTMAS TIME (IS HERE AGAIN)

In their early years, the band pandered to the Christmas market on an annual basis.

Particularly for the British, the Beatles became inextricably linked to the Christmases of the 1960s. Six of their albums were released to capitalise on the Christmas market and four of their singles were Christmas number ones. In 1963 and 1964 they presented special Christmas shows in London theatres which were a mixture of music and pantomime and had support acts ranging from the Yardbirds to Rolf Harris.

Between 1963 and 1969 they produced a flexidisc exclusively for members of their official fan club which offered spoken greetings from each Beatle and some light hearted conversation. The earliest messages were clearly scripted but as their music developed so did the discs. In 1965 they fooled around with a version of 'Auld Lang Syne' and the next year Paul wrote a mini-pantomime for the group.

'Christmas Time (Is Here Again)', the only original song written for fan club members, came out in 1967, the year that *Magical Mystery Tour* was being screened on Boxing Day. The unedited version, recorded on November 28th, was over six minutes long and parts of it were used to punctuate a satirical sketch written by all four Beatles.

Although it largely consists of a single line repeated like a musical mantra, 'Christmas Time (Is Here Again)' is illustrative of their fascination with children's songs and rhymes which began with 'Yellow Submarine' in 1966. This in part reflected nostalgia for the Liverpool of the 1940s but was also part of the psychedelic tendency to regress to simpler states of mind where it wasn't out of place for an adult to wear ripped jeans, blow bubbles and think buttercups were 'far out'.

CHRISTMAS TIME (IS HERE AGAIN)
Written: Harrison/Lennon/McCartney/Starr
Length: 3' 03"
UK single release: December 4, 1995 on 'Free As A Bird' EP
US single release: December 4, 1995 on 'Free As A Bird' EP

IN SPITE OF ALL THE DANGER

A rough recording transferred from a slightly worn 78 rpm shellac disc cut in the spring or summer of 1958, this has historical value in that it is the earliest taping of the soon-to-be Beatles as well as being the group's first songwriting effort to make it into the archives.

It was recorded on a £400 portable tape recorder at a small studio housed in the terraced home of a 63-year-old electrical goods shop owner in the Kensington district of Liverpool. The Quarry Men, which then consisted of John, Paul, George, pianist John Duff Lowe and drummer Colin Hanton, paid 17 shillings and six pence (87p) to have two songs.cut.

The first song they chose was 'That'll Be The Day', a September 1957 hit in Britain for the Crickets (with Buddy Holly), and the second was the McCartney-Harrison number 'In Spite Of All The Danger'.

"It says on the label that it was me and George but I think it was written by me and George played the guitar solo," said Paul in 1995. "It was my song. It was very similar to an Elvis song."

It was in fact very similar to a particular Elvis song – 'Trying To Get To You' – which was written by Rose Marie McCoy and Margie Singleton and recorded by Elvis on July 11 1955. It was the only Sun recording by Elvis ever to use a piano and was released as a single in September 1956.

John Duff Lowe remembers 'In Spite Of All The Danger' as being the only original song the Quarry Men played at the time.

"I can well remember even at the rehearsal at his house in Forthlin Road Paul was quite specific about how he wanted it played and what he wanted the piano to do," he says. "There was no

IN SPITE OF ALL THE DANGER

Written:	Harrison/McCartney
Length:	2' 44"
UK release:	Anthology 1 album, November 21, 1995
US release:	Anthology 1 album, November 21, 1995

question of improvising. We were told what we had to play. There was a lot of arranging going on, even back then."

It was recorded on a single microphone and Lowe thinks that it must have gone straight to disc because he can't recall waiting around for it to be transferred from tape and there are mistakes in John's vocal which would otherwise have been corrected.

The disc was then passed on from member to member and eventually came down to Lowe who kept it in a sock drawer until 1981 when a colleague suggested to him that it might have some commercial value. He had it valued by Sotheby's which led to the discovery of the disc being reported by *Sunday Times* columnist Stephen Pile in July 1981.

"Before mid-day on that Sunday Paul McCartney had called my mum in Liverpool," says Lowe. "I eventually spoke to him on the 'phone and we had long conversations over the next few days because he wanted to buy it from me.

"I was living in Worcester at the time and he sent his solicitor and his business manager up. I deposited the disc in a small brief case at the local Barclay's Bank and we met up in a small room the bank kindly let me use. The deal was done, I handed the record over and we all went home."

Although Paul didn't have a specific project in mind at the time, part of the deal was that Lowe had to assign over all rights to the track and promise not to perform the song for the next fifteen years. "That took us up to August 1996," says Lowe. "Isn't it strange that two months later the final album in the *Anthology* set came out?"

YOU'LL BE MINE

Paul and John were at their most precocious on 'You'll Be Mine', the Goons-influenced first recording of a Lennon/McCartney song.

Recorded in the summer of 1960 on a borrowed tape machine at Paul's family home at Forthlin Road this is the first recording of a Lennon and McCartney song, although that's the extent of its interest. It sounds like nothing more than a couple of minutes of musical hilarity put together by teenagers in awe of the sound of their own voices.

Without a drummer but with the addition of fourth guitarist Stuart Sutcliffe, the group were rehearsing for their upcoming stint in Hamburg and decided on an Inkspots parody with John delivering a melodramatic spoken section that owed a lot to his fascination with the Goons. Appropriately, the whole tracks concludes with a wild squeal of laughter. You can almost imagine them wetting themselves as they played it back again and again.

YOU'LL BE MINE

Written:	Lennon/McCartney
Length:	1' 38"
UK release:	Anthology 1 album, November 21, 1995
US release:	Anthology 1 album, November 21, 1995

CAYENNE

Paul has said that the instrumental 'Cayenne', or 'Cayenne Pepper' as it was originally titled, was written before he met John, probably at the age of 14 when he got his first £15 guitar. Another instrumental he wrote around the same time, 'Cat's Walk', was recorded by the Chris Barber Band in 1967 as 'Cat Call'.

When Paul committed 'Cayenne' to tape in the summer of 1960 rock'n'roll instrumentals were a regular chart phenomenon. Since January there had been hit singles by Johnny and the Hurricanes, the Ventures, Duane Eddy, Bert Weedon, Sandy Nelson, Jerry Lordan, the John Barry Seven and the Shadows.

"It's not brilliant," Paul said recently of 'Cayenne', "But when you listen to it you can hear a lot of stuff I'm going to write. So, it's interesting from that point of view."

CAYENNE
Written: McCartney
Length: 1' 13"
UK release: *Anthology 1* album, November 21, 1995
US release: Anthology 1 album, November 21, 1995

Paul wrote 'Cayenne" before even his 1957 first meeting with John.

CRY FOR A SHADOW

CRY FOR A SHADOW
Written: Harrison/Lennon
Length: 2' 22"
UK release: *Anthology 1* album, November 21, 1995
US release: Anthology 1 album, November 21, 1995

When this track was recorded in June 1961, Cliff Richard and The Shadows were Britain's premier rock and roll act. Since his first hit with 'Move It' in October 1958 Cliff had been in the Top Ten ten times and the Shadows were now making their own instrumental hits.

Although the Beatles found Cliff a bit too tame for their liking, they were early admirers of the Shadows. Paul learned the opening chords of 'Move It' from watching lead guitarist Hank Marvin's finger movements on the *Oh Boy!* TV show and, when Cliff first played the Liverpool Empire on October 12, 1958, Paul was in the audience.

'Cry For A Shadow', an instrumental intended to sound like mock Shadows, was credited to Harrison/Lennon. It was the Beatles' first composition to make it onto record when it appeared on Tony Sheridan's 1962 German album *My Bonnie* where the 'backing group' were listed as the Beat Brothers.

The composition came about by accident. Rory Storm was in Germany and had asked George to play him a recent Shadows hit – 'Apache' or 'Frightened City' – and George played something new, either because he couldn't remember the Shadows' tunes or as a joke on Storm. At first he called it 'Beatle Bop' but then, out of homage to his original inspiration, he called it 'Cry For A Shadow'.

"It doesn't sound like 'Frightened City' or 'Apache'," says Shadows guitarist Bruce Welch. "What it has in common with the Shadows is that it has the same instrumentation that we used but melodically it's nowhere near either of them.

"What I had heard was that it was done as a piss-take because at that time we had a stranglehold on the British group scene and we'd never been to Germany as almost every other group did." The song was recorded in Germany when the orchestra leader and record company producer Bert Kaempfert hired the Beatles for 300 Deutschmarks to back Sheridan on a Polydor record. Norwich-born Sheridan, a veteran of London's 2 I's coffee bar, had spent a lot of time in Germany and Kaempfert wanted him to do rocked-up versions of such standards as 'My Bonnie' and 'When The Saints Go Marching In'. The Beatles were allowed their own spot on 'Ain't She Sweet' and 'Cry For A Shadow'.

Brian Epstein, who was responsible for getting the Beatles out of leather jackets and into tailored suits, encouraged them to emulate the Shadows in their attire and on-stage courtesies. The two groups first met in 1963 at a party in London and in June of that year Hank, Bruce and Brian Locking came to Paul's 21st in Liverpool.

The band wrote 'Cry For A Shadow' in an attempt to replicate the sound of Cliff Richard's backing group, the Shadows.

LIKE DREAMERS DO

Merseybeat consisted largely of covers of recent American hits and selections from Buddy Holly, Chuck Berry, Ray Charles and Jerry Lee Lewis. The Beatles stood out initially by discovering unknown acts and obscure B-sides but even these were soon copied and became standard fare on Merseyside.

This was what pushed them into serious songwriting. It was the only guarantee of uniqueness. If you had your own material then you were set apart from the copyists.

It was this situation that prompted them into serious writing. Their goal was to come up with material that not only went down well with their audiences but which remained unique to their act. Paul has said that 'Like Dreamers Do' was one of the first of his own compositions that he tried at the Cavern. This implies that he wrote it for the Cavern audience but the Quarry Men were performing it as far back as 1958. What he probably meant was that it was one of the first songs from his back catalogue that he felt confident enough to slip into the Beatles regular set.

The early arrangement of the song, he thought was weak although "certain of the kids" at the Cavern liked it. When the Beatles came to audition for Decca on January 1st, 1962 it was one of three Lennon-McCartney songs that they included in a 15-song set (the others were 'Hello Little Girl' and 'Love Of The Loved').

By the time of their EMI audition nine months later, none of these songs were offered, all of them having been replaced by better material. Shortly afterwards they were offered to other artists, 'Like Dreamers Do' to The Applejacks, a Birmingham six-piece group with a female bassist, who reached number 20 with it in July 1964.

LIKE DREAMERS DO
Written: Lennon/McCartney
Length: 2' 35"
UK release: Anthology 1 album, November 21, 1995
US release: Anthology 1 album, November 21, 1995

HELLO LITTLE GIRL

John frequently referred to 'Hello Little Girl' as his earliest composition. Written in 1958, it became the first of his songs to be performed by the Quarry Men.

He credited its origin to the Cole Porter song 'It's De-Lovely', with its chorus of 'It's delightful, it's delicious, it's de-lovely', which was first sung by Bob Hope in the 1936 stage musical *Red, Hot and Blue* and was recorded in Britain by Carroll Gibbons and The Savoy Hotel Orpheans in 1938.

"That song always fascinated me for some reason or another," John said. "It was possibly connected to my mother. She used to sing that one. It's all very Freudian. So I made 'Hello Little Girl' out of it. It was supposed to be a Buddy Holly-style song."

There is no similarity between the two songs other than the device of repeating the title as a chorus. It may have been more the

The Beatles played 'Hello Little Girl' in their early sets before ditching it when they signed to EMI.

HELLO LITTLE GIRL

Written:	Lennon/McCartney
Length:	1' 40"
UK release:	Anthology 1 album, November 21, 1995
US release:	Anthology 1 album, November 21, 1995

playful spirit of the song and, as with 'Please Please me', the association with his mother's musical interests. The imprint of Buddy Holly is more easily detectable. In its earliest incarnation the middle eight was apparently swiped wholesale from 'Maybe Baby'.

Just as Paul's early songs always bore the hallmark of optimism, John's bore the hallmark of pessimism. Paul assumed acceptance and love where John braced himself for rejection. In 'Hello Little Girl' he attempts to attract a girl's attention but she remains unaware of him. He sends her flowers but she is unmoved. He ends up lonely about to 'lose my mind'.

Recorded for the Decca audition in January 1962 'Hello Little Girl' was already off their set list by the time they signed for EMI later in the year. "It was then offered to Gerry and the Pacemakers," remembers Tony Bramwell. "It was considered as the follow up to 'How Do You Do It?'. They recorded a demo of it (included on *Gerry and the Pacemakers; The Best of the EMI Years*, 1992) but by that time Mitch Murray had come up with 'I Like It'."

The song was then offered to The Fourmost, another Liverpool group managed by Brian Epstein. After a Sunday concert in Blackpool where the two groups had appeared, John invited The Fourmost to his house to see the lyrics. The following morning they were sent a demo tape. "We had to record on the Wednesday and so we only had two days to record it," said bass guitarist Billy Hatton. "As a matter of fact, when we were recording, we were just learning the song as we went along."

The record was a hit after its release on August 23 and reached number 7 in the British charts. It was released in America on September 16.

YOU KNOW WHAT TO DO

A languid country-flavoured song written by George and recorded on June 3, 1964. Ringo had been taken ill that morning, on the verge of a tour, and so the studio time booked to record a fourteenth and final song for the *A Hard Day's Night* album had to be used to rehearse substitute drummer Jimmy Nicol. As a result only three new demos were recorded that day – Paul's 'It's For You' (later given to Cilla Black), John's 'No Reply' and this new song from George.

Being the youngest Beatle, George always had a hard time getting his ideas to be taken seriously. This was only the second song of his to be taped by the group (the first being 'Don't Bother Me') but it was never developed and, due to misfiling, it was lost for the next three decades. If it had been worked on by the group, it would surely have been a contender for *Beatles For Sale*.

Although it is undoubtedly a formula song with no deep revelation at the core it's interesting to note that George was just twelve weeks into his courtship of Pattie Boyd. Could he have written a song at the time about wanting to be with his girl 'every hour of the day' without having her in mind?

George wrote the under-rated 'You Know What To Do' a few weeks after he first met Pattie Boyd.

YOU KNOW WHAT TO DO

Written:	Harrison
Length:	1' 58"
UK release:	Anthology 1 album, November 21, 1995
US release:	Anthology 1 album, November 21, 1995

IF YOU'VE GOT TROUBLE

John and Paul never gave Ringo their best songs but neither did they only give him their worst. However, 'If You've Got Trouble' must rate as the worst one they ever expected him to sing. Melodically, it's uninspiring. Lyrically, it's embarrassing. It's hard to believe that the team that had just written 'Ticket To Ride' and 'You've Got To Hide Your Love Away' could come up with this. Recorded in one take, it sounds as though it was also composed in one take.

The theme of the song could be roughly summarised as 'If you think you've got problems - you should see mine!' The vitriol in the song sounds like John. Did it start out as a barbed attack on Cynthia, telling her to quit complaining about his abilities as a husband and a father and to be grateful for the luxuries afforded by the Beatles' new stardom?

An interview that year in the *Saturday Evening Post* conducted by Al Aronowitz suggests such a context for the song; "Their friends say that she (Cynthia) was in awe of John when they first met and she still is; a feeling, in fact, which has grown as his stardom rockets him further into the entertainment heavens, troubling her with the occasional thought that she might be left behind. When the Beatles are on tour, she often is left behind. 'Well, she certainly doesn't seem to mind spending the money I'm making,' John says."

Intended for the *Help!* album, it was left to die after this session.

IF YOU'VE GOT TROUBLE
Written: Lennon/McCartney
Length: 2' 48"
UK release: Anthology 2 album, March 18, 1996
US release: Anthology 2 album, March 18, 1996

THAT MEANS A LOT

Written primarily by Paul, this was another song intended for *Help!* but which the Beatles were never able to record in what they considered to be a definitive version. In sessions on February 20th and March 30th, 1965 they attempted the song 24 times before finally abandoning it.

The band attempted to play 'That Means A Lot' 24 times in one 1965 session before finally giving it up.

The song takes the point of view of a third party looking in on a relationship, a device first used in 'She Loves You'. The shift in viewpoint opened up the possibility of writing in voices other than their own and expressing attitudes that were not necessarily their own.

"We found that we just couldn't sing it," summarised John some time later. "In fact, we made such a hash of it that we thought we'd better give it to someone who could do it well." That someone was P. J. Proby, an American singer who'd been invited to Britain by Brian Epstein in April 1964 to take part in a Beatles TV special, and who had become friendly with the group. Proby recorded 'That Means A Lot' and it made number 30 in the British charts in October 1965.

THAT MEANS A LOT

Written:	Lennon/McCartney
Length:	2' 26"
UK release:	Anthology 2 album, March 18, 1996
US release:	Anthology 2 album, March 18, 1996

12-BAR ORIGINAL

All four Beatles shared credit for writing the atypical, Booker T & the MG's-like number '12-Bar Original'.

Recorded between 'What Goes On' and 'I'm Looking Through You' in November 1965, was this song meant for *Rubber Soul*? Two takes were recorded, one was mixed, but neither was ever released.

It is one of the least typical Beatles' tracks and appears to be an attempt to mimic the Memphis soul sound. The obvious template is Booker T. & The MG's – keyboard player Booker T. Jones, drummer Al Jackson, bass player 'Duck' Dunn and guitarist Steve Cropper – the Stax Records session musicians who played behind such soul greats as Otis Redding, Sam and Dave, and Eddie Floyd. They had enjoyed a string of instrumental hits under their own name beginning with 'Green Onions' in 1962. '12-Bar Original', which is credited to all four Beatles, sounds like a pastiche of 'Green Onions' and its follow-up 'Jellybread' minus the distinctive keyboard playing.

The track was recorded at a point when the Beatles were striving for recognition as musicians and was also at a juncture in British pop when the heavier sounds of the Animals, Yardbirds, Kinks and Pretty Things were taking over from Tin Pan Alley.

12-BAR ORIGINAL

Written:	Harrison/Lennon/McCartney/Starr
Length:	2' 55"
UK release:	Anthology 2 album, March 18, 1996
US release:	Anthology 2 album, March 18, 1996

JUNK

Paul wrote 'Junk' while in India and first recorded it in May 1968 when all four Beatles met up at George's home on Claremont Drive, Esher, Surrey. It's this version, an acoustic demo with unfinished lyrics, that appears on *Anthology*. Paul hoped to complete it for inclusion on *Abbey Road* but instead recorded it for his first solo album, *McCartney*, which was released in April 1970.

The demo is nothing more than a rough sketch. An unfinished verse is repeated twice, he is still thinking up words for the chorus and the gaps are filled with humming and giggling.

It's impossible to determine the story because Paul's way of composing at the time was to fit interesting words to a tune he had hit upon, in this case words to do with a scrap yard and a junk shop. In the press release that went out with his solo album his only comment was; "Originally written in India, at Maharishi's camp, and completed bit by bit in London."

JUNK

Written:	McCartney
Length:	2' 24"
UK release:	Anthology 3 album, October 28, 1996
US release:	Anthology 3 album, October 28, 1996

NOT GUILTY

Recorded during the White Album sessions in August 1968 George had already spent two months in the studio with only one of his songs – 'While My Guitar Gently Weeps' – having been picked up by the group. Over 100 takes and rehearsals of this song were produced between August 7 and August 12 but for some reason it wasn't included in the final line-up.

The song didn't surface until 1979 when a re-recorded version was used on the album *George Harrison*. Structurally the song remained the same, with the exception of the addition of the lines; 'not guilty for being on your street/ Getting underneath your feet'.

Around this time George explained the song as being about the problems that were beginning to affect him as a part of the Beatles in 1968: "Paul, John, Apple, Rishikesh, Indian friends etc." Written when he was starting to be regarded as the freaky, mystical Beatle he seems to be saying, "Don't blame me for getting you involved with freak culture. Hey, I'm not asking for too much. I just want to do my job and get a bit of respect."

It's hard not to see such lines as, 'I'm not trying to be smart/ I only want what I can get' as a bitter comment on his inability to increase his presence within the group and become regarded as a songwriting equal to John and Paul.

Maybe that's why it didn't get on the album.

George expressed his resentment at seeing his songwriting relegated behind that of Paul and John in the bitter 'Not Guilty'.

NOT GUILTY
Written: Harrison
Length: 3' 22"
UK release: Anthology 3 album, October 28, 1996
US release: Anthology 3 album, October 28, 1996

WHAT'S THE NEW MARY JANE

"This was a thing I wrote half with our electronic genius Alex," said John in 1969. "It was called 'What A Shame Mary Jane Had A Pain At The Party' and it was meant for *The Beatles* album."

Written in India when the Greek-born John Alexis Mardas paid a visit, it was demoed at George's Esher home in May 1968. At this stage it was a little over two and a half minutes long and as the Beatles improvised towards the end of the track one of them shouted, "Ooh. What's the news?... What are you saying? What a shame Mary Jane had a pain at the party. What's the new Mary Jane... Oh, my God! Mary! Mary!" This gave rise to the unusual title.

The studio version, recorded by John and George with help from Yoko and Mal Evans, went on for over six minutes with a two-minute 'freak out' before the final verse. The lyric remained the same as demoed in May except for the line 'He cooking such groovy spaghetti' which came out, whether by accident or creative play, as 'He groovy such cooking spaghetti'.

The syntax of the lyric is unorthodox. There is a deliberate use of wrong tenses and wrong words which suggest that John may have been imitating the way that Indians often speak English when it is their second language. The story told is either deliberate or a coded putdown of someone in Maharishi's circle. Significantly, John had been recording 'Sexy Sadie' the day before.

At the end of the recording John can be heard saying, "Let's hear it before we get taken away". A year later he planned to have it released as a B side to 'You Know My Name (Look Up The Number)' as a Plastic Ono Band single but it was pulled at the last minute. "It was real madness," said John describing the track in 1969. "I'd like to do it again."

WHAT'S THE NEW MARY JANE
Written: Lennon/McCartney
Length: 6' 12"
UK release: Anthology 3 album, October 28, 1996
US release: Anthology 3 album, October 28, 1996

STEP INSIDE LOVE

Cilla Black, real name Priscilla White, was a Liverpool typist signed by Brian Epstein and given a contract with Parlophone. Her first single, released in February 1963, was 'Love Of The Loved', an old Quarry Men song written by Paul and used by the Beatles at their Decca Records audition. Paul turned up for the recording.

In 1964 he wrote 'It's For You' for her and then in 1968, after hearing that she was to front her own BBC TV series, he offered to write the theme song for her. Entertainment shows of the time were traditionally book-ended by big band numbers but Cilla wanted to change that.

"Paul understood what I felt," she said. "He said to me: 'I know what they're doing. They're sending you these Billy Cotton Band-type of numbers and that's not you. You're the kind of person that should invite people into your house. You should have a song that that starts off very quietly and then builds up.' "

Paul did a demo of 'Step Inside Love' at his home in Cavendish Avenue and double tracked it with his own voice. "All he had given us was one verse and a chorus with him playing on guitar," remembers director and producer Michael Hurll. "We played it that way for the first couple of weeks and then decided that we needed a second

STEP INSIDE LOVE

Written:	Lennon/McCartney
Length:	2' 30"
UK release:	Anthology 3 album, October 28, 1996
US release:	Anthology 3 album, October 28, 1996

Paul wrote 'Step Inside Love' as the theme tune for Cilla Black's 1968 BBC TV show.

verse. Paul came over to the BBC Theatre in Shepherd's Bush and sat with me and Cilla and worked on a second verse. It started off with the line 'You look tired love' because Cilla was tired after a lot of rehearsing and most of what he wrote related to what was going on that day."

The version of the song included on *Anthology* was captured in September 1968 while the Beatles were waiting to record 'I Will'. Paul begins with the chorus and slips straight into the second verse which he forgets, singing 'kiss me goodnight' instead of 'love me tonight', leaving a line out and concluding with the last line of what should have been the third verse.

'Step Inside Love' became a Top Ten hit for Cilla in Britain, was released in America in May and earned her a ban in South Africa where it was considered to be a play on a prostitute's invitation. It could have been worse. Tony Bramwell remembers that Paul's initial idea was 'Come Inside Love'.

"I quite like the song," said Paul. "It was just a welcoming song for Cilla. It was very cabaret. It suited her voice."

LOS PARANOIAS

This was nothing more than an extended studio joke initiated by Paul when, at the end of his bossa nova version of 'Step Inside Love' he announced in the voice of an MC, 'Joe Prairie and the Prairie Wall Flyers'. John responded with 'Los Paranoias' which was enough to get Paul improvising a South American spoof about Los Paranoias.

The likely inspiration was the Paraguayan group Trio Los Paraguayas led by Luis Alberto Del Parana who appeared in variety shows on British TV during the 1950s with their 'Latin American rhythms' and released a *Best Of* album in 1957.

'Los Paranoias' was no more than a Beatles' studio in-joke.

LOS PARANOIAS

Written:	Lennon/McCartney
Length:	Snippet at the end of 'Step Inside Love'
UK release:	Anthology 3 album, October 28, 1996
US release:	Anthology 3 album, October 28, 1996

TEDDY BOY

"Another song started in India," announced Paul in 1970 when 'Teddy Boy' was included on his first solo album. "It was recorded for the *Get Back* album but later not used." It was started during one of the Maharishi's lectures at Rishikesh when Paul turned to John and sang the first line in his ear and was then finished in Scotland and London.

Strictly speaking, it was never 'recorded' by the Beatles because there was no final take, no mixing and in January 1969 Paul had still not completed the lyric. What is presented on *Anthology* is a rough sketch of a song offered by Paul in the hopes that John, George and Ringo would like it. The atmosphere is so informal that Paul laughs in parts, whistles over the unwritten patches and John can be clearly heard talking to others in the studio as he played along.

This inconsequential tale of a boy called Ted who is told to be good by his mother is not one that would have warmed John's heart. He once referred to Paul's story songs as being about, "Boring people doing boring things". This is probably why, as the song ended during this session, John picked up the rhythm on his guitar and turned it into a clunky square-dance song; 'Take your partners do-si-do/ Hold them tight and don't let go'. That was his none-too-subtle comment about where 'Teddy Boy' fitted into sixties rock culture.

TEDDY BOY
Written: McCartney
Length: 3' 18"
UK release: Anthology 3 album, October 28, 1996
US release: Anthology 3 album, October 28, 1996

ALL THINGS MUST PASS

In November 1968, after finishing up his work on the *White Album*, George had gone to Woodstock to stay with Bob Dylan. Here he also spent time with The Band, Dylan's former backing group, who had just recorded *Music From Big Pink*.

This album was seen at the time as a reaction against the excesses of psychedelia and a return to the mainstream of American music. The bluntness of the group's name and the rustic simplicity of their publicity photographs suggested a swing away from surrealism and a return to the roots of American culture.

Their music was particularly appealing to seasoned musicians weary of the demands of fan hysteria. It was instrumental in the break-up of Cream, for example. "I got the tapes of *Music From Big Pink* and I thought this is what I want to play – not extended solos and maestro bullshit but just good, funky songs," he explained in 1974.

George's song 'All Things Must Pass', which he played during Beatles recording sessions in January 1969 and then recorded alone on February 25th, was an attempt to capture the feeling that the

ALL THINGS MUST PASS

Written:	Harrison
Length:	3' 05"
UK release:	Anthology 3 album, October 28, 1996
US release:	Anthology 3 album, October 28, 1996

George based 'All Things Must Pass' on a Timothy Leary poem but it failed to make it onto a Beatles album.

Band had captured on their single 'The Weight'. In fact, when George first played it through to John and Paul he openly enthused about the Band and their music.

The lyric was based on a poem from Timothy Leary's book *Psychedelic Prayers After The Tao Te Ching* (Poets Press, New York, 1966). The poem was a 'translation from English to psychedelese' of part of the 23rd chapter of the Tao that Leary had titled 'All Things Pass'; '*All things pass/ A sunrise does not last all morning/ All things pass/ A cloudburst does not last all day...*' As George was to admit; "I remembered one of these prayers and it gave me the idea for this thing."

Despite George's frequent references to the song while the others were recording it wasn't considered for either *Let It Be* or *Abbey Road*. Instead, it became the title track of his debut solo album in December 1970 which reached number 4 in the British album charts and topped the American charts.

COME AND GET IT

Apple Films, which was being run by Denis O'Dell, were planning a film of Terry Southern's 1958 novel *The Magic Christian* and O'Dell asked Paul to do the music. Paul agreed, reluctantly it now seems, and with a shooting script in hand began to write.

He started with a song to be used over a scene where Sir Guy Grand, the world's richest man, (played by Peter Sellers), throws banknotes into a vat of filth and gets pleasure from seeing respectable people wallowing in slime in the hopes of grabbing some free cash. The idea came to him late at night while at Cavendish Avenue and he came downstairs and taped it in a whisper so as not to wake Linda. When he played it back the next day he believed that he had come up with "a very catchy song".

On July 5th, 1969 one of the Apple label signings, a group called The Iveys, gave an interview to *Disc & Music Echo* in which they complained of being neglected by the Beatles. Three weeks later Paul contacted the group and on July 29th he met them at their home and offered them 'Come And Get It' which he'd recorded alone with engineer Phil MacDonald five days previously at Abbey Road. He also suggested that they might make other contributions to the film

COME AND GET IT

Written:	McCartney
Length:	2' 29"
UK release:	Anthology 3 album, October 28, 1996
US release:	Anthology 3 album, October 28, 1996

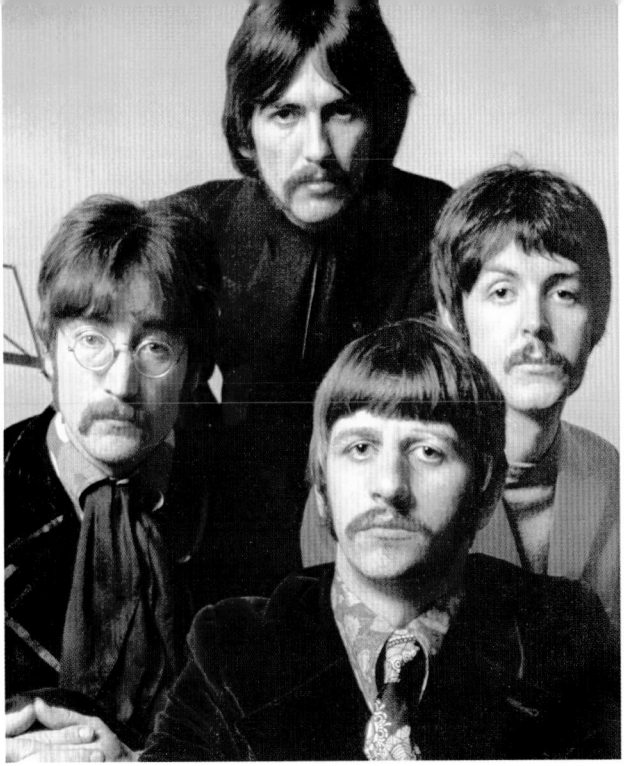

Paul denied that 'Come And Get It' detailed the Beatles' intra-band travails: "It was just a straightforward pop song," he claimed.

soundtrack as he was trying to put his energies into recording the *Abbey Road* album.

Paul produced the group on August 2nd, choosing Tom Evans to do the lead vocal and encouraging them to stick to the simplicity of his demo on which he'd played only piano, drums, bass and maracas. He told them that if they did it right he could guarantee them a hit and if they didn't do it right then he'd keep it for a Beatles single. "That challenge really made us work hard," said Evans.

By the time 'Come And Get It ' came out The Iveys were Badfinger (after John's 'Badfinger Boogie'). The single reached the top five and the group could no longer say they were neglected. The soundtrack to *The Magic Christian* contained three Badfinger songs and in a move to capitalize on this they titled their next album *Magic Christian Music*.

Asked whether 'Come And Get It' was a veiled message to those squabbling over the Beatles fortune in 1968, Paul said; "It was just a straightforward pop song with all the old innuendoes. Come and get what?"

CHRONOLOGY

1940

July 7 Ringo Starr born in Liverpool as Richard Starkey

Oct 9 John Lennon born in Liverpool as John Winston Lennon

1942

June 18 Paul McCartney born in Liverpool as James Paul McCartney

1943

Feb 25 George Harrison born in Liverpool

1956

Oct 31 Paul's mother, Mary, dies of breast cancer

1957

March John Lennon forms the Quarry Men skiffle group with school friend Pete Shotton

July 6 The Quarry Men play at the garden fete of St Peter's Church, Woolton, after which John is introduced to Paul by Ivan Vaughan

Oct 18 After weeks of rehearsals Paul McCartney makes his debut with the Quarry Men

1958

Feb George Harrison meets John and Paul and shortly afterwards is invited to join the Quarry Men

July 15 John's mother, Julia, is killed in a hit-and-run accident

1959

Aug 29 The Quarry Men play the newly opened Casbah Club which is run by Mona Best, mother of drummer Pete Best

1960

Jan John's art school friend Stuart Sutcliffe joins the group on bass guitar. They start to be known variously as the Beatals, the Silver Beetles and the Silver Beats

May London poet Royston Ellis uses the group to back him at a Liverpool reading. While staying with John and Stuart at their flat in Gambier Terrace, Ellis introduces them to the high produced by sniffing a broken-down benzedrine inhaler

May 10 The Silver Beetles audition before Britain's top rock 'n' roll manager, Larry Parnes, and Liverpool's best known pop star, Billy Fury. They aren't offered the job of backing Fury but instead get a tour of Scotland playing for Johnny Gentle

May 20 Silver Beetles begin seven-date tour with Johnny Gentle

July 9 *Record Mirror* reveals that Royston Ellis is considering bringing a Liverpool group called the Beetles to London

Aug 12 Pete Best auditions for the group and later joins on drums

Aug 17 Now known as the Beatles, the group begins its first season in Hamburg, Germany – 48 nights at the Indra Club

Oct 4 They then appear at the Kaiserkeller for a further 58 nights

1961

Feb 9 The Beatles play the Cavern Club in Mathew Street, Liverpool, for the first time

April 1 The Beatles return to Hamburg for a 13-week engagement at the Top Ten Club

June The Beatles return to Hamburg and back English guitarist-vocalist Tony Sheridan

Aug Polydor in Germany release 'My Bonnie' which is credited to Tony Sheridan and 'The Beat Brothers'

Sept During a holiday trip to Paris, Paul and John change their hairstyles into what would later become known as the 'Beatle haircut' or 'mop top'

Nov 9 Brian Epstein visits the Cavern Club and sees the Beatles for the first time

1962

Jan 1 Fifteen audition track recorded for Decca Records in London

Jan 24 The Beatles sign a management contract with Brian Epstein

April 10 Stuart Sutcliffe dies of a brain haemorrhage while in Germany with his girlfriend Astrid Kirchherr

April 13 Start of a seven-week residency at the Star-Club in Hamburg

June 4 The Beatles sign a contract with EMI in England

June 6 First session at EMI Studios in Abbey Road with producer George Martin

Aug 16 Pete Best is dismissed as drummer

Aug 18 Ringo Starr joins the Beatles. The first John, Paul, George and Ringo concert is held at Hulme Hall in Birkenhead

Aug 23 John marries Cynthia Powell at Mount Pleasant Register Office, London

Sept 3 Second session at Abbey Road

Sept 11 Third Abbey Road session at which 'Love Me Do' is re-recorded with session drummer Andy White

Oct 5 British release of 'Love Me Do', the Beatles' first single

Nov 1 Return to the Star-Club, Hamburg, for 14 nights

Nov 26 Second single, 'Please Please Me', recorded at Abbey Road

Dec 18 Final return to club dates in Hamburg – 13 nights at the Star-Club

1963

Feb 2 Start of Beatles' first British tour. They support 16-year-old Helen Shapiro

Feb 4 Last lunchtime session at the Cavern

Feb 11 Debut album *Please Please Me* recorded in just over nine hours

Mar 9 Nationwide tour with American stars Tommy Roe and Chris Montez

April 8 Julian Lennon born as John Charles Julian Lennon in Liverpool

April 18 After an appearance at London's Royal Albert Hall, Paul meets teenage actress Jane Asher for the first time

Aug 3 The Beatles' final performance at the Cavern Club where they had played almost 300 times

Sept 11 Work starts on *With The Beatles* LP

Oct 13 An appearance on the top-rated British TV show *Sunday Night At The London Palladium* helps create the phenomenon the press later dub 'Beatlemania'

Oct 25 Start of a short tour of Sweden

Nov 1 The Beatles' Autumn Tour opens in Cheltenham, Gloucestershire

Nov 4 Royal Command Performance at Prince of Wales Theatre, London, before the Queen Mother and Princess Margaret

Dec 24 'The Beatles' Christmas Show' opens at the Astoria Cinema, Finsbury Park, London for a 16-night run

1964

Jan 16 An 18-day run at the Olympia Theatre, Paris, France

Feb 7 The Beatles fly to New York where they are greeted by 3,000 screaming fans

Feb 9 First appearance on the *Ed Sullivan Show* to

an estimated audience of 73 million

Feb 11 First American concert takes place at the Washington Coliseum

Mar 2 Shooting begins on *A Hard Day's Night*

Mar 23 John's first book, *In His Own Write*, is published

June 4 Beatles leave for a tour of Denmark, Holland, Hong Kong, Australia and New Zealand with Jimmy Nicol substituting for Ringo who is hospitalized with tonsillitis and pharyngitis

June 14 Ringo re-joins the Beatles in Melbourne

July 6 World premiere of *A Hard Day's Night* at the London Pavilion

July John buys a home in Weybridge, Surrey

Aug 19 The Beatles' second visit to America but their first American tour. The first concert is at the Cow Palace in San Francisco

Aug 28 In New York City they are introduced to Bob Dylan and smoke marijuana for the first time

Oct 9 British tour begins in Bradford, Yorkshire

Dec 24 Another Beatles' Christmas Show opens for 20 nights at the Odeon Cinema, Hammersmith, London

1965

Feb 11 Ringo Starr marries Maureen Cox

Feb 23 – May 11 Filming *Help!*, the Beatles' second feature film

March – April John and George experience LSD for the first time when a dentist friend spikes their after-dinner coffees

June 12 Each Beatle is awarded an MBE in the Queen's Birthday Honours list

June 24 John's second book, *A Spaniard In The Works*, is published

July 29 World premiere of *Help!*

Aug 14 Beatles arrive in New York for their second American concert tour

Aug 15 First appearance at Shea Stadium in Queens, New York. The attendance of almost 56,000 makes it the biggest pop concert ever

Aug 27 The Beatles meet Elvis Presley at his home in Bel Air

Aug John and George take their second LSD trip in the company of actor Peter Fonda

Aug 31 Final concert of 1965 North American tour takes place at Cow Palace, San Francisco

Dec 3 The first date of what would turn out to be their final British tour

Dec 25 George gets engaged to Pattie Boyd

1966

Jan 21 George marries Pattie Boyd

Mar 4 John's interview with Maureen Cleave in which he claims that the Beatles are now "more popular than Jesus" is published in London's *Evening Standard*

April 6 – June 22 Recording *Revolver* at Abbey Road

June 24 Beginning of Far Eastern tour which goes from Germany to Japan and on to the Philippines

July John's comments about the Beatles being bigger than Jesus are appear in the American magazine *Datebook* and trigger a Beatles backlash in the Bible Belt states

Aug 12 Final tour of America begins in Chicago

Aug 29 The last-ever concert performance by John, Paul, George and Ringo takes place at Candlestick Park, San Francisco

Sept 6 – Nov 6 John films *How I Won The War* in Germany and Spain

Nov 9 John meets Japanese artist Yoko Ono for the first time, in London

Nov 24 Beatles enter Abbey Road to begin recording *Sgt. Pepper's Lonely Hearts Club Band*

1967

Jan 1 – April 2 Recording continues on *Sgt Pepper's Lonely Hearts Club Band*

April 3 Paul flies to San Francisco

June 1 *Sgt Pepper's Lonely Hearts Club Band* is released in America

June 16 Paul becomes the first Beatle to confess to having taken LSD, in a *Life* cover story

June 25 *Our World* television programme in which the Beatles sing the specially composed 'All You Need Is Love'.

July 24 Beatles sign petition for the legalization of cannabis which is published in the London *Times*

Aug 1 George and Pattie fly to Los Angeles and later on to San Francisco where they visit the Haight Ashbury district

Aug 24 All four Beatles attend a lecture given by the Maharishi Mahesh Yogi at the Hilton Hotel in London's Park Lane

Aug 25 At the personal invitation of the Maharishi the Beatles travel to Bangor, North Wales, for a summer school in Transcendental Meditation

Aug 27 Brian Epstein dies

Sept 11 – 24 *Magical Mystery Tour* is filmed

Sept 22 Beatles make the cover of *Time* magazine

Oct 18 World premiere of *How I Won The War*, starring John Lennon

Dec 5 Apple Boutique opens at 94 Baker Street, London W1

Dec 25 Paul announces his engagement to Jane Asher

Dec 26 *Magical Mystery Tour* premiered on British television (BBC)

1968

Feb 15 John, Cynthia, George and Pattie fly out to India to join the Maharishi at his ashram in Rishikesh where they will study meditation

Feb 19 Paul, Jane, Ringo and Maureen join the rest of the Beatles in India

May 15 John and Paul travel to New York to announce the formation of Apple. Paul is reunited with Linda Eastman

May John begins his affair with Yoko Ono

May 30 Beatles demo the songs written during their stay in India

May 31 – Oct 14 Recording *The Beatles*, better known as The White Album

June 20 – 24 Paul is in Los Angeles on business and again meets up with Linda Eastman

July 20 Jane Asher announces that her engagement to Paul is off

July 31 The Apple Boutique is closed down

Oct 16 George goes to California to produce Apple artist Jackie Lomax

Oct 18 John and Yoko arrested on a charge of drug possession

Nov 8 Divorce granted to John and Cynthia

Nov 10 John puts his Weybridge home on the market

1969

Jan 2 Filming begins in Twickenham for what will eventually become the documentary *Let It Be*

Feb 2 Yoko Ono and Tony Cox divorce

Feb 10 George temporarily leaves the group after disagreements with John and Paul

Mar 12 Paul marries Linda Eastman at Marylebone Registry Office in London

Mar 20 John marries Yoko Ono in Gibraltar

Mar 25 – 31 John and Yoko organize their first 'bed-in' at the Amsterdam Hilton

Mar 28 It is announced that ATV are poised to buy Northern Songs

May 26 – June 2 John and Yoko arrange a bed-in at the Queen Elizabeth Hotel in Montreal

July 1 Work begins in earnest on the *Abbey Road* album

Aug 8 Iain MacMillan shoots the celebrated cover photo of the four Beatles walking across Abbey Road

Aug 11 John and Yoko move to Tittenhurst Park, Sunningdale, Ascot

Aug 20 The last day on which all four Beatles would be together in a recording studio

Aug 31 John, George and Ringo see Bob Dylan perform at the Isle of Wight festival

Sept 13 The Plastic Ono band (John, Yoko, Eric Clapton, Klaus Voorman and Alan White) makes its live debut in Toronto

Nov 25 John returns his MBE to Buckingham Palace

1970

Jan 4 The final taping of *Let It Be*

Apr 10 Paul announces that he has left the Beatles due to "personal, business and musical differences"

May – Aug Battles over the ownership of Northern Songs and involvement of Allen Klein continue

Aug 4 Apple's press office closes down

Dec 31 Paul files a suit against The Beatles and Co to dissolve the partnership

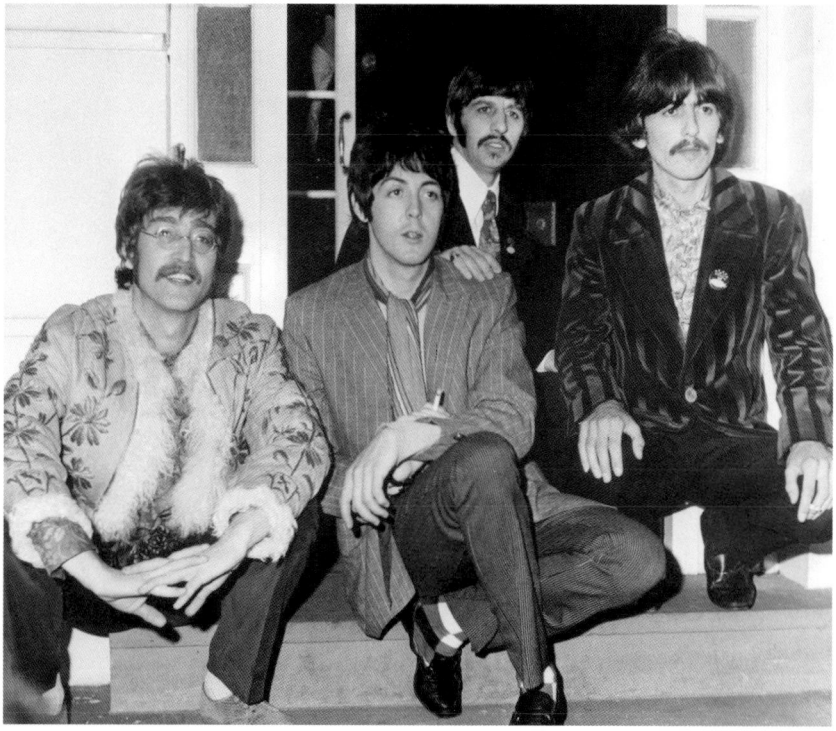

DISCOGRAPHY 1962-66

UK RELEASES

SINGLES

'Love Me Do'/'PS I Love You', October 5, 1962, Parlophone 45-R 4949.

'Please Please Me'/'Ask me Why', January 11, 1963, Parlophone 45-R 4983.

'From Me To You'/'Thank You Girl', April 11, 1963, Parlophone R 5015.

'She Loves You'/'I'll Get You', August 23, 1963, Parlophone R 5055.

'I Want To Hold Your Hand'/'This Boy', November 29, 1963, Parlophone R 5084.

'Can't Buy Me Love'/'You Can't Do That', March 20, 1964. Parlophone R 5114.

'A Hard Day's Night'/'Things We Said Today', July 10, 1964, Parlophone R 5160.

'I Feel Fine'/'She's A Woman', November 27, 1964, Parlophone R 5200.

'Ticket To Ride'/'Yes It Is', April 9, 1965, Parlophone R 5265.

'Help!'/'I'm Down', July 23, 1965, Parlophone R 5305.

'We Can Work It Out'/'Day Tripper', December 3, 1965, Parlophone R 5389.

'Paperback Writer'/Rain', June 10, 1966, Parlophone R 5452.

'Eleanor Rigby'/'Yellow Submarine', August 5, 1966, Parlophone R 5493.

EPS

Twist And Shout, July 12, 1963, Parlophone GEP 8882 (mono)– 'Twist And Shout';'A Taste Of Honey'/Do You Want To Know A Secret';'There's A Place'.

The Beatles' Hits, September 6, 1963, Parlophone GEP 8880 (mono) – 'From Me To You';'Thank You Girl'/'Please Please Me';'Love Me Do'.

The Beatles (No 1), November 1, 1963, Parlophone GEP 8883 (mono) – 'I Saw Her Standing There'; 'Misery'/'Anna (Go To Him)';'Chains'.

All My Loving, February 7, 1964, Parlophone GEP 8891 (mono) –
'All My Loving';'Ask Me Why'/'Money (That's What I Want)'/'PS I Love You'.

Long Tall Sally, June 19, 1964, Parlophone GEP 8913 (mono) –
'Long Tall Sally';'I Call Your Name'/'Slow Down'; 'Matchbox'.

Extracts From The Film A Hard Day's Night, November 6, 1964, Parlophone GEP 8920 (mono) – 'I Should Have Known Better';'If I Fell'/'Tell Me Why';'And I Love Her'.

Extracts From The Album A Hard Day's Night, November 6, 1964, Parlophone GEP 8924 (mono) – 'Any Time At All';'I'll Cry Instead'/ 'Things We Said Today';'When I Get Home'.

Beatles For Sale, April 6, 1965, Parlophone GEP 8931 (mono) – 'No Reply';'I'm A Loser'/'Rock And Roll Music';'Eight Days A Week'.

Beatles For Sale (No 2), June 4, 1965, Parlophone GEP 8938 (mono) –
'I'll Follow The Sun';'Baby's In Black'/'Words Of Love';'I Don't Want To Spoil The Party'

The Beatles' Million Sellers, December 6, 1965, Parlophone GEP 8946 (mono) –
'She Loves You';'I Want To Hold Your Hand'/'Can't Buy Me Love';'I Feel Fine'.

Yesterday, March 4, 1966, Parlophone GEP 8948 (mono only)– 'Yesterday';'Act Naturally'/'You

Like Me Too Much';'It's Only Love'.

Nowhere Man, July 8, 1966, Parlophone GEP 8948 – 'Nowhere Man';'Drive My Car'/'Michelle';'You Won't See Me'.

ALBUMS

Please Please Me, March 22, 1963, Parlophone PMC 1202 (mono), PCS 3042 (stereo) – 'I Saw Her Standing There';'Misery';'Anna (Go To Him)';'Chains';'Boys';'Ask Me Why';'Please Please Me'/'Love Me Do';'PS I Love You';'Baby It's You'; 'Do You Want To Know A Secret';'A Taste Of Honey';'There's A Place';'Twist And Shout'.

With The Beatles, November 22, 1963, Parlophone PMC 1206 (mono), PCS 3045 (stereo) – 'It Won't Be Long';'All I've Got To Do';'All My Loving';'Don't Bother Me';'Little Child';'Till There Was You';'Please Mister Postman'/'Roll Over Beethoven';'Hold Me Tight';'You Really Got A Hold On Me';'I Wanna Be Your Man';'(There's A) Devil In Her Heart';'Not A Second Time'; 'Money (That's What I Want)'.

A Hard Day's Night, July 10, 1964, Parlophone PMC 1230 (mono), PCS 3058 (stereo) – 'A Hard Day's Night';'I Should Have Known Better';'If I Fell';'I'm Happy Just To Dance With You';'And I Love Her';'Tell Me Why';'Can't Buy Me Love'/'Any Time At All';'I'll Cry Instead';'Things We Said Today';'When I Get Home';'You Can't Do That';'I'll Be Back'.

Beatles For Sale, December 4, 1964, Parlophone PMC 1240 (mono), PCS 3062 (stereo) – 'No Reply';'I'm A Loser';'Baby's In Black';'Rock And Roll Music';'I'll Follow The Sun';'Mr Moonlight'; 'Kansas City'/'Hey-Hey-Hey!'/'Eight Days A Week';'Words Of Love';'Honey Don't';'Every Little Thing';'I Don't Want To Spoil The Party'; 'What You're Doing';'Everybody's Trying To Be My Baby'.

Help! , August 6, 1965, Parlophone PMC 1255 (mono), PCS 3071 (stereo) – 'Help!';'The Night Before';'You've Got To Hide Your Love Away';'I Need You';'Another Girl'; 'You're Going To Lose That Girl';'Ticket To Ride'/'Act Naturally';'It's Only Love';'You Like Me Too Much';'Tell Me What You See';'I've Just Seen A Face';'Yesterday';'Dizzy Miss Lizzy'.

Rubber Soul, December 3, 1965, Parlophone PMC 1267 (mono), PCS 3075(stereo) – 'Drive My Car';'Norwegian Wood (This Bird Has Flown)'; 'You Won't See Me';'Nowhere Man';'Think For Yourself';'The Word';'Michelle'/'What Goes On'; 'Girl';'I'm Looking Through You';'In My Life';'Wait'; 'If I Needed Someone';'Run For Your Life'.

Revolver, August 5, 1966, Parlophone PMC 7009 (mono), PCS 7009 (stereo) – 'Taxman';'Eleanor Rigby';'I'm Only Sleeping';'Love You To';'Here, There And Everywhere';'Yellow Submarine';'She Said She Said'/'Good Day Sunshine';'And Your Bird Can Sing';'For No One';'Doctor Robert';'I Want To Tell You';'Got To Get You Into My Life'; 'Tomorrow Never Knows'.

A Collection Of Beatles Oldies, December 9, 1966, Parlophone PMC 7016 (mono), PCS 7016 (stereo) – 'She Loves You';'From Me To You';'We Can Work It Out';'Help!';'Michelle';'Yesterday';'I Feel Fine';'Yellow Submarine'/'Can't Buy Me Love';'Bad Boy';'Day Tripper';'A Hard Day's Night';'Ticket To Ride';' Paperback Writer'; 'Eleanor Rigby';'I Want To Hold Your Hand'.

US RELEASES

SINGLES

"Please Please Me'/'Ask Me Why', February 25, 1963, Vee Jay VJ 498.

'From Me To You'/'Thank You Girl', May 27, 1963, Vee Jay VJ 522.

'She Loves You'/'I'll Get You', September 16, 1963, Swan 4152.

'I Want To Hold Your Hand'/'I Saw Her Standing There', December 26, 1963, Capitol 5112.

'Please Please Me'/'From Me To You', January 30, 1964, Vee Jay VJ 581.

'Twist And Shout'/'There's A Place', March 2, 1964, Tollie 9001.

'Can't Buy Me Love'/'You Can't Do That', March 16, 1964, Capitol 5150.

'Do You Want To Know A Secret'/'Thank You Girl', March 23, 1964, Vee Jay VJ 587.

'Love Me Do'/'PS I Love You', April 27, 1964, Tollie 9008.

'Sie Liebt Dich'/'I'll Get You', May 21, 1964, Swan 4182.

'A Hard Day's Night'/'I Should Have Known Better', July 13, 1964, Capitol 5222.

'I'll Cry Instead'/'I'm Happy Just To Dance With You', July 20, 1964, Capitol 5234.

'And I Love Her"/'If I Fell', July 20, 1964, Capitol 5235.

'Matchbox'/'Slow Down', August 24, 1964, Capitol 5255.

'I Feel Fine'/'She's A Woman', November 23, 1964, Capitol 5327.

'Eight Days A Week'/'I Don't Want To Spoil The Party', February 15, 1965, Capitol 5371.

'Ticket To Ride'/'Yes It Is', April 19, 1965, Capitol 5407.

'Help!'/'I'm Down', July 19, 1965, Capitol 5476.

'Yesterday'/'Act Naturally', September 13, 1965, Capitol 5498.

'We Can Work It Out'/'Day Tripper', December 6, 1965, Capitol 5555.

'Nowhere Man'/'What Goes On', February 21, 1966, Capitol 5587.

'Paperback Writer'/Rain', May 30, 1966, Capitol 5651.

'Eleanor Rigby'/'Yellow Submarine', August 8, 1966, Capitol 5715

ALBUMS

Introducing The Beatles, July 22, 1963, Vee Jay VJLP 1062 (mono), SR 1062 (stereo) – 'I Saw Her Standing There'; 'Misery'; 'Anna (Go To Him)'; 'Chains'; 'Boys'; 'Love Me Do'/'PS I Love You'; 'Baby It's You'; 'Do You Want To Know A Secret'; 'A Taste Of Honey'; 'There's A Place '; 'Twist And Shout'.

Meet The Beatles!, January 20, 1964, Capitol T-2047 (mono), ST-2047 (stereo) – 'I Want To Hold Your Hand'; 'I Saw Her Standing There'; 'This Boy'; 'It Won't Be Long'; 'All I've Got To Do'; 'All My Loving'/'Don't Bother Me'; 'Little Child'; 'Till There Was You'; 'Hold Me Tight'; 'I Wanna Be Your Man'; 'Not A Second Time'.

Introducing The Beatles, January 27, 1964, Vee Jay VJLP 1062 (mono; no stereo release) – 'I Saw Her Standing There'; Misery'; 'Anna (Go To Him)'; 'Chains'; 'Boys'; 'Ask Me Why'/'Please Please Me'; 'Baby It's You'; 'Do You Want To Know A Secret'; 'A Taste Of Honey'; 'There's A Place'; 'Twist And Shout'.

The Beatles' Second Album, April 10, 1964, Capitol T-2080 (mono), ST-2080 (stereo) – 'Roll Over Beethoven'; 'Thank You Girl'; 'You Really Got A Hold On Me'; '(There's A) Devil In Her Heart'; 'Money (That's What I Want)'; 'You Can't Do That'/ 'Long Tall Sally'; 'I Call Your Name'; 'Please Mister Postman'; 'I'll Get You'; 'She Loves You'.

A Hard Day's Night, June 26, 1964, United Artists UA 6366 (mono), UAS 6366 (stereo) – 'A Hard Day's Night'; 'Tell Me Why'; 'I'll Cry Instead'; 'I'm Happy Just To Dance With You'; plus two soundtrack instrumental cuts by George Martin & Orchestra/ I Should Have Known Better'; 'If I Fell'; 'And I Love Her'; 'Can't Buy Me Love'; plus two soundtrack instrumental cuts by George Martin & Orchestra.

Something New, July 20, 1964, Capitol T-2108 (mono), ST-2108 (stereo) – 'I'll Cry Instead'; 'Things We Said Today'; 'Any Time At All'; 'When I Get Home'; 'Slow Down'; 'Matchbox'/'Tell Me Why'; 'And I Love Her'; 'I'm Happy Just To Dance With You'; 'If I Fell'; 'Komm, Gib Mir Deine Hand'.

The Beatles' Story, November 23, 1964, Capitol TBO-2222 (mono), STB0-2222 (stereo) – 'Interviews plus extracts from 'I Want To Hold Your Hand'; 'Slow Down'; 'This Boy'/Interviews plus extracts from 'You Can't Do That'; 'If I Fell'; 'And I Love Her'/Interviews plus extracts from 'A Hard Day's Night'; 'And I Love Her'/ Interviews plus extracts from 'Twist And Shout' (live); 'Things We Said Today'; 'I'm Happy Just To Dance With You'; 'Little Child'; 'Long Tall Sally'; 'She Loves You'; 'Boys'.

Beatles '65, December 15, 1964, Capitol T-2228 (mono), ST-2228 (stereo) – 'No Reply'; 'I'm A Loser'; 'Baby's In Black'; 'Rock And Roll Music'; 'I'll Follow The Sun'; 'Mr Moonlight'/ 'Honey Don't; 'I'll Be Back'; 'She's A Woman'; 'I Feel Fine'; 'Everybody's Trying To Be My Baby'.

The Early Beatles, March 22, 1965, Capitol T-2309 (mono), ST-2309 (stereo) – 'Love Me Do'; 'Twist And Shout'; 'Anna (Go To Him)'; 'Chains'; 'Boys'; 'Ask Me Why'/'Please Please Me'; 'PS I Love You'; 'Baby It's You'; 'A Taste Of Honey'; ' Do You Want To Know A Secret'.

Beatles VI, June 14, 1965, Capitol T-2358 (mono), ST-2358 (stereo) – 'Kansas City'/'Hey-Hey-Hey-Hey!'; 'Eight Days A Week'; 'You Like Me Too Much'; 'Bad Boy'; 'I Don't Want To Spoil The Party'; 'Words Of Love'/ 'What You're Doing'; 'Yes It Is'; 'Dizzy Miss Lizzy'; 'Tell Me What You See'; 'Every little Thing'.

Help! August 13, 1965, Capitol MAS-2386 (mono), SMAS-2386 (stereo) – 'Help!'; 'The Night Before'; 'You've Got To Hide Your Love Away'; 'I Need You'; plus three soundtrack instrumental cuts by George Martin & Orchestra/'Another Girl'; 'Ticket To Ride'; 'You're Going To Lose That Girl'; plus three soundtrack instrumental cuts by George Martin & Orchestra.

Rubber Soul, December 6, 1965, Capitol T-2442 (mono), ST-2442 (stereo) – 'I've Just Seen A Face'; Norwegian Wood (This Bird Has Flown)'; 'You Won't See Me'; 'Think For Yourself'; 'The Word'; 'Michelle'/ 'It's Only Love'; 'Girl'; 'I'm Looking Through You'; 'In My Life'; 'Wait'; 'Run For Your Life'.

"Yesterday"...And Today, June 20, 1966, Capitol T-2553 (mono), ST-2553 (stereo) – 'Drive My Car'; 'I'm Only Sleeping'; 'Nowhere Man'; 'Doctor Robert'; 'Yesterday'; 'Act Naturally'/'And Your Bird Can Sing'; 'If I Needed Someone'; 'We Can Work It Out'; 'What Goes On'; 'Day Tripper'.

Revolver, August 8, 1966, Capitol T-2576 (mono), ST-2576 (stereo) – 'Taxman'; 'Eleanor Rigby'; 'Love You To'; 'Here, There And Everywhere'; 'Yellow Submarine'; 'She Said She Said'/'Good Day Sunshine'; 'For No One'; 'I Want To Tell You'; 'Got to Get You Into My Life'; 'Tomorrow Never Knows'.

DISCOGRAPHY 1967-70

UK RELEASES

SINGLES

'Strawberry Fields Forever'/'Penny Lane', February 17, 1967, Parlophone R 5570.

'All You Need Is Love'/'Baby, You're A Rich Man', July 7, 1967, Parlophone R 5620

'Hello, Goodbye'/'I Am The Walrus', November 24, 1967, Parlophone R 5655.

'Lady Madonna'/'The Inner Light', March 15, 1968, Parlophone R 5675.

'Hey Jude'/'Revolution', August 30, 1968, Apple [Parlophone] R 5722.

'Get Back'/'Don't Let Me Down', April 11, 1969, Apple [Parlophone] R 5777.

'The Ballad Of John And Yoko'/'Old Brown Shoe', May 30, 1969, Apple [Parlophone] R 5786.

'Something'/Come Together', October 31, 1969, Apple [Parlophone] R 5814.

'Let It Be'/'You Know My Name (Look Up The Number)', March 6, 1970, Apple [Parlophone] R 5833.

'Free As A Bird'/'I Saw Her Standing There'/'This Boy'/ 'Christmas Time (Is Here Again)', December 4 1995, Apple [Parlophone] CDR 6422

'Real Love'/'Baby's In Black'/'Yellow Submarine'/'Here, There And Everywhere', March 4, 1996, Apple [Parlophone] CDR 6425

EPS

Magical Mystery Tour, December 8, 1967, Parlophone MMT-1 (mono), SMMT-1 (stereo) – 'Magical Mystery Tour'; 'Your Mother Should Know'/'I Am The Walrus'; 'The Fool On The Hill'; 'Flying'/'Blue Jay Way'.

ALBUMS

Sgt Pepper's Lonely Hearts Club Band, June 1, 1967, Parlophone PMC 7017 (mono), PCS 7027 (stereo) – 'Sgt Pepper's Lonely Hearts Club Band'; 'With A Little Help From My Friends'; 'Lucy In The Sky With Diamonds'; 'Getting Better'; 'Fixing A Hole'; 'She's Leaving Home'; 'Being For The Benefit Of Mr Kite!'/ 'Within You Without You'; 'When I'm Sixty Four'; 'Lovely Rita'; 'Good Morning Good Morning'; 'Sgt Pepper's Lonely Hearts Club Band (Reprise)'; 'A Day In The Life'.

The Beatles, November 22, 1968, Apple [Parlophone] PMC 7067-7068 (mono), PCS 7067-7068 (stereo) – 'Back In The USSR'; 'Dear Prudence'; 'Glass Onion'; 'Ob-La-Di, Ob-La-Da'; 'Wild Honey Pie'; 'The Continuing Story Of Bungalow Bill'; 'While My Guitar Gently Weeps'; 'Happiness Is A Warm Gun'/'Martha My Dear'; 'I'm So Tired'; 'Blackbird'; 'Piggies'; 'Rocky Raccoon'; 'Don't Pass Me By'; 'Why Don't We Do It In The Road'; 'I Will'; 'Julia'/'Birthday'; 'Yer Blues'; 'Mother Nature's Son'; 'Everybody's Got Something To Hide Except Me And My Monkey'; 'Sexy Sadie'; 'Helter Skelter'; 'Long Long Long'/'Revolution 1'; 'Honey Pie'; 'Savoy Truffle'; 'Cry Baby Cry'; 'Revolution 9'; 'Good Night'.

Yellow Submarine, January 17, 1969, Apple [Parlophone] PMC 7070 (mono), PCS 7070 (stereo) – 'Yellow Submarine'; 'Only A Northern Song'; 'All Together Now'; 'Hey Bulldog'; 'It's All Too Much'; 'All You Need Is Love'/ [Seven soundtrack instrumental cuts by the George Martin Orchestra].

Abbey Road, September 26, 1969, Apple [Parlophone] PCS 7088 (stereo only) – 'Come Together';'Something';'Maxwell's Silver Hammer'; 'Oh! Darling';'Octopus's Garden';'I Want You (She's So Heavy)'/'Here Comes The Sun'; 'Because';'You Never Give Me Your Money';'Sun King'/'Mean Mr Mustard';'Polythene Pam'/'She Came In Through The Bathroom Window'; 'Golden Slumbers'/'Carry That Weight';'The End'; Her Majesty'.

Let It Be, May 8, 1970, Apple [Parlophone] PCS 7096 (stereo only) – 'Two Of Us';'Dig A Pony'; 'Across The Universe';'I Me Mine';'Dig It';'Let It Be';'Maggie Mae'/'I've Got A Feeling';'The One After 909';'The Long And Winding Road';'For You Blue';'Get Back'.

Live At The BBC, November 30, 1994, Apple [Parlophone] CDPCSP 726 TC (mono) – 'From Us To You';'I Got A Woman';'Too Much Monkey Business';'Keep Your Hands Off My Baby';'I'll Be On My Way';'Young Blood';'A Shot Of Rhythm And Blues';'Sure To Fall (In Love With You)';'Some Other Guy';'Thank You Girl';'Baby It's You';'That's All Right (Mama)'; 'Carol';'Soldier Of Love';'Clarabella';'I'm Gonna Sit Right Down And Cry (Over You)';'Crying, Waiting, Hoping';'You Really Got A Hold On Me';'To Know Her Is To Love Her'; 'A Taste Of Honey';'Long Tall Sally';'I Saw Her Standing There';'The Honeymoon Song';'Johnny B Goode';'Memphis, Tennessee';'Lucille';'Can't Buy Me Love';'Till There Was You';'A Hard Day's Night';'I Wanna Be Your Man';'Roll Over Beethoven';'Things We Said Today';'She's A Woman'; 'Sweet Little Sixteen';'Lonesome Tears In My Eyes';'Nothin' Shakin'';'The Hippy Hippy Shake';'Glad All Over';'I Just Don't Understand'; 'So How Come (No One Loves Me)';'I Feel Fine';'I'm A Loser';'Everybody's Trying To Be My Baby';'Rock And Roll Music';'Ticket To Ride'; 'Dizzy Miss Lizzy';'Kansas City/'Hey! Hey! Hey!'; 'Matchbox';'I Forgot To Remember To Forget';'I Got To Find My Baby';'Ooh! My Soul';'Don't Ever Change';'Slow Down';'Honey Don't'; Love Me Do'.

Anthology 1, November 21, 1995, Apple [Parlophone] CDPCSP 727 – 'Free As A Bird'; 'That'll Be The Day';'In Spite Of All The Danger'; 'Hallelujah, I Love Her So';'You'll Be Mine'; 'Cayenne';'My Bonnie';'Ain't She Sweet';'Cry For A Shadow';'Searchin'';'Three Cool Cats';'The Sheik Of Araby';'Like Dreamers Do';'Hello Little Girl';'Besame Mucho';'Love Me Do';'How Do You Do It';'Please Please Me';'One After 909'; 'Lend Me Your Comb';'I'll Get You';'I Saw Her Standing There';'From Me To You';'Money (That's What I Want)';'You Really Got A Hold On Me'; 'Roll Over Beethoven';'She Loves You';'Till There Was You';'Twist And Shout';'This Boy';'I Want To Hold Your Hand';'Moonlight Bay';'Can't Buy Me Love';'All My Loving';'You Can't Do That';'And I Love Her';'A Hard Day's Night';'I Wanna Be Your Man';'Long Tall Sally';'Boys';'Shout';'I'll Be Back', 'You Know What To Do';'No Reply' (Demo);'Mr Moonlight';'Leave My Kitten Alone';'No Reply'; 'Eight Days A Week';'Kansas City'/'Hey! Hey! Hey!'.

Anthology 2, March 18, 1996, Apple [Parlophone] CDPCSP 728 – 'Real Love';'Yes It Is';'I'm Down'; 'You've Got To Hide Your Love Away';'If You've Got Trouble';'That Means A Lot';'Yesterday';'It's Only Love';'I Feel Fine';'Ticket To Ride'; 'Yesterday';'Help!';'Everybody's Trying To Be My Baby';'Norwegian Wood (This Bird Has Flown)'; 'I'm Looking Through You';'12-Bar Original'; 'Tomorrow Never Knows';'Got To Get You Into

My Life';'And Your Bird Can Sing';'Taxman'; 'Eleanor Rigby' (Strings Only);'I'm Only Sleeping' (rehearsal);'I'm Only Sleeping' (take 1);'Rock And Roll Music';'She's A Woman';'Strawberry Fields Forever' (Demo);'Strawberry Fields Forever' (Take 1);'Strawberry Fields Forever' (Take 7);'Penny Lane';'A Day In The Life';'Good Morning Good Morning';'Only A Northern Song';' Being For The Benefit Of Mr Kite! (Takes 1 and 2);'Being For The Benefit Of Mr Kite!' (Take 7);'Lucy In The Sky With Diamonds', 'Within You Without You' (Instrumental);'Sgt Pepper's Lonely Hearts Club Band' (Reprise); 'You Know My Name (Look Up The Number);'I Am The Walrus';'The Fool On The Hill' (Demo); 'Your Mother Should Know';'The Fool On The Hill' (Take 4);'Hello, Goodbye';'Lady Madonna'; 'Across The Universe'.

Anthology 3, October 28, 1996, Apple [Parlophone] CDPCSP 729 – 'A Beginning'; 'Happiness Is A Warm Gun';'Helter Skelter'; 'Mean Mr Mustard';'Polythene Pam';'Glass Onion';'Junk';'Piggies';'Honey Pie';'Don't Pass Me By';'Ob-La-Di, Ob-La-Da';'Good Night';'Cry Baby Cry';'Blackbird';'Sexy Sadie';'While My Guitar Gently Weeps';'Hey Jude';'Not Guilty'; 'Mother Nature's Son';'Glass Onion';'Rocky Raccoon';'What's The New Mary Jane';'Step Inside Love'/'Los Paranoias';'I'm So Tired';'I Will'; 'Why Don't We Do It In The Road';'Julia';'I''ve Got A Feeling';'She Came In Through The Bathroom Window';'Dig A Pony';'Two Of Us'; 'For You Blue';'Teddy Boy';'Rip It Up'/'Shake, Rattle and Roll'/ 'Blue Suede Shoes';'The Long And Winding Road';'Oh! Darling';'All Things Must Pass';'Mailman, Bring Me No More Blues'; 'Get Back';'Old Brown Shoe'; 'Octopus's Garden';'Maxwell's Silver Hammer';'Something'; 'Come Together';'Come And Get It';'Ain't She Sweet';'Because';'Let It Be';'I Me Mine';'The End'.

Yellow Submarine Songtrack, September 13, 1999, Apple [Parlophone] 521 4812 – 'Yellow Submarine';'Hey Bulldog';'Eleanor Rigby';'Love You To';'All Together Now';'Lucy In The Sky With Diamonds';'Think For Yourself';'Sgt. Pepper's Lonely Hearts Club Band';'With A Little Help From My Friends';'Baby You're A Rich Man';'Only A Northern Song';'All You Need Is Love';'When I'm Sixty Four';'Nowhere Man';'It's All Too Much'.

1, November 13, 2000, Apple [Parlophone] 529 9702 – 'Love Me Do';'From Me To You';'She Loves You';'I Want To Hold Your Hand';'Can't Buy Me Love';'A Hard Day's Night';'I Feel Fine';'Eight Days A Week';'Ticket To Ride';'Help!';'Yesterday'; 'Day Tripper';'We Can Work It Out';'Paperback Writer';'Yellow Submarine';'Eleanor Rigby'; 'Penny Lane';'All You Need Is Love';'Hello, Goodbye';'Lady Madonna';'Hey Jude';'Get Back'; 'The Ballad Of John And Yoko';'Something'; 'Come Together';'Let It Be';'The Long and Winding Road'.

Let It Be… Naked, November 17, 2003, Aapple [Parlophone] 595 7132 - 'Get Back';'Dig A Pony'; 'For You Blue';'The Long And Winding Road'; 'Two Of Us';'I've Got A Feeling';'One After 909'; 'Don't Let Me Down';'I Me Mine';'Across The Universe';'Let It Be'.

US RELEASES

SINGLES

'Strawberry Fields Forever'/'Penny Lane', February 13, 1967, Capitol 5810.

'All You Need Is Love'/'Baby, You're A Rich Man', 17 July 1967, Capitol 5964.

'Lady Madonna'/'The Inner Light', March 18, 1968, Apple [Capitol] 2138.

'Hey Jude'/'Revolution', August 26, 1968, Apple [Capitol] 2276.

'Get Back'/'Don't Let Me Down', May 5, 1969, Apple [Capitol] 2490.

'The Ballad Of John And Yoko'/'Old Brown Shoe', June 4, 1969. Apple [Capitol] 2531.

'Something'/'Come Together', October 6, 1969, Apple [Capitol] 2654.

'Let It Be'/'You Know My Name (Look Up The Number)', March 11, 1970, Apple [Capitol] 2764.

'The Long And Winding Road'/'For You Blue', May 11, 1970, Apple [Capitol] 2832.

'Free As A Bird'/'I Saw Her Standing There'/'This Boy'/'Christmas Time (Is Here Again)', December 4, 1995, Apple [Capitol] C2 7243 8 584 972

'Real Love'/'Baby's In Black'/'Yellow Submarine'/' Here, There And Everywhere', March 4, 1996, Apple [Capitol] C2 7243 8 585 442

ALBUMS

Sgt Pepper's Lonely Hearts Club Band, June 2, 1967, Capitol MAS-2653 (mono), SMAS-2653 (stereo) – tracks as UK release

Magical Mystery Tour, November 27, 1967, Capitol MAL-2835 (mono), SMAL-2835 (stereo) – 'Magical Mystery Tour'; 'The Fool On The Hill'; 'Flying'; 'Blue Jay Way'; 'Your Mother Should Know'; 'I Am The Walrus'/'Hello, Goodbye'; 'Strawberry Fields Forever'; 'Penny Lane'; 'Baby, You're A Rich Man'; 'All You Need Is Love'.

The Beatles, November 25, 1968, Apple [Capitol] SWBO-101 (stereo) – tracks as UK release

Yellow Submarine, January 13, 1969, Apple [Capitol] SW-153 (stereo) – tracks as UK release

Abbey Road, October 1, 1969, Apple [Capitol] SO-383 (stereo) – tracks as UK release

Hey Jude, February 26, 1970, Apple [Capitol] SW-385 (stereo) – 'Can't Buy Me Love'; 'I Should Have Known Better'; 'Paperback Writer'; 'Rain'; 'Lady Madonna'; 'Revolution'/ 'Hey Jude'; 'Old Brown Shoe'; 'Don't Let Me Down'; 'The Ballad Of John And Yoko'.

Let It Be, May 18, 1970, Apple [Capitol] AR-34001 (stereo) – tracks as UK release

Live At The BBC, November 30, 1994, Apple [Capitol] (mono) – tracks as UK release

Anthology 1, November 21, 1995, Apple [Capitol] – tracks as UK release

Anthology 2, March 18, 1996, Apple [Capitol] – tracks as UK release

Anthology 3, October 28, 1996, Apple [Capitol] – tracks as UK release

Yellow Submarine Songtrack, September 14, 1999, Apple [Capitol] – tracks as UK release

1, November 14, 2000, Apple [Capitol] – tracks as UK release

Let It Be… Naked, November 17, 2003, Apple [Capitol] – tracks as UK release

BIBLIOGRAPHY

BOOKS ABOUT THE BEATLES

Bacon, David and Maslov, Norman. *The Beatles' England*. Columbus Books, London ,1982; 910 Books, San Francisco, 1982.

Baird, Julia. *John Lennon My Brother.* Grafton, London, 1988.

Beatles, The, Anthology, Cassell & Co., London, 2000.

Beatles, The, The Beatles Lyrics. MacDonald, London, 1969.

Bedford, Carol. *Waiting For The Beatles*, Blandford Press, Newron Abbot, 1984.

Braun, Michael. *Love Me Do*. Penguin, London, 1964.

Brown, Peter. *The Love You Make*. MacMillan, London, 1983.

Coleman, Ray. *Lennon*. McGraw Hill, New York, 1984.

Dalton, David and Cott, Jonathan. *The Beatles Get Back*. Apple, London, 1969.

Davies, Hunter. *The Beatles*. Heinemann, London 1968.

Elson, Howard. *McCartney: Songwriter*. W.H.Allen, London, 1986.

Evans, Mike (ed), *The Beatles Literary Anthology*, Plexus, London, 2004.

Freeman, Robert. *The Beatles: A Private View*. Pyramid, London, 1992.

Fulpen, H.V. *The Beatles: An Illustrated Diary*. Plexus, London, 1982.

Giuliano, Geoffrey. *Blackbird*. Smith Gryphon, London, 1991.

Goldman, Albert. *The Lives Of John Lennon*. Bantam Press, London, New York.

Gottfridsson, Hans. *The Beatles from Cavern to Star Club*. Premium Publishing, Stockholm, 1997.

Harrison, George. *I Me Mine*. W.H.Allen, London, 1980.

Harry, Bill (Editor). *Mersey Beat; The Beginnings Of The Beatles*. Columbus Books, London, 1977.

The Ultimate Beatles Encyclopedia. Virgin, London, 1992.

Henke, James, *Lennon Legend*, Weidenfeld & Nicolson, London, 2003.

Lennon, Cynthia. *A Twist Of Lennon*. W.H. Allen, London 1978.

Lennon, John. *In His Own Write*. Jonathan Cape, London, 1964.

Lewisohn, Mark. *The Complete Beatles Recording Sessions*. Hamlyn, London, 1988.

The Complete Beatles Chronicle. Pyramid, London, 1992.

McCabe, Peter and Schonfeld, Robert. *Apple To The Core*. Sphere Books, London, 1972.

McCartney, Mike. *Thank U Very Much*. Weidenfeld & Nicolson, London, 1982.

Mellers, Wilfrid. *Twilight Of The Gods*. Schirmer Books, New York, 1973.

Miles, Barry. *Paul McCartney: Many Years from Now*. Secker & Warburg, London, 1997.

Miles, Barry, *The Beatles: A Diary*, Omnibus Press, London, 2002.

Norman, Philip. *Shout*, Elm Tree, London, 1981.

Pedler, Dominic, *The Songwriting Secrets Of The Beatles*, Omnibus Press, London, 2003.

Quantick, David, *Revolution: The Making of the Beatles' White Album*, Unanimous, London, 2002.

Rolling Stone magazine. *The Ballad Of John and Yoko*. Michael Joseph, London, 1982.

Salewicz, Chris. *McCartney: The Biography*. MacDonald, London, 1986.

Schafiner, Nicholas. *The Beatles Forever*. MSF Books, New York, 1978.

Schultheiss, Tom. *A Day In The Life*. Pierian Press, Ann Arbor, 1980.

Sheff, David. *The Playboy Interviews with John Lennon and Yoko Ono*. New English Library, London, 1981; Playboy Press, Chicago, 1981.

Shepherd, Billy. *The True Story of the Beatles*. Beat Publications, London, 1964.

Shotton, Pete. *John Lennon In My Life*. Stein & Day, New York, 1983.

Stuart Ryan. David, *John Lennon's Secret*, Kozmik Press Center, New York, 1982.

Taylor, Alistair. *Yesterday*. Sidgwick and Jackson, London; Pioneer Books, Las Vegas, 1989.

Wenner, Jann. *Lennon Remembers*. Straight Arrow Books, San Francisco, 1971.

Wiener, Jon. *Come Together: John Lennon In His Time*. Faber & Faber, London, 1984; Random House, New York, 1984

GENERAL BOOKS

Anthony, Gene. *Summer Of Love*. Celestial Arts, Berkeley, 1980.

Buglioso, Vincent. *Helter Skelter*. Bantam, New York, 1974.

Fein, Art. *The LA Musical History Tour*. Faber and Faber, Boston, 1990.

Gaines, Steven. *Heroes and Villains*. MacMillian, London, 1986; New American Library, New York, 1986.

Gibran, Kahlil. *Sand and Foam*, 1927.

Gillett, Charlie. *The Sound Of The City*. Sphere Books, London, 1970.

Goodman, Pete. *The Rolling Stones: Our Own Story*. Bantam, New York, 1965.

Guinness Book of Rock Stars. Guinness, London, 1989.

Hotchner, A.E. *Blown Away*. Simon and Schuster, London, 1990.

Leary, Timothy. *Flashbacks*. Heinemann, London, 1983.

Maharishi Mahesh Yogi,. *The Science of Being and the Art of Living*. International SRM Publications, London, 1963.

Mascaró, Juan. *Lamps of Fire*, Methuen, London 1958.

Marsh, Dave. *The Heart of Rock and Roll*. Penguin, London, 1989; New American Library, New York, 1989

Oldham, Andrew Loog, *Stoned*, Secker & Warburg, London, 2000.

Smith, Joe. *Off The Record*. Sidgwick and Jackson, London, 1989.

Stein, Jean. *Edie*. Jonathan Cape, London, 1982.

Turner, John M. *A Dictionary of Circus Biography* (unpublished).

White, Charles. *Little Richard*. Pan, London, 1984.

Wolfe, Tom. *The Electric Kool-Aid Acid Test*. Bantam, New York, 1968.

Worth, Fred and Tamerius, Steve. *Elvis: His Life from A-Z*. Contemporary Books, New York, 1988.

Wyman, Bill. *Stone Alone*. Viking, London, 1990

INDEX

Numbers in italics refer to captions

Allsop, Kenneth 98-100
amphetamines 177-78
Asher, Jane See McCartney, girlfriends

Beach Boys 157
Beach Boys, influence of 243
conflicts (financial) 310, 322
differences 284, 322
disliked by Russian authorities 244
drugs 213, 244, 316, 317
break-up 284, 291
earliest songs 294
jamming sessions 246, 247
Lennon/McCartney (songs by) 187, 189, 192, 195, 197, 198, 203, 204, 207, 209, 213, 216, 219, 220, 222, 223, 229, 230, 234, 235, 239, 244, 245, 247, 250, 252, 253-4, 257, 257, 259, 260, 262, 263, 265, 266, 267, 268, 269, 270, 271, 272, 273, 275, 277, 278, 279, 280, 282, 286, 287, 288, 291, 292, 293, 294, 296, 297, 301, 304, 307, 308, 309, 310, 312, 313, 314, 316, 318, 320, 321, 322, 323, 335, 339, 341, 344, 349, 350, 352; Harrison/Lennon 'Cry For A Shadow' 337; Harrison/Lennon/McCartney/Starr 290, 330, 346; Harrison/McCartney 335
MBEs 321
Shadows, admiration for 335
touring in Copenhagen 196, San Francisco 218
visiting India 240, 242
Beatles
Beatlemania 46, 52, 71, 72, 90
conquering America 40
drugs 94-5, 110-1, 141, 154, 170-1
first hit 31
first Number 1 single 19
first US Number 1 23, 64
Lennon/McCartney (songs by) 20, 23, 24-6, 27, 29, 31, 34, 37, 39, 40, 42, 44, 45, 46-7, 51, 53, 54, 56, 58, 60, 61, 63, 64, 67, 68, 71, 72, 78, 80, 89, 97, 107, 115, 121, 122
Los Angeles (visiting) 103, 170
MBEs 161
Shea Stadium 173
touring Germany 34, Paris 80, America 102-3, 177
writing songs for other artists 58
Beatles output
12-Bar Original' 346
'A Day In The Life' 184 211-2, 218
A Hard Day's Night album 32, 70-1, 72, 76, 80, 92, 111, 117; single 70, 72-74, 75, 87; film 71, 72, 74, 77, 79, 83, 84, 97
'A Little Help From My Friends' 184
'All I've Got To Do' 54-5
Abbey Road album 14, 302, *303*, 304, 306, *307*, 312, 347; film 285
'Across The Universe' 288
'All My Loving' 56-7, 80
'All Things Must Pass' 354-5
'All Together Now' 222
'All You Need Is Love' 130, 141, 214, 216-7
'And I Love Her' 70, 77, 178
'And Your Bird Can Sing' 154, 174-5
'Another Girl' 120
Anthology 326-7, 328, 347, 350
'Any Time At All' 82
'Ask Me Why' 19, 27
'Baby's In Black' 102, 107
'Baby You're A Rich Man' 218-9
'Back In The USSR' 242-4
Beatles For Sale (Beatles '65) 32, 90-1, 92, 105, 107, 109, 138
'Because' 311
'Being For The Benefit of Mr. Kite' 184, 202-3
'Birthday' 268
'Blackbird' 260-1
'Blue Jay Way' 231
'Can't Buy Me Love' 70, 80, 88
'Carry That Weight' 322
'Cayenne' 336
'Christmas Time (Is Here Again)' 332
'Come And Get It' 356
'Come Together' 302, 303-4
'Cry Baby Cry' 279
'Cry For A Shadow' 337-8
'Day Tripper' 132
'Dear Prudence' 245-6
'Dig A Pony' 287
'Dig It' 290
'Do You Want To Know A Secret' 36-7
'Doctor Robert' 155, 177
'Don't Bother Me', 59
'Don't Let Me Down' 283
'Don't Pass Me By' 264
'Drive My Car' 130, 134-5
'Eight Days A Week' 90, 92, 96-7, 102
'Eleanor Rigby' 154, 162-65, 168, 169, 309
'Every Little Thing' 108
'Everybody's Got Something To Hide Except Me And My Monkey' 271
'Fixing A Hole' 184, 198, 247
'Flying' 230
'Fool On The Hill' 228-9, 247

'For No One' 154, 176
'For You Blue' 295
'Free As A Bird' 328-30
'From Me To You' 32, 40, 42-44, 45, 46, 89, 144
'Get Back' 82, 283, 296, 353
'Getting Better' 184, 196-7
'Girl' 145-6
'Glass Onion' 247-8
'Golden Slumbers' 320
'Good Day Sunshine' 172-3
'Good Morning Good Morning' 184, 210
'Good Night' 282
'Got To Get You Into My Life' 179
Help! album 111, 117, 132, 150; single 110, 113, 115-6; film 96, 110-1, 116, 119, 121, 122, 123, 124, 127, 137, 329
'Helter Skelter' 273-4
'Her Majesty' 321
'Here Comes The Sun' 302, 310
'Here There and Everywhere' 154, 167
'Hey Bulldog' 223
'Hey Jude' 238-9, 300
'Hold Me Tight' 60
'Honey Pie' 278
'I Am The Walrus' 233-4, 247, 309
'I Call Your Name' 68
'I Don't Want To Spoil The Party' 102-3
'I Feel Fine' 92-3
'I Me Mine' 289
'I Need You' 119
'I Saw Her Standing There' 18, 20-23, 24, 112
'I Should Have Known Better' 32, 75
'I Wanna Be Your Man' 61-2, 80
'I Wanna Hold Your Hand' 40, 64, 80, 107
'I Want To Tell You' 154, 180
'I Want You' 309
'I Will' 266
'If I Fell' 70, 76
'If I Needed Someone' 152
'I'll Cry Instead' 83
'I'll Follow The Sun' 90, 104-5
'I'll Get You' 40, 51
'I'm A Loser' 33, 90, 98-100, 102
'I'm Down' 113-14
'I'm Happy Just To Dance With You' 78
'I'm Looking Through You' 147
'I'm Only Sleeping' 154, 165
'I'm So Tired' 259
'In My Life' 130, 148-51, 186, 330
'In Spite Of All Danger' 333
'It Won't Be Long' 52-3
'It's All Too Much' 224
'It's Only Love' 125
'I've Got A Feeling' 292
'I've Just Seen A Face' 126
'Julia' 267
'Junk' 347
'Lady Madonna' 223, 235-6, 237, 247
Let It Be album 14, 284-5, 290, 302; single 291, 301; film 284-5
'Like Dreamers Do' 339
'Little Child' 32, 58
'Long Long Long' 275
'Long Tall Sally 113, 114
'Los Paranoias' 352
'Love Me Do' 24, 31-3, 113
'Love You To' 166
'Lovely Rita' 209
'Lucy In The Sky With Diamonds' 184, 194-5
Magical Mystery Tour album 214-5, 225-6, 230, 232, 235, 241; film 14, 214-5, 220, 225, 229, 231, 232
'Martha My Dear' 258
'Maxwell's Silver Hammer' 307
'Mean Mr Mustard' 314
'Michelle 142
'Misery' 24-6
'Mother Nature's Son' 270
'No Reply' 101
'Norwegian Wood' 130, 136-7, 166
'Not a Second Time' 63
'Not Guilty' 348
'Nowhere Man' 130, 139, 156
'Ob-la-di Ob-la-da' 249-50
'Octopus's Garden' 308
'Oh Darling' 308
'Old Brown Shoe' 300
'One After 909' 294
'Only A Northern Song' 221
'Paperback Writer' 35, 82, 156-7, 159, 168
'Penny Lane' 184, 362-3
'Piggies' 262
Please Please Me album 19, 24; single 19, 26, 28-30, 30, 37, 45, 101, 144, 341
'Polythene Pam' 315-7
'PS I Love You' 34-5
'Rain' 158-9
'Real Love' 331
'Revolution 9' 280-1
Revolver 14, 276-7, 154-5, 169, 171, 172, 175
'Rocky Raccoon' 263
Rubber Soul 130-1, 137, 138, 153, 241, 346
'Run For Your Life' 153
'Savoy Truffle' 278
'Sexy Sadie' 272
Sgt. Pepper's Lonely Hearts Club Band 14, 15, 184-5, 190-1, 195, 196, 198, 203, 210, *211*, *212*, 221, 235, 301
Sgt Pepper's Lonely Hearts

Club Band 30, 156
'She Loves You' 46-8, 80, 130, 141, 344
'She Said She Said' 154, 170-1, 186
'She's A Woman' 94-5, 102
'She's Leaving Home' 184, 199-200
'Something' 302, 304, 305-306
'Step Inside Love' 350-1
'Strawberry Fields Forever' 184, 188-9, 247, 329; promo film 202
'Sun King' 313
'Taxman' 154, 160-1
'Teddy Boy' 353
'Tell Me What You See' 123
'Tell Me Why' 79
'Thank You Girl' 32, 40, 42, 45, 144
'That Means A Lot' 344
'The Ballad of John and Yoko' 297-299, 300
The Beatles (aka *The White Album*) 14, 214, 264
The Beatles 1967-1970
'The Continuing Story of Bungalow Bill' 253-4
'The End' 323
'The Inner Light' 237
'The Long And Winding Road' 293
'The Night Before' 117
The White Album 327, 348, 354
'There's A Place' 38-9, 158, 247
'Things We Said Today' 804, 108
'Think For Yourself' 140
'This Boy' 67, 82
'Ticket To Ride' 112, 122
'Till There Was You 77
'Tomorrow Never Knows' 181
'Two Of Us' 286
'We Can Work It Out' 130, 133
'What Goes On' 144
'What You're Doing' 109
'What's The New Mary Jane' 349
'When I Get Home' 87
'When I'm 64' 35, 207-8, 232
'While My Guitar Gently Weeps' 255, 348
'Why Don't We Do It In The Road' 265
'Wild Honey Pie' 252
'With A Little Help From My Friends' 192-3
'With Love From Me To You' 32
With The Beatles 40-1, 52, 54, 77
'Within You Without You' 184, 204-6, 247
'Yellow Submarine' 168, 221, 241; film 14, 214-5, 223
'Yer Blues' 269
'Yes It Is' 112
'Yesterday' 110, 127-9
'You Can't Do That' 88
'You Know My Name' 301
'You Like Me Too Much' 124
'You Really Got A Hold On Me' 54-5, 150
'You Won't see Me' 138
'You Never Give Me Your Money' 312
'You'll Be Mine' 335
'Your Mother Should Know' 232
'You're Going To Lose That Girl' 121
'You've Got To Hide Your Love Away' 118
Berry, Chuck 18, 22, 105, 243, 303
Best, Pete 18, 34
Black, Cilla 37, 350-1
Boone, Pat 26

Carroll, Lewis 194-5
Cavern Club 18, 20, 27, 77
Charles, Ray 18, *293*
Clapton, Eric 217, 255, 278, 295, 310

Donegan, Lonnie 64
Donovan 162, 168, 242, 260, 279
Drifters 26
Dylan, Bob 30, 54, 90, 94, 98, 118, 275, 354

Eastman, Linda 256, 266, 268, 286, 310, 312, 318-9
Ed Sullivan Show 23, 29, 64, 102, 173
Elliot, (Mama) Cass 173
Epstein, Brian 23, 36, 65, 101, *212*, 217, 219, 220, 240, 338, 341
Everly Brothers 18, 67

Faith, Adam 72
Fury, Billy 43, 72

Gordy, Berry 39

Harrison, George 18, 30, 36, 37, 78, 84, 88, 133, 140, 196, 204-5, 221, 225, 231, 235, 240, 246, 262, 268, 275, 278, 290, 300, 306-7, 310, 312, 330, 331, 348, 349, 355, 354-5
as composer 14
autobiography 166
Clapton, Eric (first meeting) 173
deteriorating relationship with Beatles 291, 348, with PM 284
drugs 132, 205, 224
Eastern thought 204, *255*, 289
George Harrison 348
Indian music, influence of 154
meditation 272
religious view 300
songs by 59, 119, 124, 140, 152, 160, 180, 204, 221, 230, 231, 237, 255, 262, 275, 278, 289, 295, 300, 302, 305, 307, 354
visiting California 231,

San Francisco 218-9
Hendrix, Jimi 93
Hollies 25
Holly, Buddy 18, 23, 104

Imagine 69
Isley Brothers 44

Jagger, Mick 217, 276
Joan Baez 51
John, Elton 23

Kramer, Billy J 37

Leary, Timothy 199, 303-4, *305*, 355
Lennon, Cynthia 193, 210
Lennon, John 14-15, 18, 21, 22, 24, 32, 28, 37, 39, 44, 47, 62, 64, 76, 79, 82, 83, 84, 88, 89, 92, 101, 102, 109, 112, 135, 139, 153, 163, 173, *189*, 192-3, 195, 196-7, 202-3, 211, 212, 221, 223, 232, 233, 247, 254, 256-7, 266, 268, 269, 270, 279, *281*, 303, 309, 310, 311, 314, 315, 340, 341, 349
adultery 136
aggressive tendencies 197
annoyed with PM 265
anti-semitism 219
anxiety 115
attitude to Christianity 145-6
childhood 52-3
contrast with McCartney's outlook 104-5
criticism of McCartney 174-5
cruelty/violence 83
death of mother 267
deteriorating relationship with Cynthia 269, 271, 288; with PM 284
diminishing role in Beatles 14,
dissatisfaction with Maharishi Mahesh Yogi 272
divorce 238, 269, 292
drugs 132, 141, 159, 181, 185, 194, 210, 256, *283*, 292
Dylan, Bob, first meeting with 90
early writing with PM 294
early years 186, 189
family break-up 52-3
girlfriends 34, 38, 52, 76
Imagine 331
influence of gospel music 31
In His Own Right 90
John Lennon/Plastic Ono Band 79
laziness 210
marriage to Cynthia 36-7, 76
marries Yoko Ono (and honeymoon) 297-9
moving to USA 271
plagiarism, 311
playing harmonica 31- 2
poetry, influenced by the *Goon Show* 195
Rape 298
sex and sleep 165
social change, views on 276-7
songs by 216, 217, 303, 329, 330, 331
songwriting, influenced by Kenneth Allsop 98-9
states of mind 188, 189, 259, 269, 329
sued for plagiarism 304
therapy 79
views on 'All You Need Is Love' 217, 'Birthday' 268, 'Dig A Pony 287, 'Hello Little Girl' 340, 'Hey Jude' 238, 'Oh Darling' 308, 'Sun King' 313, 'Teddy Boy' 353, *The Beatles* 241, 'The End' 323, 'When I'm Sixty-Four' 208; the analysis of Beatles' songs 233-4, 246-8; 'All My Loving' 57, 'And Your Bird Can Sing' 174 'Any Time At All' 82, 'Do You Want To Know A Secret' 37, 'If I Fell' 76, 'From Me To You' 44, 'Help' 115, 'Hold Me Tight, 60, 'I Wanna Hold Your Hand' 65, 'It's Only Love' 125, 'Little Child' 58, 'Thank You Girl' 45, 'Ticket To Ride' 122, 'When I get Home' 87, 'Yes It Is' 112, 'Yesterday 128; Beatles' songs 120; George Harrison's voice 37
visiting India 253, 259, 276, 279, 349; 'We're more popular than Jesus …' (quote) 146, 165
writing (significant influences on) 98-9
writing relationship with McCartney 107
Lennon, Julian 194, 238, 239
Lennon/McCartney songs see Beatles
Lyttleton, Humphrey 235
Lennon and McCartney Songbook, The 32
Lewis, Jerry Lee 18
Lynne, Jeff 30

Manson, Charles 262, 274, 281
Martin, George 20, 27, 30, 48, 71, 80, 93, 130, 136, 144, 150, 190, 195, 196, 208, 213, 214, 217, 234, 285, 294, 302, 330
McCartney, Mike 22, 60
McCartney, Paul 18, 21-3, 24, 36, 44, 47, 53, 61, 62, 64, 84, 94, 101, 102, 109, 113, 120, 127-9, 130, 133, 134-5, 138, 151, 163, 173, 175, 195, 196-7, 207-8, 209, 211, 213, 221, 222, 223, 225, 226, 228, 231, 238-9, 242-3, 249, 250, 251, 254, 260-1, 263, 268, 270, 272, 273-4, 281, 302, 305, 306, 312, 318-9, 320, 321, 331, 341, 345, 350-1, 353, 357, 356-7
conceives idea for *Sgt Pepper* 190
conflict within Beatles 291, 322
contrast with Lennon's outlook 104-5
death, rumours of 247
drugs 141, 179
Dylan, Bob, first meeting with 90
early writing with JL 294

early years 186
favourite songs 51
first solo album 285
girlfriends 23, 28, 34-5, 128-9, 258; Jane Asher 41, 56, 70, 77, 84, 108, 130, 133, 138, 142, 147, 163, 167, 176, 198, 225, 258
increasing influence in Beatles 15
interpreting Beatles' songs 28, 32
jamming for Jefferson Airplane 218
leaves Beatles 284
McCartney 347
reconciliation with JL 328
songs by 15, 260, 336, 347
MPL Communications 105
views on 'A Hard Day's Night' 74, 'Can't Buy Me Love' 81, 'I'm Happy Just To Dance With You' 78, 'I Saw Her Standing There' 21-3, 'Thank You Girl' 45, 'All We Need Is Love' 217, *Anthology* 326, 'Get Back' 296, 'Hello Goodbye' 220, 'Hey Jude' 238, 'The End' 323; Beatles' songs 265; visiting India 263, Moscow (meeting Putin) 244; San Francisco 218; writing songs 220
meditation 246-7
writing relationship with Lennon 107
Melly, George 186
Milligan, Spike 195
Motown 38, 39, 87, 179

New Musical Express 26, 29, 274, 43, 46, 69

Ono, Yoko 148, 14, 195, 210, 238, *256*, 257, 259, 267, 269, 271, 280, 283, 291, 292, 297, *299*, 303, 309, 311, 326, 328, 331, 349
Orbison, Roy 19, 28, 29, 30, 132

Petty, Tom 30
Pickett, Wilson 88
Presley, Elvis 18, 43, 48, 105, 153
psychedelia 191, 207, 214, 218, 222, 226, 279, 332, 354

Quarry Men 68, 70, 267, 333, 339, 340
Who, The 93, 273
Wings 126
Wolfe, Tom 226

Yogi, Maharishi Mahesh 224, 228, 237, 240, *241*, 242, 245, 254, 270, 272, 275, 288

PICTURE CREDITS

The publishers would like to thank the following sources for their kind permission to reproduce the pictures in this book.

Corbis: /Bettmann: 35, 61, 74, 115, 169, 176, 180; /CAT'S: 107, 179; /Waltraud Grubitzsch/epa: 15; /HO/epa: 18; /Hulton-Deutsch Collection: 26, 46, 51; / John Springer Collection: 72; /Michael Ochs Archives: 157
Getty Images: /CBS Photo Archive: 32; /Express Newspapers: 110; /Hulton Archive: 125, 165; /Keystone: 58, 81, 134; /John Loengard/Time & Life Pictures: 102; /Rolls Press/Popperfoto: 67; /Bob Whitaker: 118, 133
PA Photos: /AP: 29, 37, 42, 54, 56, 63, 78, 87, 89, 99, 101, 108, 127, 136, 138, 147, 148, 151, 158, 166; /Allaction.co.uk/Empics Entertainment: 7, 82, 128, 131; /Alpha General: 84; /Barratts: 91, 142, 155; /Bob Daugherty/AP: 93; / Empics Entertainment: 120; /PA Archive: 8, 11, 12-13, 17, 21, 23, 24, 31, 39, 40, 53, 64, 71, 77, 95, 96, 104, 112, 117, 122, 140, 152, 174; /Sport and General: 69
Rex Features: 160, 162; /Denis Cameron: 48; /Keystone USA: 145; /David Magnus: 45; /Bill Orchard: 171, 172

Alamy: /Mirrorpix: 109
Corbis: /**Bettmann:** 13, 21, 62, 169, 172, 183; /CAT'S: 164; /Beth A. Keiser: 131; /Michael Ochs Archives: 160, 176
Getty Images: /Ron Case/Keystone: 143; /John Downing/Express/Hulton Archive: 7, 36; /Evening Standard: 48; /Hulton Archive: 65; /Keystone: 179; / Marvin Lichtner/Time & Life Pictures: 76; /Michael Ochs Archives: 39; / Popperfoto: 159; /Roger Viollet Collection: 170; /Michael Webb/Keystone: 166; /Wesley/Keystone: 46
PA Photos: /AP: 29, 35, 44, 56, 58, 68, 70, 86, 90, 92, 96, 98, 100, 105, 110, 114, 117, 123, 137, 149, 151; /Allaction.co.uk/Empics Entertainment: 119, 156; /Barratts: 67, 75, 94; /Jean Cummings/Empics Entertainment: 33, 88; / Roy Cummings/Empics Entertainment: 30; /Robert W. Klein/AP: 129; /John Lindsay/AP: 17; /PA Archive: 15, 22, 43, 52, 72, 79, 80, 82, 85, 103, 120, 124, 133, 134, 144, 153, 162, 175; /Don Ryan/AP: 127; /Sport and General: 41, 107; /Topham Picturepoint: 112
Rex Features: /Christies Images Ltd: 9; /Lillian Evans: 51; /Everett Collection: 60, 181; /Keystone USA: 146, 154
Steve Turner Collection: 10, 18, 24, 27, 54, 138, 141

Every effort has been made to acknowledge correctly and contact the source and/or copyright holder of each picture and Carlton Books Limited apologises for any unintentional errors or omissions, which will be, corrected in future editions of the book.